Vocabulary Workshop

Fourth Course

Norbert Elliot

HOLT, RINEHART AND WINSTON

Austin • *New York • Orlando • Chicago • Atlanta*
San Francisco • Boston • Dallas • Toronto • London

Author

Norbert Elliot, the author and general editor of this new edition of *Vocabulary Workshop,* has a Ph.D. in English from The University of Tennessee. He is an associate professor of English at New Jersey Institute of Technology. A former site director for the National Writing Project, he has directed summer language arts institutes for kindergarten through twelfth-grade teachers in the public schools. A specialist in test development and evaluation of writing, Norbert Elliot has written books and articles on writing assessment, communication, and critical thinking. Dr. Elliot is the father of five children and is married to Lorna Jean Elliot, under whose care, he says, "everything thrives."

Contributing Writers

Raymond and Sylvia Teague collaborated on the writing of *Making New Words Your Own* and *Reading New Words in Context* for this edition of *Vocabulary Workshop.* The Teagues have been writing educational materials for eight years. After graduating from Texas Christian University, Raymond worked for the *Fort Worth Star-Telegram* as a writer and editor of news and features. He is now the newspaper's children's book editor. Sylvia earned her bachelor's and master's degrees from the University of Texas at Arlington, where she taught economics. Raymond and Sylvia have a daughter, Alexandra, who now attends college. The Teagues live on a mountaintop outside Eureka Springs, Arkansas, where they share a wonderful view, a crowded office, two cats, and an aging goldfish.

Lorna Jean Elliot wrote the *Connecting New Words and Patterns* sections for this edition of *Vocabulary Workshop.* She is a graduate of Susquehanna University, where she taught composition for several years. She earned her Masters of Arts degree in English Literature from the Bread Loaf School of English in Middlebury, Vermont. The author of an award-winning novella, Mrs. Elliot currently has her hands full as a freelance writer and as the mother of five thriving children.

CONTENTS

World Literature and Culture

MAKING NEW WORDS YOUR OWN 1

Context: Expression

Lesson 1: The First Artists 3
Lesson 2: The Stagecoach Never Stops: Westerns 7
Lesson 3: Gabriel García Márquez: "A Very Old Man with
           Enormous Wings" 11
Lesson 4: African Storytellers 15
Lesson 5: The Aliens at Grovers Mill 19
Lesson 6: William Faulkner: Voice from the South 23
Lesson 7: The Romance of Elizabeth and Robert Browning 27
Lesson 8: Zora Neale Hurston: Many-sided Writer 31
Lesson 9: Art Beyond Reality: Surrealism 35
Lesson 10: Leo Tolstoy: The Wealthy Russian Peasant 39

Context: Civilization

Lesson 11: Machiavelli: Designer of States 43
Lesson 12: Pyramids: Ancient Wonders 47
Lesson 13: Back in the Bronx 51
Lesson 14: What Was the Black Death? 55
Lesson 15: Two Russian Revolutions 59
Lesson 16: The Islamic World: A.D. 600–1300 63
Lesson 17: Before Aspirin: Medicine in the Middle Ages 67
Lesson 18: The Revolutions of Mahatma Gandhi 71
Lesson 19: Science Fiction: Into the Future 75
Lesson 20: The Industrial Revolution: Machines Make Progress 79

Context: The Environment

Lesson 21: Thinking Like a Mountain 83
Lesson 22: Why Be an Environmentalist? 87
Lesson 23: What Do We Owe the Environment? 91
Lesson 24: Laboratory Lakes for Acid Rain 95
Lesson 25: Rinsing the Ketchup Bottle: Recycling 99
Lesson 26: More Than Spilled Milk: 11 Million Gallons of Oil
           in the Sea 103
Lesson 27: Sketching in the Wild: John James Audubon 107
Lesson 28: Can Nature Be Restored? 111
Lesson 29: Wordsworth and the Lake District 115
Lesson 30: Moving Continents, If You Get My Drift 119

CONNECTING NEW WORDS AND PATTERNS 123

Lesson 1: ANALOGIES 126
Lesson 2: ANALOGIES 127
Lesson 3: ANALOGIES 128
Lesson 4: ANALOGIES 129
Lesson 5: ANALOGIES 130
Lesson 6: ANALOGIES 131
Lesson 7: ANALOGIES 132
Lesson 8: ANALOGIES 133
Lesson 9: ANALOGIES 134
Lesson 10: ANALOGIES 135
Lesson 11: ANALOGIES 136
Lesson 12: ANALOGIES 137
Lesson 13: ANALOGIES 138
Lesson 14: ANALOGIES 139
Lesson 15: ANALOGIES 140

READING NEW WORDS IN CONTEXT 141

Context: Expression

Lesson 1: Why Socrates Died 143
Lesson 2: The World Beyond: Native American Tales 149
Lesson 3: Franz Kafka's Bug 155
Lesson 4: Yukio Mishima: Japan's Literary Warrior 161
Lesson 5: India's Three Great Beliefs 167

Context: Civilization

Lesson 6: In Search of Troy and Ulysses 173
Lesson 7: Guatemala's Forgotten City 179
Lesson 8: China's Ming Dynasty: A Dream Journey 185
Lesson 9: Japan's Samurai Warriors 191
Lesson 10: A Letter from Nigeria 197

Context: The Environment

Lesson 11: Editorial: Can the Elephant Be Saved? 203
Lesson 12: The Destruction of the Rain Forests 209
Lesson 13: The Ocean Source 215
Lesson 14: Is the Earth Alive? 221
Lesson 15: Where Does All the Garbage Go? 227

MAKING NEW WORDS YOUR OWN

How We Make New Words Our Own

How do you learn new vocabulary? You probably already have some strategies for guessing the meanings of new words. When you first meet a new word, for example, you may try to figure out what it means by studying the context in which it appears. Or maybe you take a guess at the word and try substituting your guess in the sentence.

Below are three kinds of exercises that can help you develop your strategies for learning new words on your own.

EXERCISE 1   *Mapping* ✍

In these exercises, you will see a new word used in a sentence, and you will be asked to guess its meaning. You will check that guess against the dictionary definition of the word. Then you will be asked to list other forms of that word.

Here's an example of a mapping exercise:

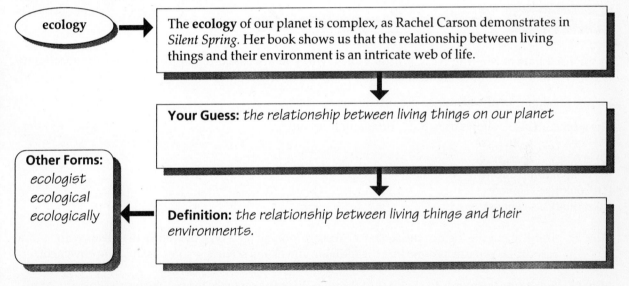

ecology → The **ecology** of our planet is complex, as Rachel Carson demonstrates in *Silent Spring*. Her book shows us that the relationship between living things and their environment is an intricate web of life.

Your Guess: *the relationship between living things on our planet*

Other Forms:
ecologist
ecological
ecologically

Definition: *the relationship between living things and their environments.*

Hint #1   Think about the word ecology. Have you heard the word before? If so, what other words do you associate it with?

Hint #2   Look for clues in the sentence. Ecology seems to be associated with the word planet and the idea that the relationship between living things is similar to a web.

Hint #3   Base your guess on an informed hunch. The example shows that the writer guesses ecology means the relationship between living things on our planet.

Hint #4   When you go to the dictionary to check your guess, be sure to read through all the definitions in order to select the one that best fits the given sentence. In the example, the writer chose the definition of ecology that seemed to make the most sense in the passage.

Hint #5   Take a moment to think about the ways that other forms of the word could be used. The writer of the example found ecologist and ecological in the dictionary and guessed that the adverb form of the word would be ecologically.

EXERCISE 2 *Context Clues*

Again, you will see the new word used in a sentence. This time, however, you're actually given a set of definitions, and you must match the new word with its meaning.

Here's an example of a context-clue exercise:

COLUMN A	**COLUMN B**
___G___. Word: ____ecology____: *n.* The relationship between living things and their environments; the science of such relationships	(G) Aldo Leopold (1866–1948) learned to think like a mountain so that he could understand and preserve the **ecology** of nature. Nature's rights, he felt, must be respected.

Hint #1 Read Column B first, and look for clues to the meaning of the word. You might imagine that thinking like a mountain would give you strong opinions about how nature should be treated. For example, as part of the earth, you would make sure that the rights of the earth were respected.

Hint #2 You should scan Column A for a likely definition of the word. In this case, the idea of relationships suggests that the sample definition is the correct one.

Hint #3 As you write the word in the blank, say it to yourself to get a sense of the sound of the word.

EXERCISE 3 *Sentence Completion*

In the final part of **Making New Words Your Own**, you are asked to supply the missing vocabulary word or words in order to create a sentence that makes sense.

Here's an example of a sentence-completion exercise:

The science of _____ allows us to _____ our natural resources.
(A) zoology . . . diminish
(B) ecology . . . preserve
(C) cultivation . . . destroy
(D) zoology . . . ignore
(E) ecology . . . exhaust

Hint #1 Think about the logic of the sentence. You are looking for a type of science that deals with natural resources. You can assume that the ultimate aim of any science is some kind of improvement.

Hint #2 Substitute the words in choices (A) through (E) in the sentence to see which pair of words completes the logic of the sentence.
• The pairs containing the word zoology can probably be ruled out, since zoology deals with animals in particular, not all natural resources.
• Cultivation has something to do with natural resources, but it is unlikely that the aim of any science is to destroy.
• Similarly, you can rule out answer (E) because the aim of ecology is not to exhaust but to preserve our natural resources. This conclusion leads to the correct answer, (B).

As you complete these three types of exercises, you will develop the ability to make an educated guess about the meaning of a word by thinking about its context.

MAKING NEW WORDS YOUR OWN

Lesson 1 | ## CONTEXT: Expression

The First Artists

Long before Picasso, before Michelangelo, even before ancient Egyptian stone carvers, there were artists. We do not know their names, but we know some of their works and the time period in which these works were created. The first artists lived in the Paleolithic or Old Stone Age, which began in Africa around 2,000,000 B.C. Prehistoric art includes paintings on the walls of caves, sculpture, pottery, baskets, and textiles.

In the following exercises, you will have the opportunity to expand your vocabulary by reading about prehistoric art. Below are ten vocabulary words that will be used in these exercises.

acquittal	condescend	elite	fortitude	mentor
assert	contemptuous	evolve	inarticulate	notoriety

EXERCISE 1 *Mapping*

Directions. In the item below, a vocabulary word is provided and used in a sentence. Take a guess at the word's meaning and write it in the box labeled **Your Guess**. Then look the word up in your dictionary and write the definition in the box labeled **Definition**. In the **Other Forms** box, write as many other forms of the word, such as adjective and noun forms, as you can think of or find in your dictionary.

Then, following the same procedure, draw your own map for each of the nine remaining vocabulary words. Use a separate sheet of paper.

1.

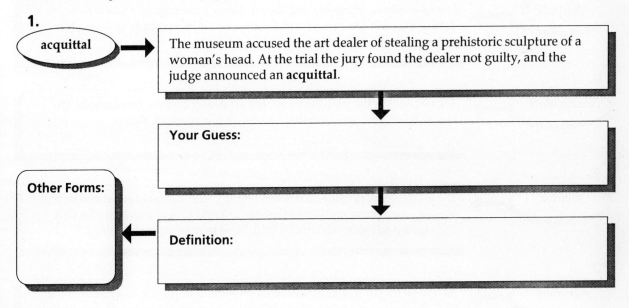

acquittal →

The museum accused the art dealer of stealing a prehistoric sculpture of a woman's head. At the trial the jury found the dealer not guilty, and the judge announced an **acquittal**.

Your Guess:

Other Forms:

Definition:

2.

assert

The museum did not have any evidence that the art dealer took the sculpture, which was carved in France around 22,000 B.C. The art dealer **asserted** his right to a free trial, and the museum could not deny his claim.

3.

condescend

The art dealer said that he was an honorable man who would not **condescend** to any form of dishonesty. Theft, he explained, was far beneath him.

4.

contemptuous

During the trial, museum officials were openly **contemptuous** of the art dealer's qualifications. The defense, however, produced witnesses who proved that the museum officials were quite wrong to show disdain for the dealer's expert knowledge.

5.

elite

"He is among the **elite** in the world of prehistoric art," one defense witness said. "Only a few select people know as much as this dealer knows about Paleolithic art and tools."

6.

evolve

The art dealer told how his interest in Paleolithic art had **evolved** over the last fifty years and also how his interest in the pottery of the Neolithic or New Stone Age (c. 8000–3000 B.C.) had gradually developed.

7.

fortitude

The newspaper article praised the art dealer's courage and moral strength during the trial. The article said he showed much **fortitude** in facing the charges from the museum.

8.

inarticulate

At one point in the trial, however, the art dealer became **inarticulate**. He was so filled with emotion that he was unable to speak clearly.

9.

mentor

The art dealer was emotional when telling about his **mentor,** whom he had accompanied on an archaeological dig in Turkey. "He was indeed a wise and trusted advisor," the dealer said, "and taught me many things."

10.

notoriety

Although the art dealer achieved an unwanted **notoriety** as a result of the trial, the museum's reputation suffered even more when it was discovered that the missing sculpture had been misplaced by a part-time employee.

EXERCISE 2   *Context Clues*

Directions. Scan the definitions in Column A. Then think about how the boldface words are used in the sentences in Column B. To complete the exercise, match each definition in Column A with the correct vocabulary word from Column B. Write the letter of your choice on the line provided; then write the vocabulary word on the line preceding the definition.

COLUMN A	COLUMN B

COLUMN A

_____ **11.** word: _____

n. patient courage in facing pain or danger; moral strength; endurance

_____ **12.** word: _____

v. to stoop to do something you think is beneath you

_____ **13.** word: _____

v. to develop gradually

_____ **14.** word: _____

n. fame, usually in an unfavorable sense; a bad reputation

_____ **15.** word: _____

v. to express or declare firmly; to defend or claim (one's rights, for example)   .

_____ **16.** word: _____

n. a setting free by judgment of a court

_____ **17.** word: _____

adj. of or suitable for a select group; *n.* a group or part of a group regarded as the best, most skilled, most powerful, and so on

_____ **18.** word: _____

n. a wise and trusted advisor; a counselor

_____ **19.** word: _____

adj. unable to speak clearly or to use words; unable to say what one thinks

_____ **20.** word: _____

adj. showing or feeling scorn; disdainful

COLUMN B

(A) One speaker **asserted** that the best Paleolithic cave paintings are at Lascaux, France; another firmly declared that the best are at Altamira, Spain.

(B) I accept the opinion of my **mentor**, who prefers the drawings of bison at Altamira. As an advisor, she has wise opinions and can be trusted.

(C) I was glad that the main speaker was not **inarticulate** and could clearly discuss why prehistoric artists painted images of animals on cave walls.

(D) He explained that the skills of prehistoric artists **evolved**, just as their concepts of pictures as symbols gradually developed.

(E) "Perhaps," he said, "the artist thought that painting a hunted animal's image would give the hunters the **fortitude** that they would need to courageously endure the hunt."

(F) Someone in the audience was **contemptuous** of the talents of prehistoric artists. Her disdain was directed at the cave paintings.

(G) The speaker felt that it was beneath him to respond to such criticisms. Nevertheless, he **condescended** to explain the primitive societies in which prehistoric artists lived and worked.

(H) "Were the people who did the cave paintings a small, **elite** group, or could just anybody paint in the caves?" I asked.

(I) The speaker said that to be an artist in a prehistoric society may have been an honor and that anyone with a bad reputation—any kind of **notoriety**—may not have been allowed to paint.

(J) Like a court jury, the members of the audience listened intently to the speaker's arguments. In the end, they decided they agreed with him and gave him an **acquittal** from any further discussion.

EXERCISE 3 *Sentence Completion* ✍

Directions. For each of the following items, circle the letter of the choice that best completes the meaning of the sentence or sentences.

21. Don't be _____ of prehistoric art; its beauty is worthy of respect, not scorn.
(A) elite
(B) inarticulate
(C) assertive
(D) fortitudinous
(E) contemptuous

22. Techniques for firing pottery _____, or developed gradually, in Near East farming villages during the Neolithic Age.
(A) asserted
(B) articulated
(C) acquitted
(D) evolved
(E) condescended

23. This author _____ that pottery is an important, visible record of a society's artistic skills. Other archaeologists have expressed that opinion, too.
(A) evolves
(B) condescends
(C) asserts
(D) represses
(E) succumbs

24. Only the _____ of the Friends of the Art Museum collect Neolithic pottery because only the most wealthy and influential people can afford it.
(A) acquittal
(B) elite
(C) mentor
(D) notoriety
(E) fortitude

25. Neolithic pottery figurines are especially valuable, according to my son's art professor, who is his trusted advisor, or _____, at college.
(A) mentor
(B) notoriety
(C) assertion
(D) acquittal
(E) elite

26. Perhaps only the _____ of Neolithic metalworkers could afford to use gold and silver. At times, however, they may have _____ to use tin or other metals that they may have considered beneath them.
(A) mentor . . . evolved
(B) acquittal . . . asserted
(C) elite . . . condescended
(D) mentor . . . acquitted
(E) notoriety . . . evolved

27. The speaker was so nervous that he was almost _____, but he ultimately was able to defend his _____ about the origins of Stonehenge.
(A) contemptuous . . . acquittal
(B) fortitudinous . . . notoriety
(C) repressive . . . fortitude
(D) contemptuous . . . elite
(E) inarticulate . . . assertion

28. Maura's _____ at art school advised her not to make copies of Neolithic pottery. Copiers gain a bad reputation, or _____.
(A) fortitude . . . elite
(B) notoriety . . . mentor
(C) elite . . . acquittal
(D) mentor . . . notoriety
(E) acquittal . . . fortitude

29. No one should be _____, or disdainful, of early prehistoric Chinese art: It is very sophisticated.
(A) contemptuous
(B) inarticulate
(C) elite
(D) whimsical
(E) prophetic

30. The courageous woman wrongly accused of smuggling precious artifacts exhibited _____ during the trial. She was found innocent, and the trial ended with _____.
(A) mentor . . . a notoriety
(B) fortitude . . . an acquittal
(C) elite . . . an assertion
(D) acquittal . . . an evolution
(E) condescension . . . an acquittal

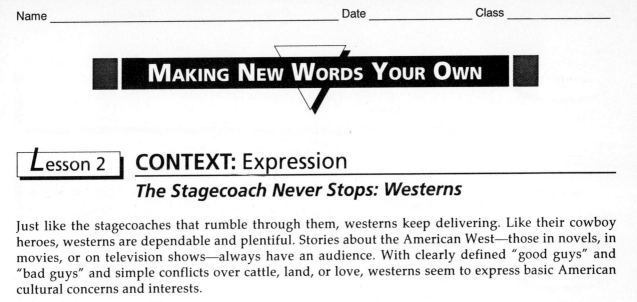

MAKING NEW WORDS YOUR OWN

Lesson 2 | **CONTEXT:** Expression

The Stagecoach Never Stops: Westerns

Just like the stagecoaches that rumble through them, westerns keep delivering. Like their cowboy heroes, westerns are dependable and plentiful. Stories about the American West—those in novels, in movies, or on television shows—always have an audience. With clearly defined "good guys" and "bad guys" and simple conflicts over cattle, land, or love, westerns seem to express basic American cultural concerns and interests.

In the following exercises, you will have the opportunity to expand your vocabulary by reading about westerns and their popularity. Below are ten vocabulary words that will be used in these exercises.

analogy	electorate	excerpt	paternal	posthumous
antiquity	ethical	heresy	pauper	prophetic

EXERCISE 1 *Mapping*

Directions. In the item below, a vocabulary word is provided and used in a sentence. Take a guess at the word's meaning and write it in the box labeled **Your Guess**. Then look the word up in your dictionary and write the definition in the box labeled **Definition**. In the **Other Forms** box, write as many other forms of the word, such as adjective and noun forms, as you can think of or find in your dictionary.

Then, following the same procedure, draw your own map for each of the nine remaining vocabulary words. Use a separate sheet of paper.

1.

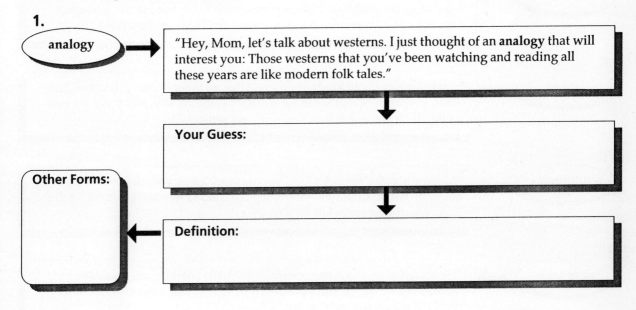

analogy → "Hey, Mom, let's talk about westerns. I just thought of an **analogy** that will interest you: Those westerns that you've been watching and reading all these years are like modern folk tales."

Your Guess:

Other Forms:

Definition:

2.

antiquity ➔ "I don't like the sound of 'all these years,' Jake. You make me sound ancient, like someone of great **antiquity**. I'm not older than the American West, you know."

3.

electorate ➔ "Mom, you're part of the **electorate**, those who have the right to vote. If you had to vote for a western movie star for president, which one would you vote for?"

4.

ethical ➔ "Well, John Wayne, of course—if he were alive—because the cowboy heroes he played always knew right from wrong. They were **ethical**. Do you remember him as Rooster Cogburn in *True Grit*?"

5.

excerpt ➔ "Yeah, and I remember how you used to read to me your favorite **excerpts** from that book. I bet you can quote them by heart even now."

6.

heresy ➔ "All I know is that John Wayne was the best western actor. If anyone were to state otherwise, it would be pure **heresy** as far as I'm concerned. You don't have a different opinion, do you?"

7.

paternal ➔ "Well, Mom, John Wayne is a **paternal** figure because he's strong and capable, as the traditional father is supposed to be. But I prefer a tougher hero, a loner, like some of the characters Clint Eastwood portrays."

8.

pauper ➔ "There's room for all kinds of different heroes in westerns, you know, Jake. Some are **paupers,** and some are wealthy; some are shy, and some are outgoing; some are wanderers, and some are settlers."

9.

posthumous ➔ "Mom, since you're such a John Wayne fan, I know you can answer this question: Did John Wayne receive a **posthumous** Academy Award, or did he receive the award while he was alive?"

10.

prophetic ➔ "He accepted an Academy Award in 1969, ten years before his death. Months before the awards I predicted he would win, which shows how good my **prophetic** abilities are."

EXERCISE 2 *Context Clues*

Directions. Scan the definitions in Column A. Then think about how the boldface words are used in the sentences in Column B. To complete the exercise, match each definition in Column A with the correct vocabulary word from Column B. Write the letter of your choice on the line provided; then write the vocabulary word on the line preceding the definition.

COLUMN A

_____ **11.** word: _____
n. a person who is very poor, especially one dependent upon public charity

_____ **12.** word: _____
n. a selected passage or scene from a literary work or piece of music; an extract; *v.* to take out or select passages; to quote

_____ **13.** word: _____
n. a likeness between different things; a similarity; a comparison

_____ **14.** word: _____
adj. pertaining to right and wrong; conforming to certain rules or standards; moral

_____ **15.** word: _____
adj. relating to someone or something that foretells events; predictive

_____ **16.** word: _____
n. a belief different from accepted doctrine

_____ **17.** word: _____
adj. inherited from or related through one's father; fatherly

_____ **18.** word: _____
n. ancient times; a thing or people of ancient times; the quality of being ancient

_____ **19.** word: _____
adj. coming after death

_____ **20.** word: _____
n. all persons having the right to vote

COLUMN B

(A) "Mom, I guess your interest in westerns is a **paternal** influence since you learned so much about them from your father."

(B) "Well, Jake, westerns can teach you a great deal about morals. The cowboy heroes and lawmen usually take **ethical** stands and do a lot of good."

(C) "I know. Read an **excerpt** from just about any western novel, such as *Shane*, and you get an idea from the passage that good triumphs over evil in westerns."

(D) "Westerns relive America's frontier days of the 1800s. Don't look to westerns for predictions of the future because they aren't **prophetic**."

(E) "Westerns are sort of American epics, like Homer's *Iliad* and *Odyssey* were to the Greeks. It's an interesting **analogy**, don't you think?"

(F) "Well, Jake, I've never thought of comparing westerns to stories of **antiquity**, but I'm sure people of ancient times had similar stories."

(G) "And westerns have a broad appeal, like a popular presidential candidate has to the general **electorate**."

(H) "Westerns show the reality of how people lived back then. They depict every kind of character: **paupers** who come to town for charity, wealthy ranchers, and mysterious loners."

(I) "Mom, do you recall a western movie about a clergyman who didn't believe the teachings of his church and so was tried for **heresy**?"

(J) "No, but I don't think I could live long enough to see all the western movies that have been made. After I'm dead and gone, there'll have to be some **posthumous** showings!"

EXERCISE 3 *Sentence Completion* ✍

Directions. For each of the following items, circle the letter of the choice that best completes the meaning of the sentence or sentences.

21. "I remember how good it felt when my father watched western movies with me. I really appreciate his _____ interest now. I wish I could tell him."
    (A) prophetic
    (B) posthumous
    (C) ethical
    (D) paternal
    (E) analogous

22. "Mom, you can't have _____ talks with your Dad; he's been dead for ten years."
    (A) ethical
    (B) prophetic
    (C) posthumous
    (D) paternal
    (E) heretical

23. "Jake, I may seem like a survivor from _____ to you, but I prefer the old westerns, which probably seem ancient to someone your age."
    (A) analogy
    (B) excerpt
    (C) electorate
    (D) heresy
    (E) antiquity

24. "Well, I know you think it's _____, but I guess I do go against your belief that old westerns are superior to newer ones."
    (A) antiquity
    (B) analogy
    (C) pauper
    (D) heresy
    (E) excerpt

25. "I guess I'm _____ after all, Jake. I predicted a long time ago that you would eventually like westerns."
    (A) ethical
    (B) paternal
    (C) posthumous
    (D) pompous
    (E) prophetic

26. "Mom, just because you sometimes feel as old as someone from _____ doesn't mean that you are _____ or can predict the future."
    (A) electorate . . . posthumous
    (B) pauper . . . prophetic
    (C) antiquity . . . prophetic
    (D) analogy . . . ethical
    (E) heresy . . . paternal

27. "Now, don't get upset like a member of the _____ throwing a candidate out at election time. Say, that's a good _____!"
    (A) heresy . . . antiquity
    (B) antiquity . . . pauper
    (C) electorate . . . analogy
    (D) pauper . . . electorate
    (E) electorate . . . heresy

28. "Mom, if I ever write an autobiography, a number of _____ from it will be about you. I don't want to tell you that I love you _____; I want to tell you while you're still alive."
    (A) excerpts . . . posthumously
    (B) analogies . . . paternally
    (C) heretics . . . ethically
    (D) electorates . . . heretically
    (E) paupers . . . paternally

29. "You know, Jake, many of my moral values came from _____ ideas in westerns. They helped me to rise from a poor background—we were practically _____—to become a successful businessperson."
    (A) paternal . . . electorates
    (B) ethical . . . analogies
    (C) posthumous . . . antiquities
    (D) ethical . . . paupers
    (E) prophetic . . . excerpts

30. "Well, I guess I'm guilty of _____ because I don't hold your belief about the ethical value of westerns. But I can recite a few _____ and quotes from famous westerns."
    (A) antiquity . . . electorates
    (B) heresy . . . excerpts
    (C) electorate . . . heresies
    (D) analogy . . . excerpts
    (E) excerpt . . . heresies

MAKING NEW WORDS YOUR OWN

Lesson 3 | CONTEXT: Expression

Gabriel García Márquez: "A Very Old Man with Enormous Wings"

Gabriel García Márquez was born in a small village near the Caribbean seacoast of Colombia, South America, in 1928. Although they were very poor, his family managed to provide him with an education that later enabled him to enter Bogotá University. His short stories and novels depict the myths, personalities, and conditions of the people with whom he grew up. García Márquez received the Nobel Prize in literature in 1982.

In the following exercises, you will have the opportunity to expand your vocabulary by reading about Gabriel García Márquez and his short story "A Very Old Man with Enormous Wings." Below are ten vocabulary words that will be used in these exercises.

amiable	bayou	indomitable	melodramatic	visage
anthropology	grimace	malleable	succumb	whimsical

EXERCISE 1 *Mapping* 👉

Directions. In the item below, a vocabulary word is provided and used in a sentence. Take a guess at the word's meaning and write it in the box labeled **Your Guess**. Then look the word up in your dictionary and write the definition in the box labeled **Definition**. In the **Other Forms** box, write as many other forms of the word, such as adjective and noun forms, as you can think of or find in your dictionary.

Then, following the same procedure, draw your own map for each of the nine remaining vocabulary words. Use a separate sheet of paper.

1.

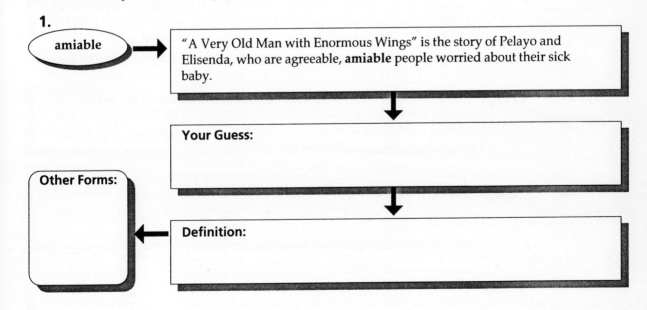

amiable → "A Very Old Man with Enormous Wings" is the story of Pelayo and Elisenda, who are agreeable, **amiable** people worried about their sick baby.

Your Guess:

Other Forms:

Definition:

2.

anthropology → People interested in **anthropology**, the study of the development and behavior of humanity, will find García Márquez's descriptions of the townspeople's reactions especially fascinating.

3.

bayou → Pelayo and Elisenda live in an area that is as marshy as a **bayou**. Days of rainfall have caused crabs to crawl into their house, and Pelayo goes out at noon to throw the crabs they have killed into the sea.

4.

grimace → On his way back to the house, Pelayo's face twists into a **grimace** of annoyance at finding an old man with enormous wings lying in the mud. Pelayo and Elisenda cannot understand the man's strange language.

5.

indomitable → Resisting the advice of a neighbor who says to kill the old man, Pelayo and Elisenda move him into the chicken coop. The old man, who has an **indomitable** spirit, is unconquered by curious, often cruel, onlookers who taunt him and throw things at him.

6.

malleable → Pelayo and Elisenda at first do not exploit the old man, but they prove to be **malleable** personalities. The constant flow of onlookers pressures them into fencing their property and charging a fee to view the old man, whom some people think is an angel.

7.

melodramatic → The old man suffers mostly in silence, except when someone prods him with a burning hot branding iron. García Márquez avoids being **melodramatic** in depicting the winged man's plight. The old man cries out in pain in the scene but is not presented in a way that is overly dramatic or emotional.

8.

succumb → Pelayo and Elisenda make a large amount of money before the townspeople **succumb** to a new temptation. They yield to the desire to see a new curiosity in town, a woman who looks like a large tarantula.

9.

visage → The old man lives on in the chicken coop until it rots away. Only his face hints at the suffering he has endured, for his **visage** is that of a dying man.

10.

whimsical → García Márquez describes the townspeople as **whimsical**, full of curious ideas or notions. Their interest in the old man is odd because they never see him as the pitiful person he is, but only as someone strangely different from themselves.

EXERCISE 2 Context Clues ✍

Directions. Scan the definitions in Column A. Then think about how the boldface words are used in the sentences in Column B. To complete the exercise, match each definition in Column A with the correct vocabulary word from Column B. Write the letter of your choice on the line provided; then write the vocabulary word on the line preceding the definition.

COLUMN A

_____ **11.** word: _____

adj. capable of being shaped by hammering or pressing; having the capacity to be changed easily; adaptive

_____ **12.** word: _____

adj. friendly; agreeable; good-natured; pleasant

_____ **13.** word: _____

n. the study of the physical, cultural, and social development and behavior of human cultures

_____ **14.** word: _____

adj. overly dramatic, emotional, or sentimental

_____ **15.** word: _____

v. to make a face showing pain, annoyance, and the like; *n*. a twisting of the face to show pain, annoyance, and the like

_____ **16.** word: _____

adj. unconquerable; unyielding; not easily overcome

_____ **17.** word: _____

v. to die; to yield or give in to an overpowering force or desire

_____ **18.** word: _____

n. a marshy inlet or outlet of a river or lake, especially in parts of the southern United States

_____ **19.** word: _____

adj. full of curious ideas or notions; odd, often in an amusing way; fanciful

_____ **20.** word: _____

n. a face or a facial expression; appearance

COLUMN B

(A) The new house that Pelayo and Elisenda build is designed to keep out the water and animals from the surroundings, which are as marshy as a **bayou**.

(B) The first people who come to see the old man **grimace** at him through the chicken wire, hoping to provoke a response with their twisted faces.

(C) The old man does not seem to be **malleable**. No matter how much pressure the people put on him to move, he resists adapting to their demands and instead sits quietly in the chicken coop.

(D) Perhaps a student of **anthropology** could explain why people in different cultures behave the way they do. For instance, why does no one help the sick and helpless old man?

(E) The old man's **visage** remains the same. His appearance suggests that he is dying, but he lives on.

(F) Throughout the years, despite neglect and abuse, the old man never gives up; he is **indomitable**.

(G) The winged man is not unpleasant, but he is not **amiable**, either. He seems to ignore the people and events around him.

(H) Pelayo and Elisenda expect the old man to **succumb** and die from old age, neglect, and exposure.

(I) There is a **whimsical** ending to the story. In an odd, fanciful scene, the old man actually grows new feathers on his wings and flies away.

(J) Elisenda, who watches the old man fly away, does not react in a **melodramatic** way. Instead, she is calmly pleased that he will no longer be an annoyance in her life.

EXERCISE 3 *Sentence Completion* ✍

Directions. For each of the following items, circle the letter of the choice that best completes the meaning of the sentence or sentences.

21. The beach near Elisenda and Pelayo's house is muddy and covered with rotten shellfish, and their courtyard is marshy, like a _____, because of the heavy rain.
  (A) grimace
  (B) visage
  (C) bayou
  (D) anthropology
  (E) whimsicality

22. The old man has the _____ of a sailor. Elisenda and Pelayo guess from his face that he is a castaway from a foreign ship wrecked by the storm.
  (A) grimace
  (B) mentor
  (C) axiom
  (D) bayou
  (E) visage

23. Because the old man has wings and cannot speak Spanish, Elisenda and Pelayo are not _____ toward him. They turn away and leave him lying in the mud.
  (A) indomitable
  (B) amiable
  (C) malleable
  (D) melodramatic
  (E) whimsical

24. They do not try to change the old man in any way, so they do not know if he is _____. With encouragement he might have adapted to their household.
  (A) amiable
  (B) indomitable
  (C) whimsical
  (D) malleable
  (E) melodramatic

25. Because the old man is _____ in the face of bad treatment, Pelayo and Elisenda begin to ignore him, believing that he can withstand anything.
  (A) indomitable
  (B) whimsical
  (C) malleable
  (D) amiable
  (E) melodramatic

26. García Márquez, a master of portraying the odd and fanciful, presents many _____ details of village life that could be of interest to _____.
  (A) melodramatic . . . a bayou
  (B) indomitable . . . an anthropologist
  (C) malleable . . . a visage
  (D) whimsical . . . an anthropologist
  (E) amiable . . . a grimace

27. Elisenda and Pelayo hope that the old man does not _____ to illness and die because they do not know how to dispose of a body in their marshy area, which is like a _____.
  (A) grimace . . . bayou
  (B) succumb . . . bayou
  (C) succumb . . . visage
  (D) grimace . . . visage
  (E) succumb . . . grimace

28. The townspeople are _____ and change whenever a more exciting, _____ circumstance presents itself.
  (A) melodramatic . . . anthropological
  (B) whimsical . . . malleable
  (C) malleable . . . melodramatic
  (D) indomitable . . . amiable
  (E) anthropological . . . indomitable

29. The townspeople hope for even a twisted _____ on the old man's _____, but he remains expressionless.
  (A) visage . . . bayou
  (B) grimace . . . visage
  (C) grimace . . . anthropologist
  (D) visage . . . bayou
  (E) bayou . . . grimace

30. The _____ nature of the townspeople is shown in their bizarre, silly suggestions about what to do with the _____ old man, who seems unable to be controlled by them.
  (A) amiable . . . grimacing
  (B) indomitable . . . melodramatic
  (C) malleable . . . amiable
  (D) anthropological . . . malleable
  (E) whimsical . . . indomitable

MAKING NEW WORDS YOUR OWN

Lesson 4   CONTEXT: Expression

African Storytellers

African literature has changed over the centuries. The literature of Africa south of the Sahara began as an oral tradition in which generations passed down stories, poems, and proverbs. In the eighteenth and nineteenth centuries, a tradition of written African literature began with the arrival of European missionaries. In the twentieth century, African writers have created a modern literature of short stories, poems, novels, and plays, not only in their own languages, but also in European languages.

In the following exercises, you will have the opportunity to expand your vocabulary by reading about traditional and modern African literature. Below are ten vocabulary words that will be used in these exercises.

apprehensive	commendable	ineffectual	mystic	personification
callous	indignant	judicious	paraphrase	verbatim

EXERCISE 1   *Mapping* ✍

Directions. In the item below, a vocabulary word is provided and used in a sentence. Take a guess at the word's meaning and write it in the box labeled **Your Guess**. Then look the word up in your dictionary and write the definition in the box labeled **Definition**. In the **Other Forms** box, write as many other forms of the word, such as adjective and noun forms, as you can think of or find in your dictionary.

Then, following the same procedure, draw your own map for each of the nine remaining vocabulary words. Use a separate sheet of paper.

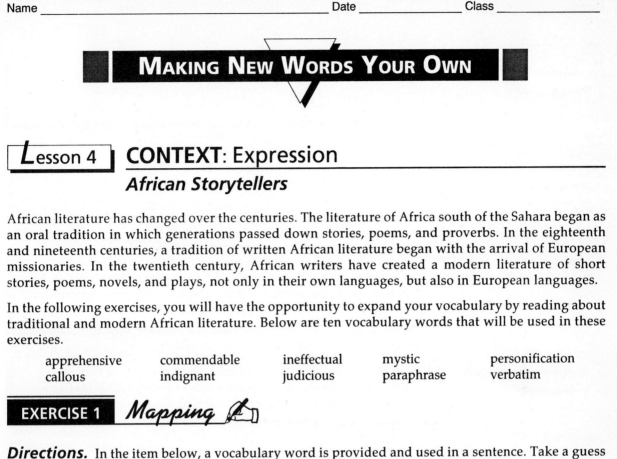

1.

apprehensive →

Listening to storytellers speak or chant traditional stories or epic poems may have helped early African peoples to be less anxious about the future. Those who were **apprehensive** may have been calmed by hearing stories about brave heroes who successfully meet life's challenges.

Your Guess:

Other Forms:

Definition:

2.

callous → Only a **callous** listener would have been insensitive to the inspirational story of the founder of the Mali empire told in the epic poem *Sundiata.* As a child, Sundiata is weak, but he grows up to be a great warrior and hunter.

3.

commendable → *Sundiata* is a **commendable** example of early African poetry. Another epic worthy of praise is *Lianja*, which tells the story of the hero of Zaire's Mongo people.

4.

indignant → It would not be fair to say that just anyone can effectively recite the epic poems of Africa. Professional storytellers would be **indignant** at such a comment. To be an effective African storyteller, one must have an excellent memory and an expressive voice and must be able to play a musical instrument.

5.

ineffectual → African audiences traditionally have been very demanding of their story-tellers. You can be sure that if an audience thinks a storyteller is **ineffectual,** he or she will be criticized for not achieving the desired effects.

6.

judicious → A **judicious** storyteller will prepare a story or poem that interests the audi-ence and is relevant to their concerns. The storyteller's good judgment in selecting the appropriate story will pay off with praise, food, and money.

7.

mystic → The storytellers in some locations have to please the **mystics** in their audi-ences. These people look for truth through spiritual insight and expect the storytellers to satisfy the gods as well as the human audience.

8.

paraphrase → You may be surprised to learn that it can take hours or even days to recite a long African epic poem. Audiences do not allow storytellers to **paraphrase** any part of an epic; they must tell the whole story in the traditional words and in the correct sequence.

9.

personification → Some popular African stories passed down by word of mouth involve **per-sonification**. In the Ashanti tale "Talk," for example, inanimate objects such as a yam, a palm branch, a stone, a fish trap, a bundle of cloth, and a stool are given human qualities.

10.

verbatim → Many stories and poems from Africa's oral literature now have been writ-ten down word-for-word, exactly as they were told by storytellers. Today's readers appreciate the efforts that were made to record these stories and poems **verbatim**.

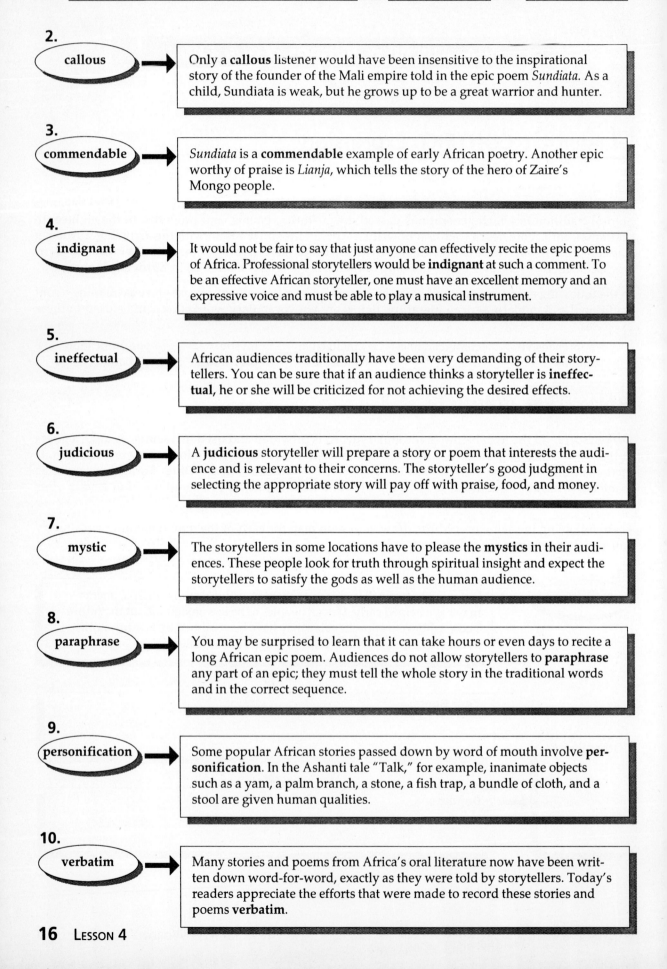

EXERCISE 2 *Context Clues* ✍

Directions. Scan the definitions in Column A. Then think about how the boldface words are used in the sentences in Column B. To complete the exercise, match each definition in Column A with the correct vocabulary word from Column B. Write the letter of your choice on the line provided; then write the vocabulary word on the line preceding the definition.

COLUMN A	COLUMN B

____ **11.** word: _____

adj. unfeeling; insensitive; thick and hardened; having calluses

____ **12.** word: _____

adj. mysterious; *n.* a person who believes that truth or God can best be known through spiritual insight; a religious seeker

____ **13.** word: _____

adj. angered by the unfairness or meanness of something

____ **14.** word: _____

adv. word-for-word; in the exact words; *adj.* following the original word–for–word

____ **15.** word: _____

v. to state a meaning in other words; *n.* a rewording of the meaning of a text or speech

____ **16.** word: _____

adj. praiseworthy; deserving approval or credit

____ **17.** word: _____

adj. showing good judgment; wise and careful; discreet; prudent

____ **18.** word: _____

n. a figure of speech in which something nonhuman is given human qualities; a person or thing that perfectly represents an idea or quality

____ **19.** word: _____

adj. unable to bring about a desired result; inadequate

____ **20.** word: _____

adj. uneasy; afraid or anxious about the future

(A) In addition to tales, the African oral tradition includes thousands of brief, wise proverbs. These short sayings are often made memorable through **personification:** Objects such as drums, rivers, and trees are given human qualities.

(B) I took my young sister, Viola, to the library's **commendable** African Stories program for children. Many people have found the program worthy of praise.

(C) When we first arrived, Viola was a bit **apprehensive** because the large poster of the trickster Anansi, a spider, made her anxious and uneasy.

(D) The **judicious** storyteller saw Viola's reaction and took down the poster. His action showed good judgment.

(E) Some past storytellers at the library have been **ineffectual,** but this one, who was born in Ghana, was very effective.

(F) The storyteller told trickster tales about the spider Anansi, a hare, and a tortoise. I'm sure that many of the children went home and **paraphrased** each story for the benefit of their parents. It would be fun to hear the little kids restating the tales in their own words.

(G) Viola, on the other hand, remembered every story word-for-word and could tell them **verbatim,** not leaving out a single sentence or detail.

(H) She became **indignant** if I said I didn't want to hear the tales again. I usually gave in to her anger, though.

(I) Mother accused me of being **callous** for becoming impatient with Viola, but I'm far from unfeeling. In fact, I bought Viola a book of African tales.

(J) Viola really liked the **mystic,** otherworldly tales from Nigeria, especially the Yoruba tales about the mysterious Elegba.

EXERCISE 3 *Sentence Completion* ✍

Directions. For each of the following items, circle the letter of the choice that best completes the meaning of the sentence or sentences.

21. To some scholars, the writings of Nigerian author Wole Soyinka perfectly represent modern African literature and are therefore the _____ of that literature's qualities.
(A) mystic
(B) judiciousness
(C) personification
(D) postulate
(E) paraphrase

22. The following is a _____ of a statement one scholar made about the Nigerian writer's works: Soyinka is concerned with what happens when tradition and progress meet in modern Africa.
(A) personification
(B) paraphrase
(C) visage
(D) mystic
(E) recourse

23. Many critics find Soyinka's writings _____. In fact, Soyinka won the Nobel Prize in literature in 1986—surely one of the highest forms of praise.
(A) apprehensive
(B) indignant
(C) ineffectual
(D) commendable
(E) callous

24. Please give me _____ account of the interview you saw with Soyinka about his recent play. I want to hear every word.
(A) a verbatim
(B) a callous
(C) an ineffectual
(D) an indignant
(E) an apprehensive

25. I tried taking notes as I watched the interview, but my hands were too _____. My pen rubbed painfully against the thick, hardened skin.
(A) commendable
(B) judicious
(C) apprehensive
(D) ineffectual
(E) calloused

26. Dr. Evans is _____ that more literature classes do not include Soyinka's writings; he is openly angry. To quote him _____, "I intend to correct such unfairness."
(A) apprehensive . . . callously
(B) verbatim . . . ineffectually
(C) indignant . . . verbatim
(D) mystic . . . apprehensively
(E) callous . . . verbatim

27. The professor's _____ financial planning enabled the class to attend Soyinka's play *A Dance of the Forests*. Such careful planning is _____ and deserves praise.
(A) callous . . . mystic
(B) mystic . . . ineffectual
(C) apprehensive . . . commendable
(D) indignant . . . verbatim
(E) judicious . . . commendable

28. One student complained that Soyinka's plots are _____, but I think they are quite effective. She must be _____, or hardened, if she cannot feel the emotional impact of Soyinka's work.
(A) verbatim . . . indignant
(B) indignant . . . mystic
(C) apprehensive . . . commendable
(D) ineffectual . . . calloused
(E) commendable . . . judicious

29. I was _____ when reading one of Soyinka's plays because I was afraid the foolish main character would not act _____.
(A) mystic . . . indignantly
(B) apprehensive . . . judiciously
(C) verbatim . . . callously
(D) apprehensive . . . ineffectually
(E) ineffectual . . . apprehensively

30. Dr. Evans says Soyinka's use of gods in *A Dance of the Forests* shows that Soyinka is at heart _____ with deep spiritual concerns. Dr. Evans gave brief _____ of two acts to help us understand Soyinka's meanings.
(A) a mystic . . . paraphrases
(B) an axiom . . . mystics
(C) a paraphrase . . . personifications
(D) a reactionary . . . acquittals
(E) a personification . . . paraphrases

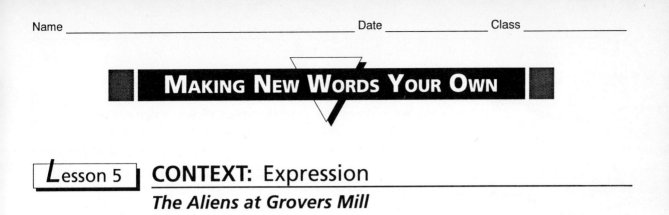

MAKING NEW WORDS YOUR OWN

| Lesson 5 | **CONTEXT:** Expression |

The Aliens at Grovers Mill

Imagine turning on the radio and hearing a news announcer explaining the details of a Martian invasion of earth. The invasion, the announcer says, is happening now at Grovers Mill, New Jersey. You believe this report to be totally accurate. What would you do? On Halloween eve in 1938, thousands of radio listeners found themselves in just such a situation, and they panicked. They didn't realize that they were hearing actor Orson Welles (1915–1985) reading a special adaptation of English writer H. G. Wells's (1866–1946) novel *The War of the Worlds.*

In the following exercises, you will have the opportunity to expand your vocabulary by reading about Orson Welles's famous radio broadcast of *The War of the Worlds.* Below are ten vocabulary words that will be used in these exercises.

affiliate	encumber	plausible	portly	rejuvenate
ecstatic	invariably	pompous	proximity	unprecedented

EXERCISE 1 *Mapping*

Directions. In the item below, a vocabulary word is provided and used in a sentence. Take a guess at the word's meaning and write it in the box labeled **Your Guess**. Then look the word up in your dictionary and write the definition in the box labeled **Definition**. In the **Other Forms** box, write as many other forms of the word, such as adjective and noun forms, as you can think of or find in your dictionary.

Then, following the same procedure, draw your own map for each of the nine remaining vocabulary words. Use a separate sheet of paper.

1.

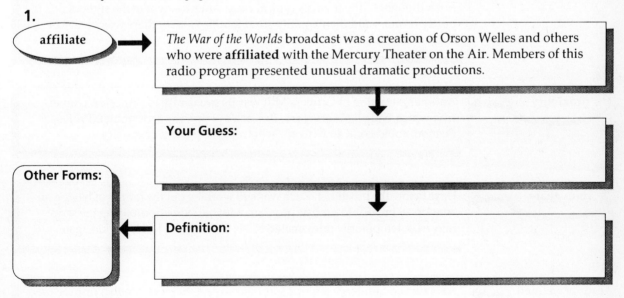

affiliate → *The War of the Worlds* broadcast was a creation of Orson Welles and others who were **affiliated** with the Mercury Theater on the Air. Members of this radio program presented unusual dramatic productions.

Your Guess:

Other Forms:

Definition:

2.

ecstatic → Welles chose writer Howard Koch to adapt *The War of the Worlds,* but the overworked Koch was not **ecstatic** about the project. Welles himself was not delighted with the project either, for he was already rehearsing for a play.

3.

encumber → Why did Welles **encumber** himself with two projects at once? An extremely talented and creative actor and director, Welles apparently liked to keep busy, even if his schedule sometimes became too heavy.

4.

invariably → Wherever he was, Koch **invariably** thought about the project. He was thinking about it continually as he took time off to visit his family in New York's Hudson Valley.

5.

plausible → Koch was thinking that he wanted the broadcast to sound **plausible**. On the way home he decided that the story needed a real setting so that the events would seem true.

6.

pompous → Koch chose the town of Grovers Mill, New Jersey, as the site of the Martian invasion. The decision was not made in some boardroom filled with **pompous**, or self-important, executives; Koch chose the place where his pencil landed on a New Jersey map.

7.

portly → He liked the sound of the name Grovers Mill. It reminded him of Grover's Corners in the play *Our Town* by Thornton Wilder (1897–1975). Perhaps Koch thought of the town as typical rural America, where the sight of **portly** farmers and their equally stout families meant there was plenty of food on the tables.

8.

proximity → Another attraction of Grovers Mill was its **proximity** to Princeton University, which had an observatory. In Koch's script, the astronomer, Professor Pierson, could come to Grovers Mill from the nearby university.

9.

rejuvenate → Days before the broadcast, Koch was still working out the format of having an announcer break into a music program with the story. Completing the script may have temporarily **rejuvenated** Koch, making him feel like a kid again.

10.

unprecedented → As it turned out, Koch's script sounded so real that it created an **unprecedented** radio event. Never before had a fictional radio program been mistaken for a real news report and so terrified its listeners.

EXERCISE 2 *Context Clues* ✍️

Directions. Scan the definitions in Column A. Then think about how the boldface words are used in the sentences in Column B. To complete the exercise, match each definition in Column A with the correct vocabulary word from Column B. Write the letter of your choice on the line provided; then write the vocabulary word on the line preceding the definition.

COLUMN A

_____ **11.** word: _____
adv. continually; perpetually; constantly; always

_____ **12.** word: _____
n. nearness; closeness; a neighboring area

_____ **13.** word: _____
n. an associated person or organization; a member; *v.* to associate or unite with a larger body

_____ **14.** word: _____
v. to make young or vigorous again; to give youthful qualities to

_____ **15.** word: _____
adj. comfortably fat or stout; large and heavy in a stately and dignified way

_____ **16.** word: _____
v. to hinder; to weigh down; to burden

_____ **17.** word: _____
adj. never done or known before; without previous example

_____ **18.** word: _____
adj. filled with rapture; transported by an exalted feeling of delight; overjoyed

_____ **19.** word: _____
adj. overly dignified; self-important; exaggerated stateliness, as in speech or manner

_____ **20.** word: _____
adj. appearing to be true; reasonable; seeming to be logical or correct

COLUMN B

(A) In 1938, people **invariably** turned to radio for affordable home entertainment. Today, many of us are perpetually turning on the TV.

(B) Regular radio listeners were **ecstatic** when their favorite programs came on and sad when they ended.

(C) Many listeners liked Orson Welles and the Mercury Theater, which was carried by radio stations that were nationwide **affiliates**, or associates, of the Columbia Broadcasting System (CBS).

(D) People may have thought they knew what to expect from Welles, but the show on Sunday night, October 30, 1938, was **unprecedented**.

(E) Welles had a dynamic, deep, clear voice during his young, lean years. It changed little as he became older and **portly**.

(F) His characterization of the radio announcer was not **pompous**, but was natural and appropriately professional.

(G) To thousands of believing listeners, the announcer's descriptions of the invading Martians sounded perfectly **plausible**.

(H) Koch's script was not **encumbered**, or weighed down, with a lot of literary description. Instead, it read like an eyewitness news story.

(I) People in the **proximity** of Grovers Mill must have been especially terrified to have the "invasion" right in their neighborhood.

(J) The broadcast frightened listeners who did not know that it was fictional, probably causing some of them to age in years with worry and terror. But it probably **rejuvenated** those listeners who knew it was a hoax, making them feel like delighted children.

EXERCISE 3 | *Sentence Completion* ☞

Directions. For each of the following items, circle the letter of the choice that best completes the meaning of the sentence or sentences.

21. My grandfather, who was a young boy at the time *The War of the Worlds* was broadcast, always became _____ when talking about it. He was like an excited child.
(A) rejuvenated
(B) unprecedented
(C) plausible
(D) affiliated
(E) portly

22. "I was _____ over the program, just as years later I was overjoyed with the movie *The War of the Worlds*," Grandpa said.
(A) plausible
(B) portly
(C) unprecedented
(D) encumbered
(E) ecstatic

23. He sometimes became _____, using overly dignified, exaggerated speech to tell about this important childhood event.
(A) unprecedented
(B) pompous
(C) portly
(D) plausible
(E) encumbered

24. "Some people back then certainly weren't _____ with the weight of common sense," Grandpa said. "Welles said at the end that the whole thing was fiction."
(A) affiliated
(B) plausible
(C) rejuvenated
(D) ecstatic
(E) encumbered

25. Grandpa was _____ man whose large stomach shook when he laughed about peoples' reaction to the broadcast.
(A) an invariable
(B) a plausible
(C) an encumbered
(D) a portly
(E) an affiliated

26. "To get out of _____ to the Martians, people rushed to train and bus stations. They didn't _____ themselves with burdensome luggage."
(A) affiliate . . . encumber
(B) rejuvenation . . . affiliate
(C) proximity . . . encumber
(D) affiliate . . . rejuvenate
(E) notoriety . . . rejuvenate

27. "Some people _____ believe the worst, and therefore they are always scared. But public reaction to the Welles broadcast was something new and _____."
(A) plausibly . . . pompous
(B) ecstatically . . . invariable
(C) pompously . . . portly
(D) invariably . . . unprecedented
(E) plausibly . . . ecstatic

28. "The script was very _____; it made the invasion seem real. But the final effect did not make CBS officials _____. They weren't delighted at all."
(A) unprecedented . . . portly
(B) plausible . . . ecstatic
(C) portly . . . unprecedented
(D) ecstatic . . . plausible
(E) portly . . . ecstatic

29. "Officials of CBS and its stations, including our local _____, were upset. Some claimed that Welles behaved _____, that he was so certain of his own importance he felt he could get away with a major hoax."
(A) affiliate . . . pompously
(B) proximity . . . ecstatically
(C) pompousness . . . plausibly
(D) rejuvenation . . . pompously
(E) plausibleness . . . ecstatically

30. "The event was _____; nothing like it had ever happened before. Radio broadcasters probably stuck to obvious fiction, nothing too _____, for some time after that!"
(A) plausible . . . portly
(B) ecstatic . . . pompous
(C) unprecedented . . . plausible
(D) pompous . . . ecstatic
(E) invariable . . . unprecedented

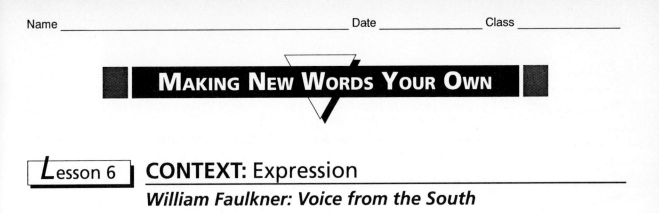

MAKING NEW WORDS YOUR OWN

| Lesson 6 | **CONTEXT:** Expression |

William Faulkner: Voice from the South

A while ago a friend said that her favorite book is William Faulkner's *As I Lay Dying* because it's darkly humorous. She said Faulkner lived from 1897 to 1962 and mostly wrote about the American South, where he lived. It sounded intriguing to me because I've always had a taste for weird humor. Assuming that Faulkner wrote only humorous books, I dropped by the library and checked out his novel *Wild Palms*. It wasn't funny; furthermore, it was confusing and hard to read. It's two completely different stories that are told in alternating chapters. The book is extremely strange, but it interested me, and I read it again. Then I read about Faulkner.

In the following exercises, you will have the opportunity to expand your vocabulary by reading about William Faulkner and his writing. Below are ten vocabulary words that will be used in these exercises.

ascertain	compassion	deteriorate	lament	painstaking
atrocious	composure	insipid	loathe	repress

EXERCISE 1 *Mapping* ✍

Directions. In the item below, a vocabulary word is provided and used in a sentence. Take a guess at the word's meaning and write it in the box labeled **Your Guess**. Then look the word up in your dictionary and write the definition in the box labeled **Definition**. In the **Other Forms** box, write as many other forms of the word, such as adjective and noun forms, as you can think of or find in your dictionary.

Then, following the same procedure, draw your own map for each of the nine remaining vocabulary words. Use a separate sheet of paper.

1.

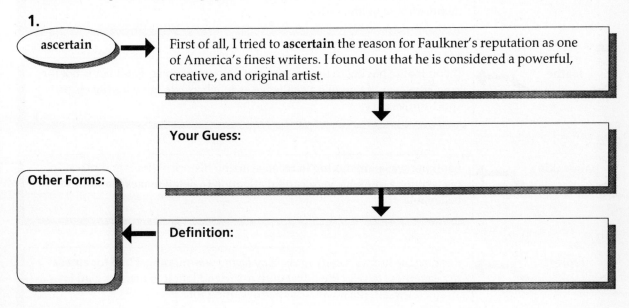

First of all, I tried to **ascertain** the reason for Faulkner's reputation as one of America's finest writers. I found out that he is considered a powerful, creative, and original artist.

Your Guess:

Other Forms:

Definition:

2.
atrocious →

Faulkner's formal education was limited as a result of his **atrocious** attendance record at school: He almost never went to class, and he dropped out completely after the tenth grade.

3.
compassion →

A friend, Phil Stone, took **compassion** on Faulkner and let him use the Stone's family library. Faulkner loved to read, and Stone's sympathetic help made it possible for Faulkner to educate himself.

4.
composure →

Faulkner had the maturity and **composure** to work at many different jobs in his early years. But he was at his calmest and most self-possessed later in his life when he was writing at his home in Oxford, Mississippi.

5.
deteriorate →

Many of Faulkner's stories and novels are about human relationships that **deteriorate**. *The Sound and the Fury,* for instance, is about the worsening relationships in a Southern aristocratic family.

6.
insipid →

Faulkner's writing is lively and spirited. I don't think it could ever be considered **insipid,** because he wrote about people who were far from dull and lifeless. His characters lead funny, tragic, happy, sad, and violent lives.

7.
lament →

Faulkner spoke against federal interference in the racial policies of the South, but his writings are often a **lament** for the mistreatment of blacks in the South. His sorrow and regret over their situation is clearly demonstrated in his stories.

8.
loathe →

If you **loathe** having to figure out what you are reading, Faulkner is not for you. However, if you like a challenge as much as I do, give his novels or short stories a try.

9.
painstaking →

Faulkner was **painstaking** in reconstructing historical times and places in his writing. I think his very careful attention to detail makes his stories believable.

10.
repress →

Because the library's copy of *As I Lay Dying* was missing, I had to **repress** my eagerness to read the novel until my friend lent it to me. I'm glad I restrained myself; the novel was worth waiting for.

EXERCISE 2 *Context Clues* ✍

Directions. Scan the definitions in Column A. Then think about how the boldface words are used in the sentences in Column B. To complete the exercise, match each definition in Column A with the correct vocabulary word from Column B. Write the letter of your choice on the line provided; then write the vocabulary word on the line preceding the definition.

COLUMN A	COLUMN B

COLUMN A

_____ **11.** word: _____

adj. flavorless; dull or unexciting; lifeless

_____ **12.** word: _____

adj. very careful; diligent; requiring great care; meticulous

_____ **13.** word: _____

v. to become worse or less valuable; to diminish

_____ **14.** word: _____

v. to regret; to express sorrow or mourning over; to grieve; *n.* an expression of grief; a song or poem expressing grief

_____ **15.** word: _____

n. pity for someone else's suffering, along with a desire to help; deep sympathy

_____ **16.** word: _____

v. to find out; to determine; to learn; to make certain

_____ **17.** word: _____

v. to hold back; to keep or put down; to restrain

_____ **18.** word: _____

v. to feel intense dislike or disgust; to detest

_____ **19.** word: _____

n. self-possession; calmness

_____ **20.** word: _____

adj. exceedingly bad; wicked or cruel; abominable

COLUMN B

(A) My **composure** was shaken when I realized I had forgotten to write a required report on Plato. I dropped my Faulkner reading, wrote the Plato paper, and was soon my usual calm self again.

(B) I'll never **lament** my mistake in thinking Faulkner was a humorous writer. How could I regret discovering my favorite author?

(C) At times, Faulkner needed money so badly that he had to hold back, or **repress,** his desire to write novels. Instead, he wrote screenplays for Hollywood.

(D) Faulkner was not as **painstaking** with screenplays as he was with his other writing. He didn't think scripts for films required as much thoughtfulness and care.

(E) Sometimes Faulkner's sentences go on and on, and it is hard to **ascertain** where they will end. Eventually, however, you do determine how to read his sentences.

(F) *Absalom, Absalom!* and other Faulkner novels are filled with the flavor of the South. They make other books I have read seem as **insipid** as weak tea in comparison.

(G) Some of Faulkner's books describe **atrocious** happenings such as lynchings, murders, and assaults. But these horrible, cruel events are important parts of the stories.

(H) Faulkner had reason to **loathe** the way blacks were treated in the South, and his disgust is evident in his writing.

(I) Faulkner wrote of Southern customs and manners that were beginning to **deteriorate**, and he gave reasons for the decline.

(J) One of my favorite aspects of Faulkner's writing is the **compassion** he shows for all sorts of people. I feel that his deep sympathy is sincere.

EXERCISE 3 Sentence Completion ✍

Directions. For each of the following items, circle the letter of the choice that best completes the meaning of the sentence or sentences.

21. Although Faulkner _____ school when he was young, he did like to read. He therefore educated himself.
(A) deteriorated
(B) loathed
(C) ascertained
(D) lamented
(E) repressed

22. It is not always easy to _____ Faulkner's meaning, but reading carefully will help you discover it.
(A) lament
(B) repress
(C) loathe
(D) ascertain
(E) deteriorate

23. Faulkner stayed calm, showing great _____ when he gave his acceptance speech for the Nobel Prize in literature in 1950.
(A) repression
(B) compassion
(C) composure
(D) deterioration
(E) loathing

24. If I become a writer, I'll try to be extremely careful with details so that my writing will be as _____ as Faulkner's.
(A) insipid
(B) compassionate
(C) atrocious
(D) repressive
(E) painstaking

25. I like exciting stories that are filled with life, not dull, _____ ones.
(A) insipid
(B) painstaking
(C) compassionate
(D) lamenting
(E) repressing

26. In *As I Lay Dying*, a sorrowful family _____ the death of a family member, but spends its time doing _____, unimportant things.
(A) loathes . . . deteriorated
(B) ascertains . . . repressive
(C) represses . . . painstaking
(D) laments . . . insipid
(E) deteriorates . . . compassionate

27. Faulkner, mourning the condition of blacks in the South, _____ their plight and wrote about the _____ they had to endure at the hands of controlling whites.
(A) ascertained . . . compassion
(B) repressed . . . deterioration
(C) lamented . . . repression
(D) loathed . . . composure
(E) deteriorated . . . atrociousness

28. *Sartoris* is a _____, sympathetic look at the steady _____ of the life of a war veteran, whose mental condition gradually worsens.
(A) loathsome . . . compassion
(B) compassionate . . . deterioration
(C) painstaking . . . insipidity
(D) repressive . . . composure
(E) lamentable . . . ascertainment

29. Faulkner was not satisfied with *Sanctuary*. He did not want to diminish his literary status and allow his reputation to _____, so he revised the novel to meet his exacting, _____ standards.
(A) deteriorate . . . painstaking
(B) repress . . . atrocious
(C) ascertain . . . insipid
(D) lament . . . compassionate
(E) loathe . . . lamentable

30. Faulkner took a stand against the abominable, _____ acts committed against some Southerners by showing deep sympathy and _____ for the victims.
(A) compassionate . . . composure
(B) loathsome . . . repression
(C) repressive . . . composure
(D) painstaking . . . deterioration
(E) atrocious . . . compassion

MAKING NEW WORDS YOUR OWN

Lesson 7 | CONTEXT: Expression

The Romance of Elizabeth and Robert Browning

There really is poetry in the romance of Elizabeth and Robert Browning. Both Elizabeth Barrett Browning (1806–1861) and her husband Robert Browning (1812–1889) are ranked among England's greatest poets. They are equally famous for their romance, including their elopement; for Elizabeth's love poems to Robert, published as *Sonnets from the Portuguese;* and for their sixteen years of marital happiness.

In the following exercises, you will have the opportunity to expand your vocabulary by reading selected thoughts about the romance of Elizabeth and Robert Browning from various students. Below are ten vocabulary words that will be used in these exercises.

aesthetic	cliché	emphatically	paradox	recipient
charisma	conceive	martial	prolific	wan

EXERCISE 1 *Mapping*

Directions. In the item below, a vocabulary word is provided and used in a sentence. Take a guess at the word's meaning and write it in the box labeled **Your Guess**. Then look the word up in your dictionary and write the definition in the box labeled **Definition**. In the **Other Forms** box, write as many other forms of the word, such as adjective and noun forms, as you can think of or find in your dictionary.

Then, following the same procedure, draw your own map for each of the nine remaining vocabulary words. Use a separate sheet of paper.

1.

aesthetic → What I find most appealing about the Brownings is their **aesthetic** awareness. They both must have been extremely sensitive to beauty in nature and in the arts.

↓

Your Guess:

↓

Other Forms:

Definition:

2.

charisma → Robert first fell in love with Elizabeth through her poetry. In her poems she showed a **charisma**, a special charm, that captured Robert's—as well as the general public's—imagination and devotion.

3.

cliché → It may be a **cliché** to say that with the Brownings it was "love at first sight," but I think that the expression, though overused, is appropriate.

4.

conceive → I can't **conceive** how Robert Browning had the nerve to write to Elizabeth after reading her books of poetry and to say, "I do . . . love these books with all my heart—and I love you, too." That is just beyond my grasp!

5.

emphatically → I'm glad that Elizabeth and Robert married, even though her father had declared **emphatically** that none of his twelve children should marry. He had no right to forcefully impose such a rule on his children.

6.

martial → Well, I was disappointed in *Sonnets from the Portuguese* because I don't care for all this romance stuff. I thought the poems were about a Portuguese warrior, but they are far from **martial** poems!

7.

paradox → "The more things change, the more they stay the same" is a **paradox** that comes to mind after reading about the Brownings' romance. That seemingly contradictory statement suggests that, while the world has changed much since the 1800s, love has not.

8.

prolific → The Brownings had a happy marriage, but they were not **prolific** parents. They had only one child, Robert Wiedeman Barrett-Browning, who was known as Pennini or Pen.

9.

recipient → After the Brownings had been married three years, Elizabeth gave Robert the manuscript of the sonnets she had written about him. He must have been a proud **recipient** of those sonnets.

10.

wan → Elizabeth Browning was a semi-invalid and spent a lot of time indoors, where she read and wrote. As a result of not being outdoors much, I imagine that she probably often looked sickly pale, or **wan**.

EXERCISE 2 *Context Clues* ✍

Directions. Scan the definitions in Column A. Then think about how the boldface words are used in the sentences in Column B. To complete the exercise, match each definition in Column A with the correct vocabulary word from Column B. Write the letter of your choice on the line provided; then write the vocabulary word on the line preceding the definition.

COLUMN A	COLUMN B

COLUMN A

_____ **11.** word: _____
adj. military; suggesting war; warlike

_____ **12.** word: _____
n. an overused idea or expression; a trite saying

_____ **13.** word: _____
adj. producing a great deal of something; producing many young or much fruit

_____ **14.** word: _____
adj. sickly pale or faint; colorless

_____ **15.** word: _____
adj. artistic; having to do with art or beauty; sensitive to art and beauty

_____ **16.** word: _____
n. a special quality of leadership or a special charm that captures the public imagination and inspires devotion

_____ **17.** word: _____
n. a person who receives something

_____ **18.** word: _____
adv. forcefully; assertively

_____ **19.** word: _____
n. a statement that may be true but that seems to say contradictory things

_____ **20.** word: _____
v. to imagine or develop as an idea; to understand or grasp; to become pregnant with

COLUMN B

(A) The Brownings were **prolific** authors and produced many poems, partly because they both began writing at a very early age.

(B) I wonder how the thirteen-year-old Elizabeth **conceived** the idea for her epic poem *The Battle of Marathon.* How could a young girl come up with such an ambitious idea?

(C) The poem's **martial** title certainly is not in keeping with Elizabeth Browning's image as a love poet.

(D) I'm sure you have heard the expression "All's fair in love and war." Although a **cliché**, the expression applies to Elizabeth's first epic poem.

(E) Love, as I'm sure the Brownings discovered, is often full of **paradoxes**, for emotions can be contradictory.

(F) The image of Elizabeth as a **wan**, or sickly, poet who only read and wrote is not completely accurate. She actually was quite active in social causes.

(G) This woman, famous for her love sonnets, **emphatically** endorsed women's issues and also forcefully protested against slavery.

(H) I envy the Brownings' **aesthetic** life in Florence, Italy, where they were surrounded by much art and beauty.

(I) Poets today do not inspire public devotion as they once did. One can only imagine the **charisma** of a Robert Browning. His charms would probably be lost on contemporary people.

(J) From what we've read, it sounds as if the Brownings were certainly worthy **recipients** of all the honors and love they received.

EXERCISE 3 *Sentence Completion* ✍

Directions. For each of the following items, circle the letter of the choice that best completes the meaning of the sentence or sentences.

21. Elizabeth Browning's line "How do I love thee? Let me count the ways" may be considered a _____ today because it is overused.
(A) charisma
(B) conception
(C) paradox
(D) recipient
(E) cliché

22. In the sonnet that starts "How do I love thee? Let me count the ways," Elizabeth _____, or forcefully, declares her love.
(A) aesthetically
(B) conceivably
(C) emphatically
(D) martially
(E) prolifically

23. The poet obviously has much love to give, and if you ask me, her beloved was a lucky _____ of her affections.
(A) recipient
(B) cliché
(C) paradox
(D) emphasis
(E) charisma

24. Although some love poems I have read contain contradictory statements, that sonnet doesn't contain any _____.
(A) clichés
(B) paradoxes
(C) postulates
(D) recipients
(E) mentors

25. I would look as _____ as a sick person if I had to express my love as openly as Elizabeth Browning did!
(A) aesthetic
(B) martial
(C) prolific
(D) wan
(E) whimsical

26. Can you possibly imagine, or _____ of, yourself as the _____ of someone's love sonnets?
(A) harass . . . recipient
(B) conceive . . . paradox
(C) repress . . . cliché
(D) conceive . . . recipient
(E) grimace . . . charisma

27. Some people, such as the Brownings, enjoy _____ lives and artistic pursuits, but I would become colorless and _____ living such a life.
(A) paradoxical . . . aesthetic
(B) wan . . . martial
(C) aesthetic . . . wan
(D) martial . . . paradoxical
(E) conceivable . . . wan

28. In contrast to the Brownings, I _____ state, with all the force in me, that I want an adventurous life. You may see me in _____ garb as an army officer someday.
(A) aesthetically . . . prolific
(B) conceivably . . . emphatic
(C) martially . . . clichéd
(D) prolifically . . . wan
(E) emphatically . . . martial

29. My sister's goal is to "follow in the footsteps" of the Brownings (forgive the _____, or trite saying) so that she can become a _____ poet with many successful books.
(A) cliché . . . prolific
(B) recipient . . . martial
(C) paradox . . . prolific
(D) recipient . . . clichéd
(E) charisma . . . conceivable

30. In the portrait of Elizabeth Browning, the painter succeeded in capturing that special charm that we call _____. The beautiful background certainly suggests her _____ nature.
(A) paradox . . . charismatic
(B) charisma . . . aesthetic
(C) emphasis . . . wan
(D) cliché . . . aesthetic
(E) recipient . . . prolific

MAKING NEW WORDS YOUR OWN

Lesson 8 | CONTEXT: Expression

Zora Neale Hurston: Many-sided Writer

Zora Neale Hurston (1891?–1960) was always her own person—talented and prolific, hardworking and outspoken. She was born in Eatonville, Florida, where her father was a carpenter and served as the minister and mayor. When her mother died, Hurston left home and worked as a maid and later as a secretary while attending college. She began writing plays and stories and for a time was part of the black cultural revival known as the Harlem Renaissance.

In the following exercises, you will have the opportunity to expand your vocabulary by reading about Zora Neale Hurston, writer of novels, short stories, plays, folk tales, and works of anthropology. Below are ten vocabulary words that will be used in these exercises.

fabricate	mediocre	opportune	reactionary	zealous
impediment	mien	qualm	stamina	zephyr

EXERCISE 1 *Mapping* 👈

Directions. In the item below, a vocabulary word is provided and used in a sentence. Take a guess at the word's meaning and write it in the box labeled **Your Guess**. Then look the word up in your dictionary and write the definition in the box labeled **Definition**. In the **Other Forms** box, write as many other forms of the word, such as adjective and noun forms, as you can think of or find in your dictionary.

Then, following the same procedure, draw your own map for each of the nine remaining vocabulary words. Use a separate sheet of paper.

1.

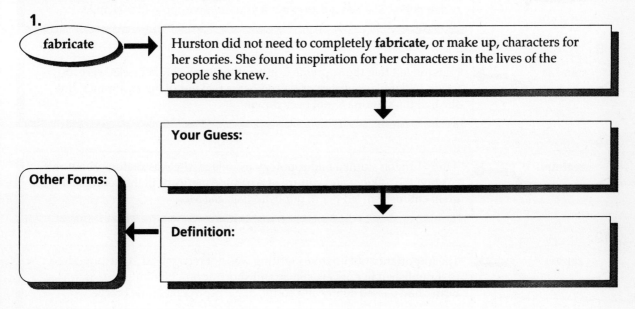

fabricate → Hurston did not need to completely **fabricate**, or make up, characters for her stories. She found inspiration for her characters in the lives of the people she knew.

Your Guess:

Other Forms:

Definition:

2.
impediment → Hurston did not let having to work hard at low-paying jobs be an **impediment** to getting an education. She overcame all obstacles and attended Howard University and Barnard College.

3.
mediocre → There is variety in Hurston's writing, and none of her writing is **mediocre**. It is all above average.

4.
mien → From the love and humor shown in her writing, a reader probably imagines Hurston as having a pleasant **mien,** or appearance and manner.

5.
opportune → Unfortunately, the time in which Hurston wrote was not an **opportune** one for African American writers. There was very little interest in literature about black families and folklore, and thus her literary career was not well timed.

6.
qualm → Hurston may have had **qualms** about moving from a small town in Florida to New York City. It is natural to feel slightly doubtful and uneasy when facing a major change in your life and surroundings.

7.
reactionary → Some people accused Hurston of having **reactionary** ideas when she opposed the desegregation ruling in 1954, but she was not advocating a return to an earlier policy. She was not an extreme conservative opposed to change.

8.
stamina → Hurston felt that the Supreme Court ruling implied that blacks were inferior. Older black writers criticized her, a real test of her endurance, but she had the **stamina** to not back down.

9.
zealous → After Hurston studied anthropology in college, she was **zealous** about recording the folklore and culture of African Americans in the South. Her great enthusiasm led her to publish *Mules and Men*.

10.
zephyr → The importance of Hurston's writing was not recognized at the time she first published her novels, plays, and short stories. Her influence as a writer had passed subtly and softly, like a **zephyr** or gentle breeze.

EXERCISE 2 Context Clues ✍

Directions. Scan the definitions in Column A. Then think about how the boldface words are used in the sentences in Column B. To complete the exercise, match the definition in Column A with the correct vocabulary word from Column B. Write the letter of your choice on the line provided; then write the vocabulary word on the line preceding the definition.

COLUMN A	COLUMN B

COLUMN A

_____ **11.** word: _____
n. bearing; appearance; manner

_____ **12.** word: _____
n. an uneasiness, misgiving, or doubt; a slight feeling of sickness or nausea

_____ **13.** word: _____
adj. intensely devoted; eager; enthusiastic

_____ **14.** word: _____
n. a speech disorder; an obstruction of some kind

_____ **15.** word: _____
n. a gentle wind; a mild breeze

_____ **16.** word: _____
adj. only average or ordinary; medium; neither bad nor good

_____ **17.** word: _____
adj. advocating a return to an earlier social, political, or economic policy or condition; *n*. one who advocates a return to an earlier policy or condition

_____ **18.** word: _____
v. to build or manufacture; to make up or invent (as a story or an excuse)

_____ **19.** word: _____
n. vigor; strength; endurance

_____ **20.** word: _____
adj. right for the purpose; advantageously timed

COLUMN B

(A) Hurston's use of natural dialogue enlivens her stories. She captures dialects and regional expressions easily. She is even able to imitate speech **impediments** such as stuttering and stammering.

(B) Because Hurston wrote stories about crude situations and people, some critics thought her work was merely **mediocre**, rather than exceptional.

(C) It is a shame that Hurston could not have written during a more **opportune** time, such as now, when there is a great appreciation for African American stories and writers. Today, her work would be very timely.

(D) In her writing, Hurston describes appearances and manners so that the reader can picture each character's **mien**.

(E) Hurston's stories are often earthy, telling of violence and marital difficulties, but you should have no **qualms** about reading them. Any doubts you have will vanish after a few pages.

(F) She **fabricated** a reputation as a controversial and outspoken person, but Hurston also built a reputation as a skilled and hard-working author.

(G) Hurston was **zealous** about her work. Her devotion and enthusiasm are evident in her collection of short stories, *The Eatonville Anthology*.

(H) Florida's African Americans of the 1920s and 1930s live on in Hurston's writing. Readers can almost feel each **zephyr** that gently blows across Eatonville and smell the scents carried on the breeze.

(I) A reader can appreciate the people and conditions of Hurston's time without being **reactionary** about them. There is little sense in returning to the conditions that existed then.

(J) Hurston had great **stamina**. Her strength and endurance were demonstrated by the fact that, in addition to writing her many books, she worked as a staff writer, a maid, a librarian, a journalist, a part-time teacher, and a professor of drama.

EXERCISE 3 *Sentence Completion* ✍

Directions. For each of the following items, circle the letter of the choice that best completes the meaning of the sentence or sentences.

21. The folklore stories Hurston wrote down were _____ that had been made up long ago by anonymous storytellers.
(A) qualms
(B) zephyrs
(C) impediments
(D) fabrications
(E) mediocrities

22. Hurston seemingly had no _____ about telling about life as it really was. If she had doubts, she overcame them.
(A) impediments
(B) opportunities
(C) qualms
(D) miens
(E) stamina

23. The lack of opportunities for black writers, the lack of interest and appreciation by the public, and her politics and lifestyle all served as obstacles, or _____, to Hurston's goals.
(A) qualms
(B) fabrications
(C) opportunities
(D) zephyrs
(E) impediments

24. In spite of the hardships she endured, Hurston was often fortunate. It was _____, for example, that Hurston had other jobs offered to her, since she made little money writing.
(A) zealous
(B) reactionary
(C) opportune
(D) mediocre
(E) fabricated

25. The _____ of certain individuals in Hurston's hometown must have been etched in her memory. Their appearances are described in detail in her stories.
(A) qualms
(B) miens
(C) zephyrs
(D) impediments
(E) mediocrities

26. Hurston's autobiography, *Dust Tracks on the Road,* shows her to be a _____ individual whose dedication gave her a great deal of _____, or endurance.
(A) zealous . . . stamina
(B) mediocre . . . fabrication
(C) reactionary . . . zephyrs
(D) pallid . . . mediocrity
(E) qualmish . . . impediment

27. Hurston achieved only a _____ reputation in her lifetime, not an exceptional one. Recently, however, her writings have been _____ received by an enthusiastic audience.
(A) reactionary . . . opportunistically
(B) mediocre . . . zealously
(C) zealous . . . opportunely
(D) reactionary . . . zealously
(E) fabricated . . . opportunistically

28. Hurston now has many _____ fans, but she died almost unknown. Many people had _____ about her work—misgivings that are hard to understand today.
(A) opportune . . . fabrications
(B) mediocre . . . miens
(C) reactionary . . . zephyrs
(D) staminal . . . impediments
(E) zealous . . . qualms

29. Hurston eventually lost her _____, health, and will to live. Her life force, once as strong as a gale, became little more than a _____.
(A) impediment . . . mediocrity
(B) mediocrity . . . fabrication
(C) stamina . . . zephyr
(D) qualms . . . reactionary
(E) mien . . . zealousness

30. This talented woman, who was once accused of being backward-looking, even _____, who had faced and overcome all sorts of _____, is buried in an unmarked grave in a segregated cemetery in Fort Pierce, Florida.
(A) mediocre . . . qualms
(B) mien . . . reactionaries
(C) opportunistic . . . fabrications
(D) reactionary . . . impediments
(E) qualmish . . . zephyrs

MAKING NEW WORDS YOUR OWN

Lesson 9 | CONTEXT: Expression

Art Beyond Reality: Surrealism

Many art viewers would say that something really strange happened to art in the 1920s—surrealism. Painters in the surrealist movement attempted to portray the unconscious mind as revealed in dreams. As you might expect, surrealist art is characterized by irrational, illogical, fantastic images. Sometimes these images are quite unsettling; they make the viewer uncomfortable. One of the movement's founders was French poet and art critic André Breton (1896–1966).

In the following exercises, you will have the opportunity to expand your vocabulary by reading about the surrealist movement in art and about two of the leading surrealist artists. Below are ten vocabulary words that will be used in these exercises.

axiom	compliance	indestructible	mutable	prevalent
compatible	inanimate	innate	perception	recourse

EXERCISE 1 — *Mapping*

Directions. In the item below, a vocabulary word is provided and used in a sentence. Take a guess at the word's meaning and write it in the box labeled **Your Guess.** Then look the word up in your dictionary and write the definition in the box labeled **Definition.** In the **Other Forms** box, write as many other forms of the word, such as adjective and noun forms, as you can think of or find in your dictionary.

Then, following the same procedure, draw your own map for each of the nine remaining vocabulary words. Use a separate sheet of paper.

1.

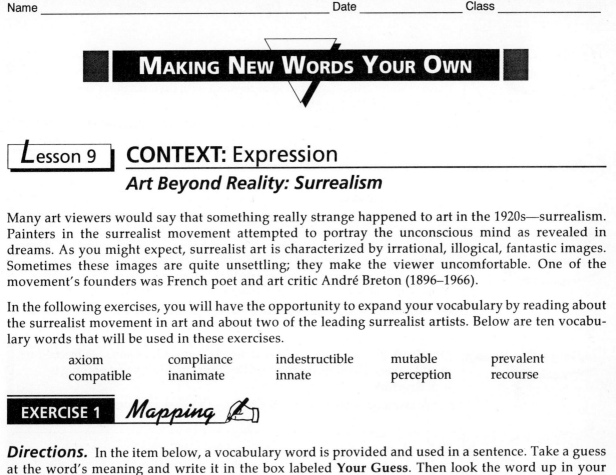

axiom → Surrealism and its forerunner, dadaism, overturned the **axiom** "Art mirrors life." Such established principles about art were contrary to André Breton's *Manifesto of Surrealism,* published in 1924.

Your Guess:

Other Forms:

Definition:

2.

compatible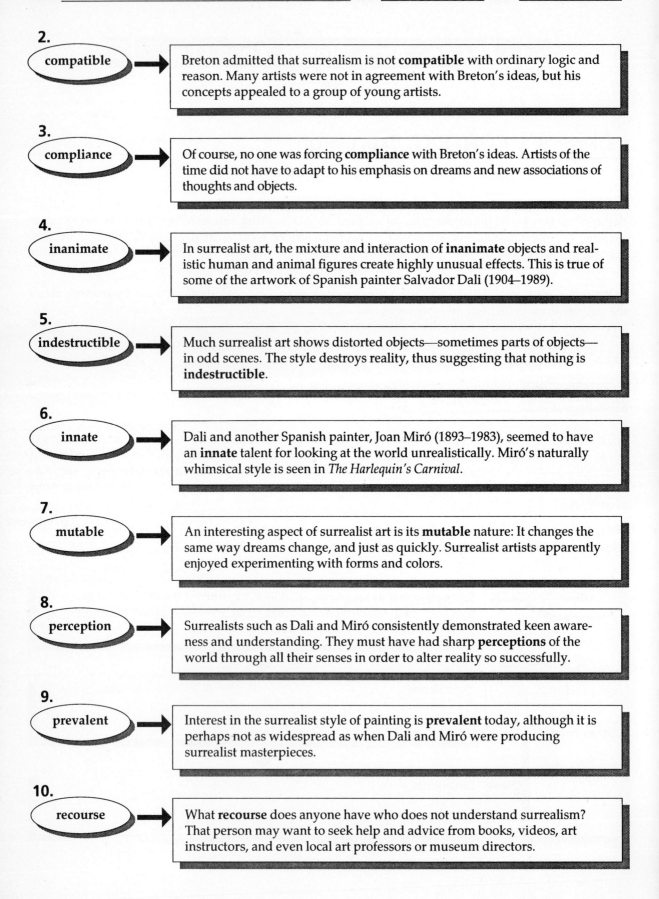

Breton admitted that surrealism is not **compatible** with ordinary logic and reason. Many artists were not in agreement with Breton's ideas, but his concepts appealed to a group of young artists.

3.

compliance

Of course, no one was forcing **compliance** with Breton's ideas. Artists of the time did not have to adapt to his emphasis on dreams and new associations of thoughts and objects.

4.

inanimate

In surrealist art, the mixture and interaction of **inanimate** objects and realistic human and animal figures create highly unusual effects. This is true of some of the artwork of Spanish painter Salvador Dali (1904–1989).

5.

indestructible

Much surrealist art shows distorted objects—sometimes parts of objects—in odd scenes. The style destroys reality, thus suggesting that nothing is **indestructible**.

6.

innate

Dali and another Spanish painter, Joan Miró (1893–1983), seemed to have an **innate** talent for looking at the world unrealistically. Miró's naturally whimsical style is seen in *The Harlequin's Carnival*.

7.

mutable

An interesting aspect of surrealist art is its **mutable** nature: It changes the same way dreams change, and just as quickly. Surrealist artists apparently enjoyed experimenting with forms and colors.

8.

perception

Surrealists such as Dali and Miró consistently demonstrated keen awareness and understanding. They must have had sharp **perceptions** of the world through all their senses in order to alter reality so successfully.

9.

prevalent

Interest in the surrealist style of painting is **prevalent** today, although it is perhaps not as widespread as when Dali and Miró were producing surrealist masterpieces.

10.

recourse

What **recourse** does anyone have who does not understand surrealism? That person may want to seek help and advice from books, videos, art instructors, and even local art professors or museum directors.

EXERCISE 2   *Context Clues* ✍

Directions. Scan the definitions in Column A. Then think about how the boldface words are used in the sentences in Column B. To complete the exercise, match each definition in Column A with the correct vocabulary word from Column B. Write the letter of your choice on the line provided; then write the vocabulary word on the line preceding the definition.

COLUMN A	COLUMN B

COLUMN A

_____ **11.** word: _____
adj. inborn; natural

_____ **12.** word: _____
n. a person or thing looked to for help, safety, and so on; a turning for help, safety, and the like, to a person or thing

_____ **13.** word: _____
adj. capable of change; inconstant

_____ **14.** word: _____
n. the act of adapting to or giving in; a tendency to yield; conformity with official requirements

_____ **15.** word: _____
adj. not capable of being destroyed

_____ **16.** word: _____
adj. widespread; in general use; having general acceptance

_____ **17.** word: _____
adj. able to get along; agreeing; in agreement with; harmonious

_____ **18.** word: _____
n. an observation, a concept, or an awareness gained by use of the senses; an understanding or impression of something; appreciation; discernment

_____ **19.** word: _____
n. a statement assumed to be true; a self-evident truth; an established principle

_____ **20.** word: _____
adj. dull; spiritless; lifeless

COLUMN B

(A) What is your **perception** of the work of surrealist artist Salvador Dali? Do you understand, for instance, his depictions of the human body?

(B) For artistic purposes, Dali certainly found the human body **mutable:** He freely changed its basic form in a number of paintings.

(C) Dali's view in the painting *Soft Construction with Boiled Beans: Premonition of Civil War* seems to be not only that humanity is not **indestructible,** but that it is capable of its own destruction.

(D) The painting clearly illustrates Dali's ability to defy reality on canvas. Such an ability can't, I think, be learned: It must be inborn, or **innate.**

(E) In that disturbing painting, Dali shows **compliance,** or agreement, with the surrealist belief that feelings and ideas must be expressed.

(F) Don't you think Dali's paintings prove the old **axiom** "Beauty is in the eye of the beholder"?

(G) Of course, Dali's paintings are **inanimate** objects, yet they are hardly lifeless or spiritless.

(H) Although surrealism was a popular movement in its day, the surrealist style never became **prevalent** in the art world. It was confined to a small group of artists.

(I) Frankly, I have never been **compatible** with anyone who likes surrealist art, but maybe we can learn to get along.

(J) Perhaps you are my last **recourse** for help in learning to appreciate surrealist art.

EXERCISE 3   *Sentence Completion*

Directions. For each of the following items, circle the letter of the choice that best completes the meaning of the sentence or sentences.

21. Our art teacher said that his favorite painter is Joan Miró. Miró's humor is _____ or harmonious with his own.
(A) prevalent
(B) innate
(C) inanimate
(D) compatible
(E) mutable

22. "I used to think Miró had an _____ artistic talent, but I now believe that his skills were learned."
(A) axiomatic
(B) innate
(C) incompatible
(D) indestructible
(E) inanimate

23. We are lucky that Miró was not rigid and unchanging but instead flexible. His _____ nature enabled him to work in many different media, from painting to sculpture and ceramics.
(A) innate
(B) compatible
(C) inanimate
(D) indestructible
(E) mutable

24. "Follow your dreams" is a self-evident truth, _____, that applies to Miró.
(A) an axiom
(B) a recourse
(C) a compatibility
(D) a perception
(E) a compliance

25. "Miró's desire to be an artist was _____, and we should be glad that his desire was too strong to be destroyed," Mr. Alvarez said.
(A) compatible
(B) prevalent
(C) indestructible
(D) inanimate
(E) prolific

26. "I enjoy the way the _____ shapes actually seem to come to life in some Miró paintings," Mr. Alvarez said. "They seem to have a vibrant quality that is naturally their own, _____ spirit that is very appealing."
(A) innate . . . a compatible
(B) inanimate . . . a mutable
(C) indestructible . . . a prevalent
(D) compatible . . . a perceptive
(E) inanimate . . . an innate

27. "Certain images were _____, or often used, in Miró's paintings. Perhaps they were _____ symbols that changed with his ideas."
(A) innate . . . compatible
(B) prevalent . . . indestructible
(C) axiomatic . . . mutable
(D) prevalent . . . mutable
(E) indestructible . . . innate

28. "Your _____ of Miró is largely that of a humorous painter, isn't it? That observation is certainly _____, or in complete agreement, with my own," Mr. Alvarez said.
(A) recourse . . . prevalent
(B) axiom . . . mutable
(C) perception . . . compatible
(D) compliance . . . inanimate
(E) prevalence . . . mutable

29. "You will be in _____ with class requirements if you write an essay about a Miró painting. Tell me your _____ of it, explaining what you understand it to mean."
(A) compliance . . . perception
(B) recourse . . . compliance
(C) compatibility . . . axiom
(D) axiom . . . recourse
(E) perception . . . personification

30. "If you need help, your best _____ will be to consult reference works at the library." Mr. Alvarez said. "In your essays, tell me if you think the _____ 'Art for art's sake' applies to Miró's work."
(A) perception . . . recourse
(B) recourse . . . axiom
(C) axiom . . . compliance
(D) recourse . . . compliance
(E) compliance . . . axiom

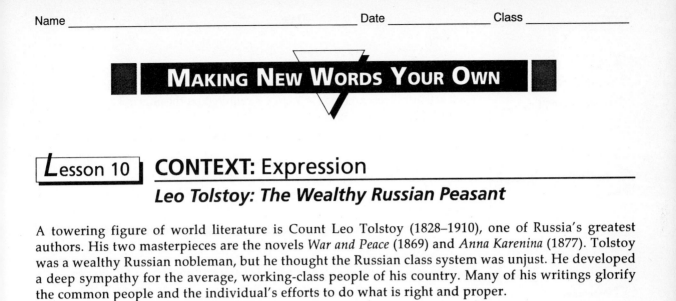

MAKING NEW WORDS YOUR OWN

| Lesson 10 | **CONTEXT: Expression** |

Leo Tolstoy: The Wealthy Russian Peasant

A towering figure of world literature is Count Leo Tolstoy (1828–1910), one of Russia's greatest authors. His two masterpieces are the novels *War and Peace* (1869) and *Anna Karenina* (1877). Tolstoy was a wealthy Russian nobleman, but he thought the Russian class system was unjust. He developed a deep sympathy for the average, working-class people of his country. Many of his writings glorify the common people and the individual's efforts to do what is right and proper.

In the following exercises, you will have the opportunity to expand your vocabulary by reading about Leo Tolstoy's life and works. Below are ten vocabulary words that will be used in these exercises.

encompass	incentive	pivotal	retribution	transcend
implacable	militant	postulate	stringent	transitory

| EXERCISE 1 | *Mapping* |

Directions. In the item below, a vocabulary word is provided and used in a sentence. Take a guess at the word's meaning and write it in the box labeled **Your Guess**. Then look the word up in your dictionary and write the definition in the box labeled **Definition**. In the **Other Forms** box, write as many other forms of the word, such as adjective and noun forms, as you can think of or find in your dictionary.

Then, following the same procedure, draw your own map for each of the nine remaining vocabulary words. Use a separate sheet of paper.

1.

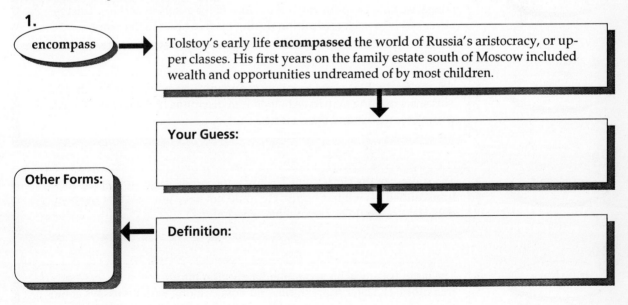

encompass → Tolstoy's early life **encompassed** the world of Russia's aristocracy, or upper classes. His first years on the family estate south of Moscow included wealth and opportunities undreamed of by most children.

Your Guess:

Other Forms:

Definition:

2.
implacable →

Implacable biographers have probed all aspects of Tolstoy's boyhood. Their relentless research has sometimes centered on the effects Tolstoy's parents' deaths had on him.

3.
incentive →

After his parents' deaths, Tolstoy was raised by relatives. I wonder if his private tutors set up **incentive** programs to encourage the young Tolstoy to study and learn.

4.
militant →

After three years at Kazan University, Tolstoy returned home to manage the family estate. Although he wanted to improve the conditions of the peasants, he was not a **militant,** or an activist, for the cause.

5.
pivotal →

Becoming a soldier at the age of twenty-three was a **pivotal** event in Tolstoy's life. It was crucial to his development as an author because while in the army he started writing about his life.

6.
postulate →

You would be incorrect to **postulate** that Tolstoy did not do well during his service in the Crimean War. On the contrary, evidence shows that he was a good and dedicated soldier.

7.
retribution →

The Russian army routinely punished soldiers who disobeyed orders or otherwise failed to perform, but because of his excellent service, Tolstoy never received such **retribution** during his five years in the army.

8.
stringent →

Tolstoy no doubt learned to follow **stringent** rules while in the military. This strict training may have helped him discipline himself when he was writing his novels and short stories.

9.
transcend →

The success of the stories that Tolstoy wrote while in the army probably **transcended** his wildest hopes. He could not have guessed that the result of his labors would go beyond his expectations.

10.
transitory →

The fame Tolstoy achieved immediately after his army service was not **transitory.** His later short stories and novels, along with his essays about art and philosophy, firmly established his lasting reputation.

EXERCISE 2 Context Clues 🖎

Directions. Scan the definitions in Column A. Then think about how the boldface words are used in the sentences in Column B. To complete the exercise, match each definition in Column A with the correct vocabulary word from Column B. Write the letter of your choice on the line provided; then write the vocabulary word on the line preceding the definition.

COLUMN A	COLUMN B

_____ **11.** word: _____
adj. aggressive in support of a belief or cause; *n.* an individual prepared to fight for a cause; an activist

_____ **12.** word: _____
adj. passing quickly; lasting only a short time; temporary

_____ **13.** word: _____
n. motivation; encouragement; *adj.* motivating; encouraging

_____ **14.** word: _____
v. to contain or include; to surround

_____ **15.** word: _____
n. an assumption; a basic principle; *v.* to assume without proof

_____ **16.** word: _____
adj. tight in finances or credit; strict; severe

_____ **17.** word: _____
adj. relentless; not capable of being pacified or appeased

_____ **18.** word: _____
n. something given to make up for a wrong done; punishment

_____ **19.** word: _____
adj. on which something turns or depends; crucial; vitally important

_____ **20.** word: _____
v. to rise above or go beyond the limits of; to exceed; to surpass

(A) What was my **incentive** for reading *War and Peace*? I was motivated by my cousin's claim that my mother's side of the family is very distantly related to Leo Tolstoy.

(B) The novel is long because it **encompasses** so much of Russian life during the early 1800s. It even includes Napoleon's invasion of Russia in 1812.

(C) **Pivotal** to the story are the lives of three aristocratic families. The story especially revolves around two characters, Andrey and Pierre.

(D) As you would expect, some of the characters are strong and **implacable**, while others are weak and easily pacified.

(E) Among Tolstoy's basic principles is the **postulate** that people should be of service to others. That belief comes across in the novel.

(F) The number of characters in *War and Peace*—more than five hundred—certainly **transcends**, or goes beyond, the number in any other novel I've read.

(G) There are, of course, many characters in the novel whose roles are **transitory**; they are each in the story for only a short time.

(H) Some of the war heroes in the novel become very aggressive in supporting their sides. They actually are too **militant** for my tastes.

(I) My favorite character was Natasha, so I didn't want her to suffer any **retributions** in the story. I didn't care so much if other characters were punished, though.

(J) Reading *War and Peace* was a welcome break from my work at the bank, where I keep track of the **stringent**, or tight, money markets.

EXERCISE 3   Sentence Completion ✍

Directions. For each of the following items, circle the letter of the choice that best completes the meaning of the sentence or sentences.

21. During the last thirty years of his life, Tolstoy had a new _____, or motivation, for writing.
(A) incentive
(B) retribution
(C) militant
(D) postulate
(E) transcendence

22. In his novels, Tolstoy _____ that love and nonviolence are basic principles that have influenced many people.
(A) encompasses
(B) transcends
(C) postulates
(D) personifies
(E) fabricates

23. Tolstoy imposed strict rules on his own behavior; some members of his family found his self-discipline too _____.
(A) transitory
(B) pivotal
(C) incentive
(D) apprehensive
(E) stringent

24. "To do good" was a _____ point in the philosophy that Tolstoy developed in the late 1870s; his life revolved around that idea.
(A) transcendent
(B) transitory
(C) stringent
(D) pivotal
(E) mediocre

25. Ironically, some people thought Tolstoy had become too _____, or aggressive, in support of his philosophy of love.
(A) incentive
(B) pivotal
(C) plausible
(D) transitory
(E) militant

26. Tolstoy looked at the world that _____ him and found it disturbing. He tried to understand life's basic principles, or _____.
(A) transcended . . . militants
(B) encompassed . . . postulates
(C) grimaced . . . incentives
(D) postulated . . . retributions
(E) excerpted . . . postulates

27. His inner struggles were so difficult and painful that they must have seemed like _____. If the time was punishing, however, it was also _____ and eventually passed.
(A) postulate . . . incentive
(B) militant . . . stringent
(C) retribution . . . transitory
(D) compliance . . . incentive
(E) incentive . . . militant

28. Tolstoy became _____ in his desire to live right and equally relentless in his desire to live simply. He applied _____ standards to himself, denying himself luxuries.
(A) transitory . . . implacable
(B) pivotal . . . incentive
(C) incentive . . . transitory
(D) implacable . . . stringent
(E) transitory . . . stringent

29. Tolstoy's writings provided _____ for many people to become followers. Those motivated to follow his ideas were peaceful rather than _____ in their support.
(A) incentives . . . militant
(B) retributions . . . implacable
(C) postulates . . . transitory
(D) incentives . . . stringent
(E) militants . . . pivotal

30. The Indian leader Mohandas K. Gandhi found Tolstoy's writings influential, even _____. They were important in developing his ideas to urge people to _____, or rise above, violence.
(A) transitory . . . postulate
(B) militant . . . transcend
(C) pivotal . . . encompass
(D) implacable . . . fabricate
(E) pivotal . . . transcend

Name _____ Date _____ Class _____

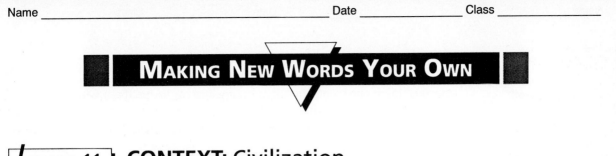
Lesson 11   CONTEXT: Civilization

Machiavelli: Designer of States

The recent breakup of some of the countries in eastern Europe started me thinking: If different ethnic groups and political units wanted to be independent of one another, why did they form into countries to begin with? There seem to be many reasons, and some of them came from the ideas of one man, Niccolo Machiavelli (1469–1527). Machiavelli, one of the most famous thinkers of the Renaissance, lived in Florence, Italy. He wrote *The Prince*, a book that has greatly influenced what has happened in Europe and its colonies for centuries.

In the following exercises, you will have the opportunity to expand your vocabulary by reading about Niccolo Machiavelli and his influence on the formation of modern countries. Below are ten vocabulary words that will be used in these exercises.

autonomy	devastation	latitude	precarious	wane
besiege	inclement	perseverance	vulnerable	wreak

EXERCISE 1   Mapping

Directions. In the item below, a vocabulary word is provided and used in a sentence. Take a guess at the word's meaning and write it in the box labeled **Your Guess**. Then look the word up in your dictionary and write the definition in the box labeled **Definition**. In the **Other Forms** box, write as many other forms of the word, such as adjective and noun forms, as you can think of or find in your dictionary.

Then, following the same procedure, draw your own map for each of the nine remaining vocabulary words. Use a separate sheet of paper.

1.

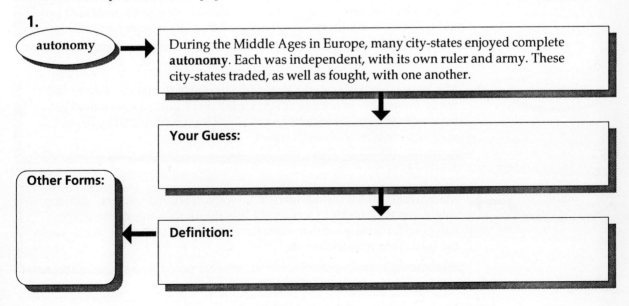

During the Middle Ages in Europe, many city-states enjoyed complete **autonomy**. Each was independent, with its own ruler and army. These city-states traded, as well as fought, with one another.

Your Guess:

Other Forms:

Definition:

2.

besiege

Because each city-state stood alone, it was easy for attacking armies to **besiege** them one by one by surrounding and capturing them. Many Italian city-states were lost in this way to the French and Spanish armies.

3.

devastation

The **devastation** caused by such attacks made some people think it would be wise for the city-states to band together to try to resist such complete destruction.

4.

inclement

Niccolo Machiavelli had no mercy for the weakness of the Italian city-states. His **inclement** attitude made him a champion of Italian unification, and he wrote *The Prince* as a manual for the ruler who would be strong enough to unite Italy into one state.

5.

latitude

Machiavelli felt that the Italians would not do well with too much **latitude** in government. Therefore, he urged that, for the good of the state, freedoms be restricted by an absolute ruler.

6.

perseverance

Machiavelli resented the Catholic Church's **perseverance** in meddling in the affairs of the city-states. He felt that the church's persistence in urging people to turn away from public affairs weakened the people and the city-states.

7.

precarious

Machiavelli felt that the Church was putting the city-states in an uncertain, even dangerous, situation by entrusting government to supernatural powers. He suggested that the only way the Italians could save themselves from their **precarious** position was to separate government from the authority of the Church.

8.

vulnerable

Machiavelli also advocated a strong military force so that the state would not be **vulnerable** to outside attack. He felt that a unified state would be better able to resist injury and destruction if it were protected by drafted male citizens who were well trained.

9.

wane

Machiavelli wanted the influence of mercenaries (hired soldiers), corrupt rulers, and the Church to **wane** until only the prince—the absolute ruler—had power. He believed that only after these influences had declined would the state reach its full strength.

10.

wreak

Machiavelli believed that the ruling prince should have cunning and strength enough to **wreak** punishment on those who threatened the state. This ability to inflict vengeance would strengthen both the state and the ruler, he claimed.

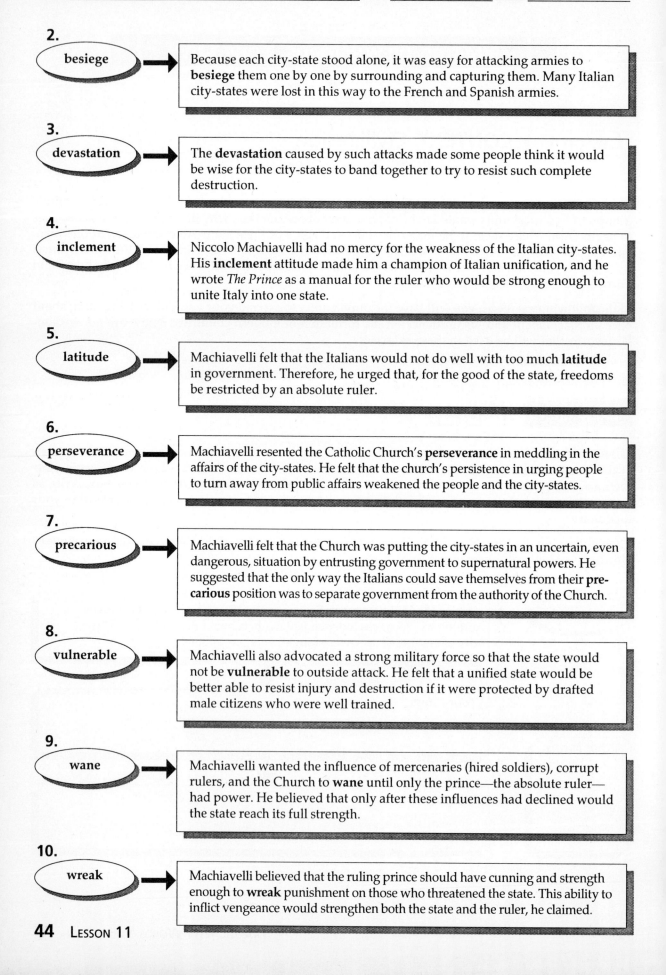

EXERCISE 2 *Context Clues* ✍

Directions. Scan the definitions in Column A. Then think about how the boldface words are used in the sentences in Column B. To complete the exercise, match each definition in Column A with the correct vocabulary word from Column B. Write the letter of your choice on the line provided; then write the vocabulary word on the line preceding the definition.

COLUMN A	COLUMN B

COLUMN A

_____ **11.** word: _____
adj. unsafe; insecure; uncertain; dangerous

_____ **12.** word: _____
n. destruction; desolation

_____ **13.** word: _____
adj. easily injured or hurt physically or emotionally; open to criticism or attack

_____ **14.** word: _____
v. to crowd around in order to press with requests; to harass; to beset; to surround in order to capture

_____ **15.** word: _____
v. to inflict (as vengeance or punishment); to express (as anger or hatred)

_____ **16.** word: _____
n. the act or habit of holding to a course of action or belief; persistence; steadfastness

_____ **17.** word: _____
n. independence; the condition of having self-government

_____ **18.** word: _____
v. to decrease gradually; to decline in power, importance, or size

_____ **19.** word: _____
adj. without mercy; rough or stormy; harsh

_____ **20.** word: _____
n. freedom; scope

COLUMN B

(A) Machiavelli wrote that a ruler who followed the guidelines in *The Prince* would be **besieged** by citizens who crowded around him with requests.

(B) Machiavelli had many good ideas, but he didn't allow much **latitude** for common citizens, whom he did not think were worthy of much freedom.

(C) Many European city-states used the ideas in *The Prince* to change from small, **vulnerable** units to unified nations that were much more resistant to harm and injury.

(D) Each city-state traded its **autonomy** for the security of a powerful, centrally controlled state. This loss of independence gave rise to the development of countries such as we know today.

(E) Machiavelli saw the ruler as always in a **precarious** position, full of uncertainty and danger. He would be threatened on all sides by schemers.

(F) To prevent such people from **wreaking** havoc on the state, the prince should be a master of deception, Machiavelli says, willing to trick others in order to prevent them from inflicting injury on the state.

(G) Machiavelli did not seem to consider the **devastation** that results from dishonesty and deceit. He believed that the end always justifies the means, even when the end destroys someone.

(H) Because Machiavelli had a very low opinion of common people, I consider his ideas about them to be **inclement**. In many ways he was harsh and unforgiving—a man without mercy.

(I) The **perseverance** of some of Machiavelli's ideas is evident today in the United States, for we maintain a separation of church and state, and at times we use the draft system.

(J) The current urge to break up countries in Europe may **wane** when the benefits of unification are reconsidered. I would not be surprised to see a decline in this trend. After all, Machiavelli's ideas changed European political thought before.

EXERCISE 3   *Sentence Completion* ✍

Directions. For each of the following items, circle the letter of the choice that best completes the meaning of the sentence or sentences.

21. The word *Machiavellian* is now used to mean someone who is crafty and deceitful. Some people, however, think that this term is harshly negative, that it represents _____ view of Machiavelli and his philosophy.
    - (A) a precarious
    - (B) an inclement
    - (C) a waning
    - (D) an autonomous
    - (E) a vulnerable

22. Today, any politician who is crafty or deceitful is _____. He or she is open to attack and may be voted out of office.
    - (A) latitudinal
    - (B) autonomous
    - (C) inclement
    - (D) vulnerable
    - (E) perseverant

23. It is still true that countries that want to maintain their _____ must be able to defend themselves, for independence is often won through strength.
    - (A) autonomy
    - (B) perseverance
    - (C) devastation
    - (D) inclemency
    - (E) vulnerability

24. It is sad that the strength of a nation is often judged by its ability to inflict punishment on its enemies and _____ vengeance on those who threaten it.
    - (A) besiege
    - (B) wane
    - (C) devastate
    - (D) persevere
    - (E) wreak

25. Now, just as in Machiavelli's time, those in power are _____ by people who want benefits, help, and influence. The constant onslaught of requests must be exhausting.
    - (A) devastated
    - (B) waned
    - (C) persevered
    - (D) besieged
    - (E) wreaked

26. All citizens deserve some _____—most people will not abuse their right to freedom. A government should never be _____ toward its people, for all citizens deserve fair, merciful treatment.
    - (A) devastation . . . vulnerable
    - (B) autonomy . . . vulnerable
    - (C) latitude . . . inclement
    - (D) inclemency . . . waning
    - (E) vulnerability . . . besieging

27. Machiavelli pointed out how _____ the positions of unstable city-states were and how easily they could be _____, or attacked, by much stronger neighbors.
    - (A) besieged . . . wreaked
    - (B) perseverant . . . devastated
    - (C) precarious . . . besieged
    - (D) autonomous . . . waned
    - (E) inclement . . . persevered

28. Today, even large, unified countries are _____; they are open not only to injury but also to full-scale _____.
    - (A) latitudinal . . . autonomy
    - (B) precarious . . . inclemency
    - (C) inclement . . . latitude
    - (D) autonomous . . . perseverance
    - (E) vulnerable . . . devastation

29. The persistence, or _____, of Machiavelli's theories shows that his philosophy is still appealing to those who fear that, without strong rulership, a country's position will be unstable and _____.
    - (A) devastation . . . vulnerable
    - (B) perseverance . . . precarious
    - (C) autonomy . . . latitudinal
    - (D) inclemency . . . autonomous
    - (E) precariousness . . . inclement

30. Someday aggression will _____, and after this decline, people will enjoy the _____ to live freely, without fear.
    - (A) wane . . . latitude
    - (B) persevere . . . inclemency
    - (C) wreak . . . devastation
    - (D) besiege . . . autonomy
    - (E) devastate . . . perseverance

MAKING NEW WORDS YOUR OWN

Lesson 12 — CONTEXT: Civilization

Pyramids: Ancient Wonders

The pyramids of ancient Egypt are truly wondrous. They are, in fact, one of the Seven Wonders of the World, awe-inspiring ancient structures made by human beings. Pyramids were royal burial tombs. True pyramids, those with four triangular sides that meet in a point at the top, were first built around 2600 B.C. during Egypt's Fourth Dynasty. The most famous pyramid—and one that still exists—is known as the Great Pyramid of Cheops. It originally towered 481.4 feet on a base that covered an area of approximately 13 acres.

In the following exercises, you will have the opportunity to expand your vocabulary by reading about the pyramids of ancient Egypt. Below are ten vocabulary words that will be used in these exercises.

appease	balmy	commence	facsimile	pretext
archaic	beguile	espionage	invincible	vigilant

EXERCISE 1 — *Mapping*

Directions. In the item below, a vocabulary word is provided and used in a sentence. Take a guess at the word's meaning and write it in the box labeled **Your Guess**. Then look the word up in your dictionary and write the definition in the box labeled **Definition**. In the **Other Forms** box, write as many other forms of the word, such as adjective and noun forms, as you can think of or find in your dictionary.

Then, following the same procedure, draw your own map for each of the nine remaining vocabulary words. Use a separate sheet of paper.

1.

appease → The whole class wanted more time to study and discuss Egypt's famous pyramids, especially the methods used in constructing them, but we didn't know if Mr. Sims would give in to our requests. To **appease** us, he agreed to hold a round-table discussion about pyramids.

Your Guess:

Other Forms:

Definition:

2.

archaic

"As you would expect, the construction methods were **archaic**," Mr. Sims said, "but though they seem outdated to us, they were effective."

3.

balmy

"Workers in the hot desert probably appreciated any **balmy** winds that blew in to make the temperature more pleasant," Alana noted.

4.

beguile

"I've read about tomb robbers," Nick said. "Do you think some robbers **beguiled** construction bosses by deceiving them about the real reasons they were working on the pyramids?"

5.

commence

"It's not likely," Mr. Sims said, "because, as far as we can tell, pyramids were built mainly by slave labor. I'm not sure robbers would undertake such hard work. Once they **commenced** work, they probably wouldn't be able to get out of it for months or even years."

6.

espionage

"Still," Whitney said, "there could have been some **espionage** going on. You know, some workers might have been spying and finding out secret plans about burial chambers—where the really valuable items were kept."

7.

facsimile

Mr. Sims laughed. "Would the workers have stolen plans, hired scribes to make **facsimile** plans, and then have given these duplicates to would-be tomb robbers? That would certainly be a lot of trouble to go to."

8.

invincible

"Some of those Egyptian pharaohs thought themselves **invincible**—that no one and nothing could conquer them," Greta said. "I'm surprised they ever thought they would die and would need these enormous tombs!"

9.

pretext

"The Egyptians believed that the pharaoh needed a magnificent place in which to spend the afterlife," Art explained. "But I've always suspected that building a burial tomb may have been merely some sort of **pretext** by a pharaoh. For example, the pharaoh may have said he needed a burial tomb, but he really wanted a spectacular monument to himself."

10.

vigilant

"It is true that pharaohs had to be **vigilant** concerning their place in history," Mr. Sims said. "But no matter how alert and wary a pharaoh was, his great works and even his name could be erased from the land by later rulers."

EXERCISE 2 *Context Clues*

Directions. Scan the definitions in Column A. Then think about how the boldface words are used in the sentences in Column B. To complete the exercise, match each definition in Column A with the correct vocabulary word from Column B. Write the letter of your choice on the line provided; then write the vocabulary word on the line preceding the definition.

COLUMN A	COLUMN B

____ **11.** word: _____
adj. mild and pleasant; soothing

____ **12.** word: _____
n. an exact reproduction or copy;
adj. duplicate; copied exactly

____ **13.** word: _____
adj. alert; watchful; wary

____ **14.** word: _____
v. to begin; to initiate; to start

____ **15.** word: _____
adj. no longer in general use; old-
fashioned; belonging to an earlier period;
ancient

____ **16.** word: _____
adj. not to be overcome; unconquerable

____ **17.** word: _____
v. to cheat or deceive; to mislead by
tricking or cheating

____ **18.** word: _____
v. to soothe or pacify; to satisfy, especially
by giving in to demands

____ **19.** word: _____
n. a false reason concealing a real one; an
excuse

____ **20.** word: _____
n. spying

(A) Mr. Sims showed us a miniature plastic **facsimile** of the Great Pyramid of Cheops. It was an excellent likeness.

(B) He **commenced** his explanation of the pyramid's three chambers, including its large underground chamber, but was interrupted and had to stop shortly after he began.

(C) "Didn't rooms within the pyramids contain valuables that the pharaohs hoped would **appease** hard-to-satisfy gods?" Alana asked.

(D) "Yes. Workers were especially **vigilant** while sealing off these rooms. They watched carefully to be sure no one saw them."

(E) "See," Whitney said, "I knew there was **espionage** going on, that some workers spied on others."

(F) "I wonder if any advisors **beguiled** pharaohs into thinking they could be trusted and then robbed the storerooms?" Nick asked.

(G) "I can see some sneaky advisor returning to a secret chamber on the **pretext** of checking valuables, but really planning to steal them," Whitney remarked.

(H) "It's kind of sad to think that pharaohs who were **invincible** in life and never defeated in battles might be robbed after death," Art said.

(I) "Huge wooden boats that look **archaic** to us but were modern to the Egyptians were buried with the pharaohs," Mr. Sims said.

(J) Alana still worried about the weather in Egypt. "Was it **balmy** inside the pyramids or was it unpleasant from trapped air?"

EXERCISE 3 *Sentence Completion*

Directions. For each of the following items, circle the letter of the choice that best completes the meaning of the sentence or sentences.

21. "Are you really this interested in pyra-mids, or is your interest just _____ to post-pone Friday's test?" Mr. Sims asked.
    (A) a facsimile
    (B) a pretext
    (C) an appeasement
    (D) an espionage
    (E) a commencement

22. "The rest of our discussion on pyramids will _____ at the beginning of class tomor-row and end on Thursday."
    (A) appease
    (B) beguile
    (C) besiege
    (D) commence
    (E) condescend

23. "I certainly want to _____ your thirst for knowledge about pyramids. By the time we finish, I think you'll be satisfied. By the way, the word *pyramid* probably is Greek for 'wheaten cake.'"
    (A) appease
    (B) besiege
    (C) commence
    (D) condescend
    (E) beguile

24. "I'll show you some pictures of _____ tools that may have been used by ancient pyra-mid builders. They would have liked our modern tools—their work would have gone faster with advanced equipment."
    (A) balmy
    (B) vigilant
    (C) facsimile
    (D) archaic
    (E) invincible

25. "Alana, I want you to draw us a picture of pyramid workers enjoying a mild, pleas-ant, _____ day in the desert."
    (A) vigilant
    (B) invincible
    (C) balmy
    (D) facsimile
    (E) archaic

26. "Whitney, write a story about Egyptian _____. Invent a clever _____ that your spy uses to disguise the fact that he is really doing undercover work."
    (A) pretext . . . espionage
    (B) vigilance . . . facsimile
    (C) facsimile . . . pretext
    (D) appeasement . . . vigilance
    (E) espionage . . . pretext

27. "Nick, develop a skit in which a deceitful architect successfully _____ a pharaoh about pyramid plans. The architect can re-veal how he _____, or began, his scheme."
    (A) commences . . . beguiled
    (B) appeases . . . beguiled
    (C) beguiles . . . commenced
    (D) commences . . . appeased
    (E) beguiles . . . appeased

28. "Greta, you could satisfy course require-ments and _____ demands for more visuals by making some kind of _____ of a pyra-mid. Be sure your copy is realistic."
    (A) commence . . . espionage
    (B) appease . . . facsimile
    (C) ravage . . . pretext
    (D) beguile . . . facsimile
    (E) commence . . . beguilement

29. "Art, find out why the _____ pharaohs could not be overcome and what ancient or _____ weapons they used."
    (A) vigilant . . . balmy
    (B) balmy . . . facsimile
    (C) archaic . . . balmy
    (D) invincible . . . archaic
    (E) facsimile . . . appeasing

30. "The rest of the class can _____ other projects, but get approval before begin-ning. Some could report on why archae-ologists were _____, or wary, when first exploring the pyramids."
    (A) commence . . . vigilant
    (B) beguile . . . facsimile
    (C) appease . . . balmy
    (D) beguile . . . invincible
    (E) appease . . . archaic

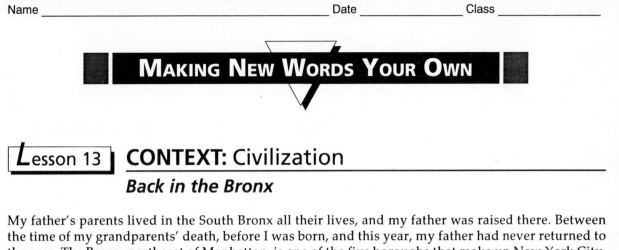

MAKING NEW WORDS YOUR OWN

Lesson 13 **CONTEXT:** Civilization

Back in the Bronx

My father's parents lived in the South Bronx all their lives, and my father was raised there. Between the time of my grandparents' death, before I was born, and this year, my father had never returned to the area. The Bronx, northeast of Manhattan, is one of the five boroughs that make up New York City. In recent years it has developed a reputation as a war zone of poverty and violence, but my father believed the neighborhood where he lived would still be there. It turned out he was right.

In the following exercises, you will have the opportunity to expand your vocabulary by reading about a visit to the South Bronx. Below are ten vocabulary words that will be used in these exercises.

coffer	hieroglyphic	innovation	retainer	subsidize
edifice	inaccessible	juncture	rivulet	tawny

EXERCISE 1 *Mapping*

Directions. In the item below, a vocabulary word is provided and used in a sentence. Take a guess at the word's meaning and write it in the box labeled **Your Guess**. Then look the word up in your dictionary and write the definition in the box labeled **Definition**. In the **Other Forms** box, write as many other forms of the word, such as adjective and noun forms, as you can think of or find in your dictionary.

Then, following the same procedure, draw your own map for each of the nine remaining vocabulary words. Use a separate sheet of paper.

1.

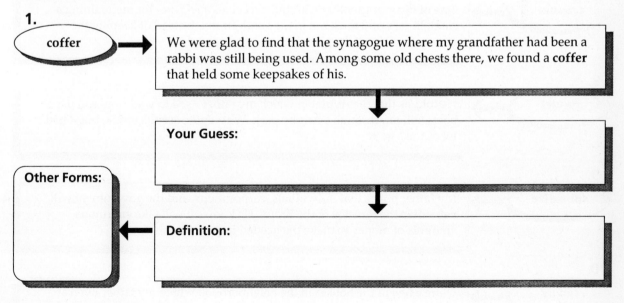

We were glad to find that the synagogue where my grandfather had been a rabbi was still being used. Among some old chests there, we found a **coffer** that held some keepsakes of his.

Your Guess:

Other Forms:

Definition:

2.

edifice → The synagogue had been a nice building, but I don't think it was ever an elaborate **edifice**. Now it is quite run down, as are many other buildings in the area.

3.

hieroglyphic → Over the door, words are carved into the stone. Some people might think they are **hieroglyphics,** or picture writing, but they aren't—they're words written in Hebrew.

4.

inaccessible → The Bronx was somewhat **inaccessible** until railroad lines were built in the middle and late 1800s to connect the small Bronx villages with one another and with Manhattan.

5.

innovation → An **innovation** in transportation, the subway eventually extended to the Bronx. This new form of travel encouraged developers in the early 1900s to build apartment buildings in the Bronx.

6.

juncture → At this **juncture,** or point of time, thousands of Europeans were immigrating to New York, primarily to the Lower East Side of Manhattan. As that area became overcrowded, many people moved instead to the rapidly developing Bronx.

7.

retainer → One of my grandmother's brothers receives a **retainer** for maintaining a small library and museum in the South Bronx. Instead of keeping the money for himself, he gives it to homeless people.

8.

rivulet → He told us that the **rivulet** in which my father used to wade and sail paper boats still ran through a nearby park. We went to see the brook, but it had a lot of trash in it.

9.

subsidize → My father hopes that individuals, corporations, and the government will **subsidize** the renewal of the Bronx. He knows it will take enormous amounts of money to make the needed improvements.

10.

tawny → Quite a few of the houses in the neighborhood where my father lived are still there and are well kept. The white houses contrast with the nearby **tawny**-colored apartments, whose tan brickwork is cracked and loose.

EXERCISE 2 *Context Clues* 👉

Directions. Scan the definitions in Column A. Then think about how the boldface words are used in the sentences in Column B. To complete the exercise, match each definition in Column A with the correct vocabulary word from Column B. Write the letter of your choice on the line provided; then write the vocabulary word on the line preceding the definition.

COLUMN A

_____ **11.** word: _____

n. a point where things are joined; a crossing; a point in time; a crisis point

_____ **12.** word: _____

adj. brownish-yellow; tan

_____ **13.** word: _____

n. a picture or symbol representing a word, syllable, or sound, used by the ancient Egyptians and others, instead of alphabetical letters; a method of writing using these pictures or symbols; picture writing; *adj.* pertaining to a system of writing that uses pictures or symbols

_____ **14.** word: _____

v. to aid or assist with a grant of money; to support; to promote

_____ **15.** word: _____

adj. not easily reached or approached; out of the way

_____ **16.** word: _____

n. a box or chest, especially one used to hold money or other valuables

_____ **17.** word: _____

n. a small stream; a brook

_____ **18.** word: _____

n. a building or structure, especially an imposing or elaborate one

_____ **19.** word: _____

n. a fee paid in advance for services; a servant; an attendant

_____ **20.** word: _____

n. a new way to do something; something new

COLUMN B

(A) In 1959, tolls collected from the interstate highway system **subsidized** the building of the Cross Bronx Expressway, which cut through many established neighborhoods.

(B) This **innovation** destroyed huge areas of housing and separated neighborhoods that had once been close knit.

(C) The expressway made it easier to leave and to enter the Bronx, but it separated other areas, making them **inaccessible** to one another.

(D) The freeway also did away with **junctures** of streets where bakeries, grocery stores, delicatessens, and all sorts of other businesses had come together and thrived.

(E) Once the area began to decline, it deteriorated rapidly. Graffiti, which my father says is a modern form of **hieroglyphics**, or picture writing, was defiantly scrawled on every surface.

(F) What began as a mere **rivulet** became a raging river of destruction; houses and apartments were torn down or burned.

(G) Landlords were given **retainers** by public agencies to accept tenants on welfare. But, because the landlords were paid whether or not they took care of their buildings, many let the housing decay.

(H) Many **edifices** that had given the area a look of elegance and prosperity were now abandoned, run-down buildings.

(I) But just looking at the brownish-yellow rubble, I could tell that the buildings had once been attractive. I wanted to be able to put the **tawny** bricks back together and rebuild the stores and churches and schools.

(J) I told my great-uncle how I felt. He took some old pictures from a **coffer**—the chest contained hundreds of photos—and showed me how some of his favorite buildings had looked years ago.

EXERCISE 3 *Sentence Completion* 🖎

Directions. For each of the following items, circle the letter of the choice that best completes the meaning of the sentence or sentences.

21. We went to the Bronx Zoo, a wonderful place with many animals, including gray elephants, brightly colored birds, and _____ lions.
    - (A) hieroglyphic
    - (B) tawny
    - (C) inaccessible
    - (D) subsidized
    - (E) atrocious

22. We also went to the New York Botanical Gardens. The Bronx River, which is much more than a mere _____, is an outstanding feature of the site.
    - (A) a retainer
    - (B) an innovation
    - (C) an edifice
    - (D) a rivulet
    - (E) a coffer

23. An elegant Bronx _____ that can be toured is the Van Courtland House, built in 1748.
    - (A) juncture
    - (B) rivulet
    - (C) innovation
    - (D) coffer
    - (E) edifice

24. You can imagine the mansion occupied by a lively family and their _____ who helped with the work.
    - (A) edifices
    - (B) retainers
    - (C) subsidies
    - (D) hieroglyphs
    - (E) coffers

25. Then we went to Poe Cottage, where Edgar Allan Poe lived during the last three years of his life. I had hoped it would have heavy wooden _____ filled with Poe's handwritten manuscripts. What treasure chests those would be!
    - (A) rivulets
    - (B) edifices
    - (C) coffers
    - (D) hieroglyphics
    - (E) retainers

26. At this point, or _____, we stopped for a rest at an old cafe.
    - (A) retainer
    - (B) edifice
    - (C) juncture
    - (D) innovation
    - (E) rivulet

27. Another _____ that interested us was the Bartow-Pell Mansion, built on land that was purchased from the Siwanoy Indians in 1654. This region must have been nearly _____ at that time because of dense woods.
    - (A) coffer . . . hieroglyphic
    - (B) juncture . . . tawny
    - (C) innovation . . . tawny
    - (D) edifice . . . inaccessible
    - (E) rivulet . . . inaccessible

28. I probably could read _____ more easily than I could find my way around the Bronx. I was confused by the many twists and turns and _____ of the streets.
    - (A) hieroglyphics . . . junctures
    - (B) coffers . . . innovations
    - (C) edifices . . . retainers
    - (D) rivulets . . . hieroglyphics
    - (E) innovations . . . coffers

29. At first, the Bronx seemed remote, but now it doesn't seem at all _____. In fact, when I grow up, I'd like to raise money to _____ some renewal project there.
    - (A) hieroglyphic . . . evolve
    - (B) tawny . . . loathe
    - (C) inaccessible . . . subsidize
    - (D) innovative . . . assert
    - (E) tawny . . . lament

30. Visiting the magnificent old _____ was a great experience, topped only by attending a game at Yankee Stadium. Compared to the old buildings, Yankee Stadium seemed like a complete _____, a new kind of structure never seen before.
    - (A) rivulets . . . hieroglyphic
    - (B) edifices . . . innovation
    - (C) coffers . . . edifice
    - (D) retainers . . . juncture
    - (E) innovations . . . rivulet

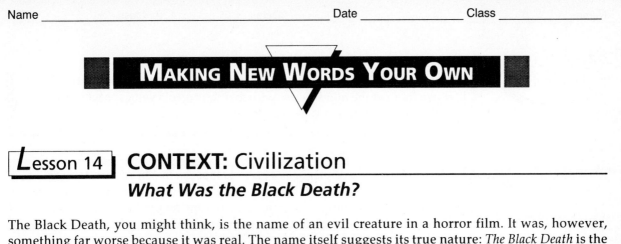

MAKING NEW WORDS YOUR OWN

Lesson 14 | CONTEXT: Civilization
What Was the Black Death?

The Black Death, you might think, is the name of an evil creature in a horror film. It was, however, something far worse because it was real. The name itself suggests its true nature: *The Black Death* is the term given to the destructive plague that raged across Asia, the Middle East, and Europe during the fourteenth century. This disease killed millions—in Europe alone, as much as a third of the population may have fallen to the contagious, deadly illness.

In the following exercises, you will have the opportunity to expand your vocabulary by reading about the Black Death. Below are ten vocabulary words that will be used in these exercises.

apex	canine	influx	obliterate	perceive
bourgeois	defunct	meager	ossify	ravage

EXERCISE 1 | *Mapping*

Directions. In the item below, a vocabulary word is provided and used in a sentence. Take a guess at the word's meaning and write it in the box labeled **Your Guess**. Then look the word up in your dictionary and write the definition in the box labeled **Definition**. In the **Other Forms** box, write as many other forms of the word, such as adjective and noun forms, as you can think of or find in your dictionary.

Then, following the same procedure, draw your own map for each of the nine remaining vocabulary words. Use a separate sheet of paper.

1.

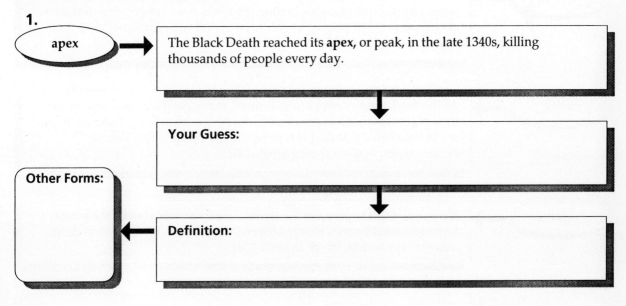

The Black Death reached its **apex,** or peak, in the late 1340s, killing thousands of people every day.

Your Guess:

Other Forms:

Definition:

2.

bourgeois →

The Black Death paid no attention to a person's class or values. It struck down those of the middle class with their **bourgeois** values as well as those of the lower and upper classes of society.

3.

canine →

The cause of bubonic plague is a bacteria that can live in a flea's stomach. The plague was spread by fleas, but apparently not the fleas on **canines**. As far as can be determined, these fleas' hosts were rats, not dogs.

4.

defunct →

In hundreds of European villages, daily affairs ground to a halt because of the Black Death. The villages became **defunct** as their populations died.

5.

influx →

With the trade between the ports of Europe, Asia, and the Middle East came the **influx** of this disease. When the ships flowed into port, infected rats came, too.

6.

meager →

The masses had **meager** resources and equally scanty medical knowledge to combat the plague. In Europe, many people were already physically weak because of recent famines.

7.

obliterate →

The plague originated in the Gobi Desert of Mongolia and was originally spread by nomadic peoples. During the 1300s, it was impossible to **obliterate** the plague. The plague, unable to be wiped out, completely destroyed huge populations in Asia and the Middle East.

8.

ossify →

As the Black Death swept across Europe, many people became **ossified** in their responses to the destruction. Some people became rigid and unchanging in their belief that God was justly punishing humanity; others became numb to the suffering around them.

9.

perceive →

It is not difficult to **perceive** the terrible legacy of death left by the plague. From historical records we can observe, for example, one thousand deaths a day in Alexandria, Egypt, in early 1348.

10.

ravage →

The effect of the Black Death was to **ravage** the populations of Europe, Asia, and the Middle East. The damage affected people of all social classes.

EXERCISE 2 *Context Clues* ✍

Directions. Scan the definitions in Column A. Then think about how the boldface words are used in the sentences in Column B. To complete the exercise, match each definition in Column A with the correct vocabulary word from Column B. Write the letter of your choice on the line provided; then write the vocabulary word on the line preceding the definition.

COLUMN A	COLUMN B

_____ **11.** word: _____
n. any animal belonging to the dog family; *adj.* of or like a dog

_____ **12.** word: _____
v. to change into bone; to harden like bone; to become rigid, hardhearted, or opposed to change

_____ **13.** word: _____
adj. noticeably lacking in quantity, quality, or extent; scanty; lean; thin

_____ **14.** word: _____
v. to destroy or devastate; *n.* the act of devastating; great damage

_____ **15.** word: _____
n. the highest point of something; vertex; the culmination or point of climax

_____ **16.** word: _____
adj. no longer in existence or functioning; dead

_____ **17.** word: _____
v. to become aware of or to understand by means of the senses; to detect; to observe; to grasp the meaning of

_____ **18.** word: _____
adj. of or like the middle class—often referring to a focus upon material things and respectability; *n.* a middle-class person; the middle class

_____ **19.** word: _____
n. a flowing in, as of people or things

_____ **20.** word: _____
v. to destroy completely; to wipe out; to erase

(A) It is the year 1348, and I, Jean Chapelle, **perceive** a terrible thing happening—the plague is killing people all around me. All my senses bring evidence of the destruction.

(B) I walk with my **canine**—he is still a puppy— through the narrow streets of our neighborhood. The dog barks at the many rats.

(C) Mr. Delville, who has lost his wife and brother, wanders the streets with an expressionless face. He has not expressed any sadness or grief over the deaths; I believe that he is in such shock that his feelings have **ossified,** become as rigid and hardened as bone.

(D) My neighbor was a singer and had reached great heights. At the **apex** of her career, she was known all over France.

(E) Now she is not permitted visitors, and the Black Death is destroying her beautiful voice as it **ravages** her body.

(F) This plague has **obliterated** the world I knew as a child; it has erased the normal, happy working scenes of the neighborhood.

(G) Even the bakery, once the heart of our neighborhood, is **defunct,** for last month the baker and his wife died of the plague.

(H) The baker was such a jolly, hard-working man. He was proud of his skills and his **bourgeois,** or middle-class, background.

(I) The quality of my daily life has lessened greatly. It has become **meager** because it lacks such people as the baker and his wife.

(J) At night I dream that the plague has ended and that there is an **influx** of new residents who restore our part of Paris, returning it to its former state. But I would give anything to have those I knew and loved return to life.

EXERCISE 3 *Sentence Completion* ✍

Directions. For each of the following items, circle the letter of the choice that best completes the meaning of the sentence or sentences.

21. It is, perhaps, difficult for us to _____ the horrors of the Black Death and to understand its extensive effects.
    (A) obliterate
    (B) ossify
    (C) commence
    (D) ravage
    (E) perceive

22. Most of us even have trouble imagining the carriers, the fleas on rats, because we usually think of fleas on _____ and felines.
    (A) apexes
    (B) influxes
    (C) canines
    (D) ravages
    (E) perceptions

23. We need an extensive knowledge of geography to trace the plague's route from Asia across Europe. A _____ knowledge will not be sufficient.
    (A) meager
    (B) bourgeois
    (C) defunct
    (D) perceivable
    (E) canine

24. Can you picture the _____ of traders and merchants who poured into cities and helped spread the plague?
    (A) apex
    (B) influx
    (C) obliteration
    (D) canine
    (E) ravage

25. Perhaps you can get an idea of the _____ of the plague if you know that it damaged human-population figures far more than any war ever has.
    (A) bourgeois
    (B) canines
    (C) influxes
    (D) ravages
    (E) apexes

26. At its height, its _____, the plague _____ a large portion of the population of India every day, wiping out entire villages.
    (A) ravage . . . obliterated
    (B) influx . . . perceived
    (C) apex . . . obliterated
    (D) canine . . . ravaged
    (E) apex . . . perceived

27. The plague had been _____ in Europe since A.D. 744. But it broke out again in 1347 and once again started _____ entire cities.
    (A) defunct . . . obliterating
    (B) bourgeois . . . ossifying
    (C) meager . . . perceiving
    (D) canine . . . obliterating
    (E) perceived . . . ossifying

28. It must have been especially difficult for the lower class and even the _____ to cope with the _____, the widespread destruction, caused by the plague. But even the upper classes had few resources to cope with the disease.
    (A) canine . . . bourgeois
    (B) apex . . . canines
    (C) ravage . . . influxes
    (D) influx . . . apexes
    (E) bourgeois . . . ravages

29. Some observant people _____ that fewer people had the plague in the country than in towns. As a result, rural areas experienced _____ of city people.
    (A) ravaged . . . an apex
    (B) perceived . . . an influx
    (C) ossified . . . a canine
    (D) ravaged . . . an influx
    (E) obliterated . . . a bourgeois

30. I would have had _____ abilities—practically none at all, in fact—to cope with such a tragedy. My defense is to _____ and hide behind a rigid exterior.
    (A) defunct . . . ravage
    (B) meager . . . obliterate
    (C) canine . . . perceive
    (D) meager . . . ossify
    (E) bourgeois . . . ravage

MAKING NEW WORDS YOUR OWN

Lesson 15 CONTEXT: Civilization
Two Russian Revolutions

My mother is a professor of Russian history at a large university. All my life I've heard about Russian politics, culture, and current events. The information has come in handy for papers I've written for several classes. Now my history teacher has asked me to write a comparison of two Russian revolutions: the one in 1917 that established communism in the country and the more peaceful one that occurred recently and led to the breakup of the Soviet Union. Of course, I immediately went to my mother for advice.

In the following exercises, you will have the opportunity to expand your vocabulary by reading about two Russian revolutions. Below are ten vocabulary words that will be used in these exercises.

buffet	ensue	facilitate	lapse	steppe
delectable	expedient	hors d'oeuvre	palatable	succulent

EXERCISE 1   Mapping

Directions. In the item below, a vocabulary word is provided and used in a sentence. Take a guess at the word's meaning and write it in the box labeled **Your Guess**. Then look the word up in your dictionary and write the definition in the box labeled **Definition**. In the **Other Forms** box, write as many other forms of the word, such as adjective and noun forms, as you can think of or find in your dictionary.

Then, following the same procedure, draw your own map for each of the nine remaining vocabulary words. Use a separate sheet of paper.

1.

(buffet) →
> My mother went to the **buffet** in our dining room where, instead of dishes and napkins in the drawers and cupboards, she keeps photographs and keepsakes from Russia. She showed me pictures of czars (emperors) and serfs (peasants) and told me how difficult life was for the serfs during the czars' tyrannical rule.

Your Guess:

Other Forms:

Definition:

2.

delectable →

My mother likes children and considers her picture of the last czar's family to be a **delectable** treasure. I, too, think it is a delightful photograph.

3.

ensue →

When Nicholas II and his wife, Alexandra, had their picture taken with their family, they had no idea of the sad events that would **ensue**. Soon after the picture was taken, the Communists seized power and murdered the czar and his family.

4.

expedient →

Since the purpose of the revolution in 1917 was to replace the autocratic government with a communist one, the Bolsheviks did not think it was **expedient** to let any of the czar's family survive. It was more to the Communists' advantage to kill the royal family.

5.

facilitate →

In order to **facilitate** the changes in the country, the Communists killed people who opposed them. My mother says that, although these horrible killings may have made the changes easier, they certainly made life difficult.

6.

hors d'oeuvre →

A few days later a dinner was given for a visiting professor from Russia, and my mother invited me to accompany her. **Hors d'oeuvres** were served before the meal, and I ate several of these appetizers.

7.

lapse →

After I was introduced to the professor, I hoped he didn't notice the **lapse** in my manners. I forgot to offer to shake hands.

8.

palatable →

Still eating the **palatable** food (the appetizers were delicious), I asked the professor whether he felt that the recent changes in Russia would be greater than those caused by the revolution of 1917.

9.

steppe →

The professor said he thought that recent changes were affecting people in the cities, but he didn't know if they would make a difference in rural areas, such as the vast, nearly treeless plains called **steppes**.

10.

succulent →

A stranger who had overheard my question pointed to a **succulent** growing in a pot in the corner of the room and said, "Just as the leaves of this plant absorb water and store it in order to grow, so will the people of Russia absorb the ideas of capitalism and freedom in order to expand their lives."

EXERCISE 2　Context Clues ✍

Directions. Scan the definitions in Column A. Then think about how the boldface words are used in the sentences in Column B. To complete the exercise, match each definition in Column A with the correct vocabulary word from Column B. Write the letter of your choice on the line provided; then write the vocabulary word on the line preceding the definition.

COLUMN A	COLUMN B

_____ **11.** word: _____

v. to come next, or follow; to happen as a consequence

_____ **12.** word: _____

adj. juicy; not dry or dull; having fleshy plant tissue that conserves moisture; *n.* a plant that has such tissues

_____ **13.** word: _____

v. to make easier or more convenient; to aid or assist in

_____ **14.** word: _____

n. a vast, almost treeless plain in southeastern Europe or Asia

_____ **15.** word: _____

n. a food served as an appetizer, either before a meal or with drinks

_____ **16.** word: _____

adj. suitable; advantageous; based on self-interest

_____ **17.** word: _____

adj. acceptable to the mind; fit to be eaten; pleasant tasting; pleasing

_____ **18.** word: _____

n. a piece of dining room furniture with cupboards and drawers; a meal set out so that people may serve themselves

_____ **19.** word: _____

v. to fall from a higher level (as of manners) to a lower; to pass gradually; to come to an end; *n.* a slight, temporary error or slip; a fall from a better to a worse condition

_____ **20.** word: _____

adj. pleasing; delightful; delicious

(A) The professor frowned at the stranger's remark and chose another **hors d'oeuvre** from the tray of appetizers.

(B) He then said that he did not know what would **ensue** because too many changes were being attempted at once. He said it would be impossible to predict what would follow.

(C) As we served ourselves from the **buffet**, choosing from among the variety of foods set out for us, the professor excused himself and moved on to talk to someone else.

(D) I was pleased to find that the food was **delectable**. As I sampled the delicious dishes, I listened in on nearby conversations.

(E) One woman said that she thinks other democracies, such as the United States, should do what they can to **facilitate** the changes taking place in Russia. Money and technology would make the changes go more smoothly and easily.

(F) One man said he was ashamed to be eating such an array of **succulent** foods when many people in Russia had nothing more tasty and exciting to eat than dry bread.

(G) An anthropologist said he had visited the **steppes** of Russia, and the people there had a unique culture that was well suited to their vast and virtually treeless surroundings.

(H) The anthropologist said it was unlikely that this culture would **lapse** or even change very much as a result of the recent political upheavals because it had survived other changes in the past.

(I) The dean of the history department remarked that the Russians would find recent changes more **palatable**, or agreeable, if they could experience some immediate benefits.

(J) I found it **expedient** to listen and not talk; it allowed me to take advantage of the fact that people around me knew much more about the situation than I did.

EXERCISE 3 *Sentence Completion* ☞

Directions. For each of the following items, circle the letter of the choice that best completes the meaning of the sentence or sentences.

21. The _____ food was no longer tempting me. Although it was delicious, I think I had overeaten.
    (A) expedient
    (B) lapsable
    (C) ensuing
    (D) facilitative
    (E) delectable

22. Not one _____ was in sight. The appetizers had been very popular, and the guests had eaten every one.
    (A) hors d'oeuvre
    (B) buffet
    (C) succulent
    (D) delectability
    (E) steppe

23. Workers came to remove the food and tables that had been set up for the _____, and the guests, no longer able to serve themselves, stood around the room visiting.
    (A) succulent
    (B) steppe
    (C) buffet
    (D) lapse
    (E) juncture

24. Two men started loudly discussing the breakup of the Soviet Union. It sounded as if an argument might _____ at any moment.
    (A) lapse
    (B) ensue
    (C) facilitate
    (D) succumb
    (E) repress

25. Then one of the men gestured emphatically and accidentally knocked over the large _____ in the corner. Both men laughed as they stood the plant upright again.
    (A) steppe
    (B) buffet
    (C) hors d'oeuvre
    (D) electorate
    (E) succulent

26. My mother says that when she goes to Russia again, she will take me everywhere, from the cities of Moscow to the desolate and vast _____. Who knows what will _____ from that? I may major in Russian history.
    (A) steppes . . . ensue
    (B) buffet . . . facilitate
    (C) succulent . . . lapse
    (D) hors d'oeuvre . . . ensue
    (E) buffet . . . lapse

27. It would _____ my understanding of Russia to learn the language. It would be especially helpful if I plan to spend time in rural areas such as the _____, far away from the cities where many people speak English.
    (A) ensue . . . buffet
    (B) lapse . . . steppe
    (C) ensue . . . hors d'oeuvre
    (D) facilitate . . . steppes
    (E) lapse . . . succulent

28. Everyone had a different explanation for the _____ of communism; there seemed to be no one reason for its decline or for the _____ breakup of the country.
    (A) steppe . . . facilitating
    (B) buffet . . . ensuing
    (C) lapse . . . ensuing
    (D) facilitator . . . lapsing
    (E) succulent . . . facilitating

29. Many of the arguments were _____. The most appealing ideas will be very helpful, _____ the writing of my paper.
    (A) succulent . . . ensuing
    (B) palatable . . . facilitating
    (C) expedient . . . lapsing
    (D) delectable . . . ensuing
    (E) palatable . . . lapsing

30. My mother and I left the party at a suitable, _____ moment. I hoped I would have no memory _____; I would hate to lose the information I had learned.
    (A) succulent . . . buffets
    (B) delectable . . . hors d'oeuvres
    (C) palatable . . . steppes
    (D) expedient . . . lapses
    (E) delectable . . . expediencies

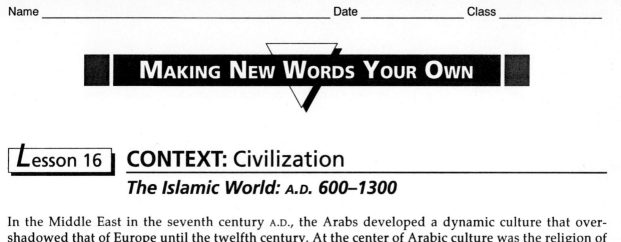

MAKING NEW WORDS YOUR OWN

Lesson 16 **CONTEXT:** Civilization

The Islamic World: A.D. 600–1300

In the Middle East in the seventh century A.D., the Arabs developed a dynamic culture that over-shadowed that of Europe until the twelfth century. At the center of Arabic culture was the religion of Islam. The founder of this religion was Mohammed (570–632), a spiritual, military, and political leader. He began uniting his followers, known as Muslims, under one faith. Mohammed's successors expanded the empire across the Middle East to Gibraltar in the west, India in the east, and across Africa.

In the following exercises, you will have the opportunity to expand your vocabulary by reading about Mohammed and the Islamic world from A.D. 600–1300. Below are ten vocabulary words that will be used in these exercises.

abound	astute	erratic	quantitative	requisite
aptitude	conducive	pastoral	recur	zenith

EXERCISE 1 *Mapping*

Directions. In the item below, a vocabulary word is provided and used in a sentence. Take a guess at the word's meaning and write it in the box labeled **Your Guess**. Then look the word up in your dictionary and write the definition in the box labeled **Definition**. In the **Other Forms** box, write as many other forms of the word, such as adjective and noun forms, as you can think of or find in your dictionary.

Then, following the same procedure, draw your own map for each of the nine remaining vocabulary words. Use a separate sheet of paper.

1.

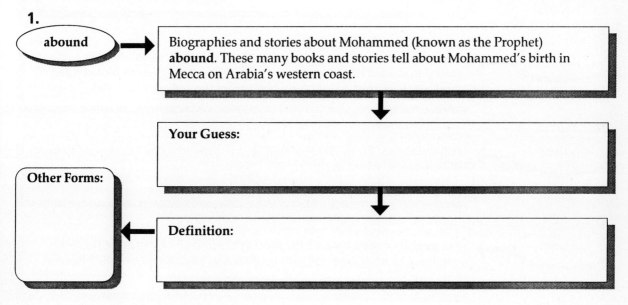

abound → Biographies and stories about Mohammed (known as the Prophet) **abound**. These many books and stories tell about Mohammed's birth in Mecca on Arabia's western coast.

Your Guess:

Other Forms:

Definition:

2.
aptitude → Although Mohammed apparently did not have a formal education, he seems to have had a good **aptitude** for business because he learned the merchant trade.

3.
astute → It is entirely possible that Mohammed was an **astute**, or shrewd, merchant, but at about the age of forty, he gave up his career as a merchant and became a religious hermit.

4.
conducive → Mohammed, who was familiar with the teachings of Judaism and Christianity, found solitude to be **conducive** to understanding proper faith. He also found meditation to be helpful.

5.
erratic → The responses to Mohammed's teachings were at first **erratic**. Some people responded favorably, while others resisted his claim that "there is no God but Allah, and Mohammed is his Prophet."

6.
pastoral → Mohammed is not thought of as a **pastoral** preacher who went into the country to convert people. He is identified with the cities of Mecca and Medina.

7.
quantitative → His success could be measured not only in **quantitative** ways—the number of followers of Islam—but also in a qualitative way: the improvement in people's lives.

8.
recur → Ramadan **recurs** every year as the ninth month of the Muslim lunar calendar. Ramadan is remembered as the time during which Mohammed received the Koran, Islam's holy book, from the archangel Gabriel.

9.
requisite → Following the "Five Pillars of Faith" is a **requisite** part of Muslim religious duties. The required duties include giving to the poor.

10.
zenith → The **zenith** of any Muslim's life is a trip to Mecca. The trip is the highest point of a Muslim's earthly path because Mecca is considered the Muslims' holy city.

EXERCISE 2 *Context Clues* ✍

Directions. Scan the definitions in Column A. Then think about how the boldface words are used in the sentences in Column B. To complete the exercise, match each definition in Column A with the correct vocabulary word from Column B. Write the letter of your choice on the line provided; then write the vocabulary word on the line preceding the definition.

<table>
<tr><td>

COLUMN A

_____ **11.** word: _____
adj. capable of being measured or expressed as a numerical amount

_____ **12.** word: _____
n. the highest point of any course or path; peak; the point in the sky directly above an observer

_____ **13.** word: _____
adj. showing keen judgment; shrewd; crafty

_____ **14.** word: _____
v. to return in thought or speech; to happen or appear again; to occur at intervals

_____ **15.** word: _____
adj. favorable; helpful; tending to promote as a result

_____ **16.** word: _____
adj. irregular; not steady; uncertain

_____ **17.** word: _____
v. to teem; to exist in large numbers; to have plenty

_____ **18.** word: _____
adj. relating to a simple country way of life; relating to shepherds; rural

_____ **19.** word: _____
n. a necessity; a requirement;
adj. absolutely necessary; required by circumstances

_____ **20.** word: _____
n. a talent; a natural ability; the ability to learn

</td><td>

COLUMN B

(A) The **zenith** of Muslim civilization occurred between the ninth and tenth centuries A.D.; achievements during this peak period were impressive and long-lasting.

(B) This fairly peaceful period was **conducive** to advances in commerce and agriculture and was also favorable to advances in education and medicine.

(C) Examples of the Islamic style in architecture **abound** throughout the world. Among the many examples is the Taj Mahal in India.

(D) It would be difficult to give a **quantitative** account of the Arabic words in our vocabulary today. They number in the thousands.

(E) The spellings of such Arabic words as *bazaar* and *traffic* may have been **erratic** over the centuries, but they are more stable now.

(F) Reading Muslim poetry is a **requisite** in some literature classes; reading stories from the *Arabian Nights* is sometimes a requirement, too.

(G) **Astute** Muslims helped preserve the writings of the ancient Greeks. Modern scholars are grateful for the Muslims' keen judgment.

(H) Many Muslims had **aptitudes** for music, and their talents were supported by the rulers.

(I) If you study the architecture built during the seventh through twelfth centuries in the Middle East and Europe, you will find that certain similarities **recur,** such as round domes and elaborate tiles. These features appear again and again.

(J) Córdova, the Muslim capital of Spain, was not a **pastoral** setting by any means; it was the second largest city in Europe.

</td></tr>
</table>

EXERCISE 3 *Sentence Completion* ✍

Directions. For each of the following items, circle the letter of the choice that best completes the meaning of the sentence or sentences.

21. I imagine myself in the place that I've been reading about. This lesson has been _____ to—that is, has helped promote—an imaginary trip to the ancient Islamic world.

(A) erratic
(B) pastoral
(C) quantitative
(D) astute
(E) conducive

22. How do I get there? I imagine myself looking up at the _____, the point in the sky directly above me, and there I am.

(A) aptitude
(B) latitude
(C) zenith
(D) influx
(E) requisite

23. I find myself first on the edge of a _____ village where I'm surrounded by sheep.

(A) pastoral
(B) quantitative
(C) requisite
(D) astute
(E) conducive

24. Fortunately, I meet a man with _____ for giving directions, as I have no talent along those lines, and he tells me how to reach Medina.

(A) a zenith
(B) a facsimile
(C) a requisite
(D) an aptitude
(E) an axiom

25. Mohammed has just finished speaking when I arrive, but I hope the opportunity to hear him will _____. I'd like another chance.

(A) wane
(B) recur
(C) lapse
(D) abound
(E) ossify

26. People who are anxious to spread the Muslim faith _____; they are everywhere. The time seems _____, or favorable, to spreading the faith to many lands.

(A) abound . . . astute
(B) recur . . . erratic
(C) abound . . . conducive
(D) commence . . . conducive
(E) recur . . . pastoral

27. You could say that my trip schedule is _____ because I'm not certain where I will be next. It may be _____ field where a battle is taking place.

(A) astute . . . a conducive
(B) requisite . . . a quantitative
(C) pastoral . . . an erratic
(D) conducive . . . an astute
(E) erratic . . . a pastoral

28. Now I'm in Córdova, where the number of beautiful buildings is so great that they cannot be _____ estimated. This city must reflect the _____, the peak, of Muslim architecture.

(A) pastorally . . . zenith
(B) erratically . . . aptitude
(C) quantitatively . . . zenith
(D) erratically . . . requisite
(E) astutely . . . aptitude

29. I'm making a _____ trip to a mosque, a necessity while here. Mosques certainly _____ in this city; I've seen dozens.

(A) requisite . . . abound
(B) astute . . . recur
(C) pastoral . . . abound
(D) conducive . . . perceive
(E) erratic . . . beguile

30. An observer who is _____, or keen, would notice on this trip how a sense of excitement and change _____. It can be felt everywhere, all the time.

(A) pastoral . . . abounds
(B) conducive . . . recurs
(C) requisite . . . ravages
(D) astute . . . abounds
(E) erratic . . . recurs

MAKING NEW WORDS YOUR OWN

Lesson 17 | CONTEXT: Civilization

Before Aspirin: Medicine in the Middle Ages

The other day I read something about the Black Death in the Middle Ages and wondered why so many people had died. Weren't there medicines in those days? And what were the doctors doing while people died by the thousands? After doing some research, I found these answers: not many and not much. I'm glad I wasn't around then, when medicine was not scientific. There were only six medical schools in Europe in the fourteenth century, and they taught medical procedures that were rather scary—and mostly ineffective.

In the following exercises, you will have the opportunity to expand your vocabulary by reading about medical practices in the Middle Ages. Below are ten vocabulary words that will be used in these exercises.

annihilate	decimate	diversion	flagrant	purge
concession	disperse	evade	insolence	sadistic

EXERCISE 1   Mapping

Directions. In the item below, a vocabulary word is provided and used in a sentence. Take a guess at the word's meaning and write it in the box labeled **Your Guess**. Then look the word up in your dictionary and write the definition in the box labeled **Definition**. In the **Other Forms** box, write as many other forms of the word, such as adjective and noun forms, as you can think of or find in your dictionary.

Then, following the same procedure, draw your own map for each of the nine remaining vocabulary words. Use a separate sheet of paper.

1.

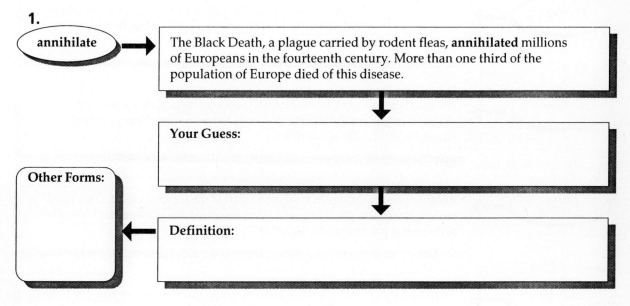

annihilate →

The Black Death, a plague carried by rodent fleas, **annihilated** millions of Europeans in the fourteenth century. More than one third of the population of Europe died of this disease.

Your Guess:

Other Forms:

Definition:

2.

concession →

Although no immediate medical improvements were made during the Middle Ages, many people grant that modern medicine began at that time. They are willing to make this **concession** because of the interest in curing diseases that arose as a result of the Black Death.

3.

decimate →

In the fourteenth century, medical personnel probably unintentionally killed as many people as were **decimated** by disease and injury. Physicians were often clergymen who were trained in theory but were given no clinical training.

4.

disperse →

Surgeons, considered inferior to physicians, were the ones who actually treated patients, usually by bleeding them. I'll bet it was easy to **disperse** patients from a waiting room when the treatment was made known. I know I'd have been driven away!

5.

diversion →

Patients often found that medical treatment offered little more than a temporary **diversion,** or distraction, from their health problems. Often, they only got worse after treatment.

6.

evade →

Surgeons could not **evade** the task of setting broken bones and performing operations, since patients sought medical help from those who had practical experience. Physicians probably avoided such work by rambling on about theory.

7.

flagrant →

Hospitals existed only to isolate patients, not to cure them. Staff members were **flagrant** in their disregard of the patients' well-being. In addition to the glaringly bad treatment, there was no regard for sanitation.

8.

insolence →

The **insolence** of some of the hospital workers caused many patients to abandon treatment. Indirectly, this rude behavior may have eventually forced hospitals to begin caring for patients.

9.

purge →

Apothecaries, or druggists, were also a part of the medical world. They filled prescriptions from physicians and also prescribed drugs themselves, usually herbal mixtures designed to **purge** or eliminate disease from a patient.

10.

sadistic →

All in all, medical treatment bordered on being **sadistic,** not because the practitioners were cruel, but because so little was known of the cause and treatment of disease and injury. Sometimes the "cure" was worse than the disease!

EXERCISE 2   *Context Clues* ✍

Directions. Scan the definitions in Column A. Then think about how the boldface words are used in the sentences in Column B. To complete the exercise, match each definition in Column A with the correct vocabulary word from Column B. Write the letter of your choice on the line provided; then write the vocabulary word on the line preceding the definition.

COLUMN A	COLUMN B

_____ **11.** word: _____

n. quality or instance of being disrespectful and insulting; impudence

(A) Did you know that barbers in the Middle Ages were also medical practitioners who bled people and set simple bone fractures? I think I might have **evaded** going to a barber for a haircut since they only cut hair as a sideline.

_____ **12.** word: _____

adj. having an unnatural love of cruelty; extremely cruel

(B) Reading about medicine in the Middle Ages started out as a simple **diversion**, but it has begun to take all my time.

_____ **13.** word: _____

n. a turning aside, as of traffic or attention; a game or pastime; a recreation

(C) I did take time to run over to the refreshment **concession** to buy a fruit-juice popsicle, but then the stick made me want to find out when tongue depressors first came into use.

_____ **14.** word: _____

v. to destroy completely; to vanquish; to make ineffectual or unimportant; to kill

(D) I need to **purge** my mind of all of this, but I don't really want to rid myself of all the information I've gathered.

_____ **15.** word: _____

v. to remove undesirable elements from; to rid; to remove by cleansing; *n.* the removal of members by a higher authority

(E) Physicians of the Middle Ages would probably have considered it **insolence** if someone had told them how little they actually helped people. Still, it wouldn't be rudeness to point this out; it would simply be the truth.

_____ **16.** word: _____

v. to break up and scatter or spread; to dispel

(F) After the Black Death **annihilated** so many people, physicians lost much of their reputation as healers. Surgeons, with their practical knowledge, saved more lives and thus became more respected. As a result, medical schools introduced anatomy classes and practical training.

_____ **17.** word: _____

n. an act of granting or yielding; something granted or yielded; a privilege, such as the right to use land, granted for a specific purpose

(G) Hospitals cleaned up their act. They began to stop the spread of diseases, instead of **dispersing** them among the general public.

_____ **18.** word: _____

adj. glaringly bad; notorious; outrageous

(H) Cities, too, acted to eliminate **flagrant** practices, such as glaringly bad sewage disposal, that threatened the public health.

_____ **19.** word: _____

v. to destroy or kill a large part of

(I) Knowledge of medical cures advanced slowly, but plagues no longer **decimated** or destroyed large segments of the population.

_____ **20.** word: _____

v. to escape or avoid something, especially by using deceit or cleverness; to avoid doing or answering something directly

(J) Today we need to solve the problems that lead to starvation, another **sadistic** killer that seems to enjoy inflicting pain.

EXERCISE 3 Sentence Completion ✍

Directions. For each of the following items, circle the letter of the choice that best completes the meaning of the sentence or sentences.

21. How could people ____ the knowledge that diseases spread from one person to another, or avoid the realization that unsanitary conditions contributed to illness?
(A) annihilate
(B) evade
(C) decimate
(D) disperse
(E) purge

22. What ____ practice it was to remove blood from sick people! Did medical practitioners in the Middle Ages enjoy being cruel?
(A) a concessionary
(B) an insolent
(C) an evasive
(D) a sadistic
(E) a flagrant

23. To barber-surgeons, cutting hair must have seemed like a pleasant ____, compared to setting a broken bone.
(A) concession
(B) insolence
(C) purge
(D) dispersion
(E) diversion

24. The plague ____ the population; it took Europe centuries to recover from losing so many people.
(A) decimated
(B) waned
(C) dispersed
(D) evaded
(E) fabricated

25. At some point apothecaries had to yield their rights to prescribe medications themselves. I wonder when they made that ____?
(A) annihilation
(B) dispersion
(C) concession
(D) insolence
(E) decimation

26. City officials could not avoid, or ____, their responsibility to ____ the city of unhealthful conditions, thus removing the threat of disease.
(A) annihilate . . . decimate
(B) decimate . . . evade
(C) purge . . . decimate
(D) evade . . . purge
(E) disperse . . . annihilate

27. Improved sanitation helped to ____ cities of the fleas that carried the plague by making their hosts, the rats, ____, scattering far and wide.
(A) evade . . . decimate
(B) annihilate . . . evade
(C) evade . . . annihilate
(D) decimate . . . purge
(E) purge . . . disperse

28. Will future generations look back at our medical practices and regard them as the ____ acts of a cruel civilization?
(A) sadistic
(B) flagrant
(C) dispersed
(D) insolent
(E) purged

29. It would be wonderful if medical science could ____ all diseases that threaten to ____ populations. If they could utterly destroy such illnesses, they would save the lives of thousands of people.
(A) purge . . . evade
(B) evade . . . disperse
(C) annihilate . . . decimate
(D) decimate . . . evade
(E) disperse . . . purge

30. The ____, outrageous medical conditions of the Middle Ages are gone. Most medical practitioners do not avoid the challenges of their practice; they do not ____ taking responsibility for their patients' health.
(A) sadistic . . . purge
(B) flagrant . . . evade
(C) diversionary . . . decimate
(D) concessionary . . . annihilate
(E) insolent . . . purge

MAKING NEW WORDS YOUR OWN

Lesson 18 | CONTEXT: Civilization
The Revolutions of Mahatma Gandhi

The name of one man comes immediately to mind when India's struggle for independence is discussed—Mohandas K. Gandhi (1869–1948), also respectfully called Mahatma ("Great Soul") by the Indian people. As a religious and a political leader, Gandhi was a quietly powerful force for Indian independence from Great Britain. Independence came in 1947, in large part due to Gandhi's inspiring personality and his use of nonviolent resistance against British policies and practices.

In the following exercises, you will have the opportunity to expand your vocabulary by reading about Mohandas K. Gandhi in South Africa and India. Below are ten vocabulary words that will be used in these exercises.

clemency	inhibition	mannerism	mettle	submission
harass	mandatory	meticulous	protocol	ultimatum

EXERCISE 1 *Mapping*

Directions. In the item below, a vocabulary word is provided and used in a sentence. Take a guess at the word's meaning and write it in the box labeled **Your Guess**. Then look the word up in your dictionary and write the definition in the box labeled **Definition**. In the **Other Forms** box, write as many other forms of the word, such as adjective and noun forms, as you can think of or find in your dictionary.

Then, following the same procedure, draw your own map for each of the nine remaining vocabulary words. Use a seperate sheet of paper.

1.

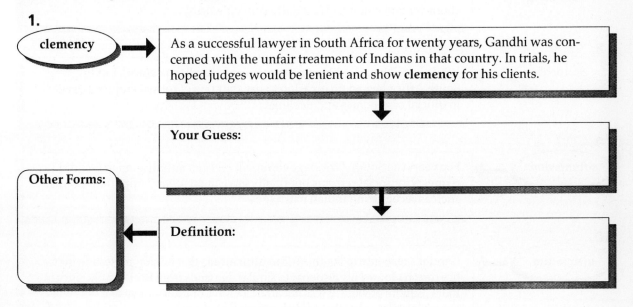

clemency → As a successful lawyer in South Africa for twenty years, Gandhi was concerned with the unfair treatment of Indians in that country. In trials, he hoped judges would be lenient and show **clemency** for his clients.

Your Guess:

Other Forms:

Definition:

2.

harass → While in South Africa, Gandhi was **harassed** because of his race; as a result, he strongly identified with others who were repeatedly troubled and annoyed by bigots.

3.

inhibition → Partly because of his own natural **inhibition** to hold back violent responses to injustice, Gandhi developed and used his nonviolent resistance technique in South Africa.

4.

mandatory → It certainly was not a **mandatory** part of Gandhi's legal duties in South Africa to protest social discrimination. His actions were voluntary—and sometimes they landed him in jail.

5.

mannerism → In the face of threats, Gandhi had a distinctive personal trait, or **mannerism,** that probably upset South African authorities—namely, his peaceful and calm attitude. When beaten, Gandhi employed a policy of passive resistance.

6.

meticulous → Born into a middle-class Indian family, Gandhi studied law at University College in London. As a young lawyer in South Africa, it is likely that he was **meticulous**, being extremely careful with the details of each case.

7.

mettle → Gandhi's social work in South Africa and his imprisonments there in the years before his involvement in India's independence movement tested his character and courage. His **mettle** proved worthy.

8.

protocol → While in college, Gandhi may have learned English **protocol,** but in South Africa he had no occasion to use the code of formal etiquette used in official ceremonies and dealings.

9.

submission → For years the South African government resisted **submission** to Gandhi's requests for social reforms but finally gave in on several important points, such as recognizing Indian marriages.

10.

ultimatum → Gandhi's response to South African **ultimatums** that he stop protesting injustice foreshadowed his response to similar demands from British authorities in India. Gandhi obviously was not afraid of force or punishment and was willing to resist demands that he discontinue his actions.

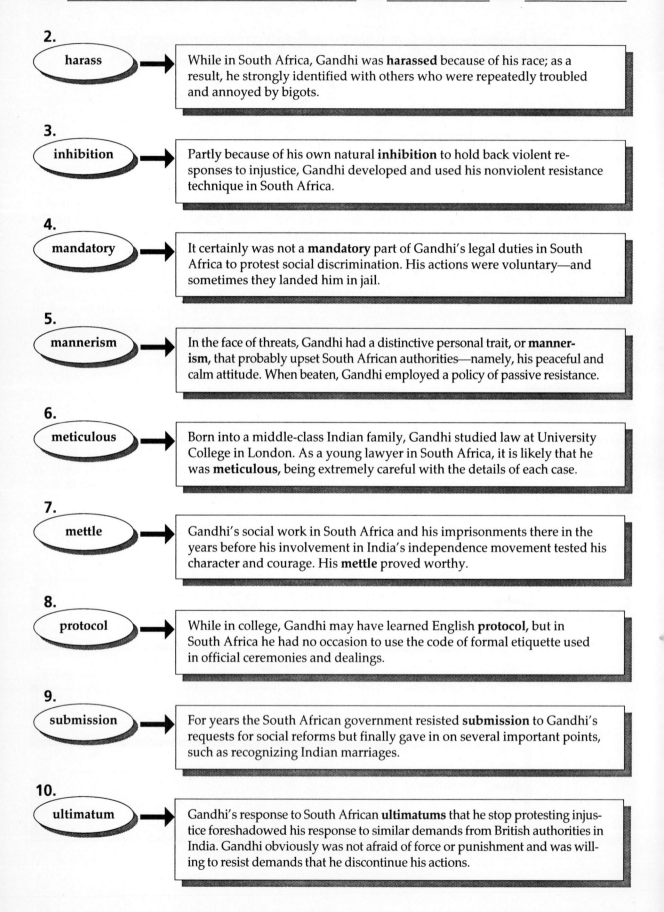

EXERCISE 2 *Context Clues* ✍

Directions. Scan the definitions in Column A. Then think about how the boldface words are used in the sentences in Column B. To complete the exercise, match each definition in Column A with the correct vocabulary word from Column B. Write the letter of your choice on the line provided; then write the vocabulary word on the line preceding the definition.

COLUMN A

_____ **11.** word: _____

n. the code prescribing formal etiquette and precedence for official ceremonies and dealings, as with diplomats and the military; an original draft or record of a negotiation or document

_____ **12.** word: _____

v. to trouble, worry, annoy, or irritate; to attack repeatedly

_____ **13.** word: _____

n. quality of character; courage; spirit

_____ **14.** word: _____

n. a final demand or proposition, especially one whose refusal implies an end to negotiations or the risk of force

_____ **15.** word: _____

n. leniency or mercy, especially toward an enemy; a lenient or merciful act; mildness

_____ **16.** word: _____

n. a distinctive personal trait; an idiosyncrasy; an exaggerated or unnatural style or habit, as in speech or dress

_____ **17.** word: _____

n. the act of holding back; an inner belief, feeling, or force that checks one's actions, thoughts, or feelings; restraint

_____ **18.** word: _____

adj. extremely careful; overly precise or fussy about details; painstaking

_____ **19.** word: _____

n. obedience; the act of giving in; humbleness

_____ **20.** word: _____

adj. required; obligatory

COLUMN B

(A) When Gandhi returned to India, he realized that India could not remain in **submission** to Great Britain and be obedient to unfair laws and policies.

(B) Gandhi saw that the Indian people had taken repeated verbal and physical abuse from the British but that now they were being not only **harassed** but also brutally attacked and killed.

(C) The **clemency** given the British general who ordered the Amritsar massacre of Indians in 1919 was a factor in Gandhi's joining the independence movement. He felt the leniency was undeserved.

(D) Millions of Indians showed their **mettle** by courageously following Gandhi's call for nonviolent resistance toward Great Britain.

(E) Gandhi became involved in the **meticulous,** or painstaking, political negotiations necessary to bring independence to India.

(F) Gandhi helped convince Indian National Congress members to give up the **inhibitions** that had restrained a call for complete independence.

(G) While not officially required, it was almost **mandatory** that Gandhi's followers boycott British goods and wear only Indian cloth.

(H) Gandhi adopted the **mannerism** of wearing only simple Indian clothes. This habit emphasized his bond with the common people.

(I) To accomplish certain goals, Gandhi sometimes issued **ultimatums** that were often followed by lengthy fasts. He threatened to starve himself to death if his demands were not met.

(J) In London in 1931, Gandhi participated in a high-level conference where **protocol** was observed. At this conference, diplomats behaved according to strict codes.

EXERCISE 3 Sentence Completion ✍

Directions. For each of the following items, circle the letter of the choice that best completes the meaning of the sentence or sentences.

21. Gandhi's famous march to the sea in 1930 is a dramatic example of his _____. The whole world responded to his spirit and courage.
    - (A) ultimatum
    - (B) inhibition
    - (C) protocol
    - (D) mettle
    - (E) clemency

22. The British government made it _____ that Indians pay a tax on salt. With his followers, Gandhi decided to protest this requirement.
    - (A) mandatory
    - (B) submissive
    - (C) inhibitive
    - (D) meticulous
    - (E) mettlesome

23. Instead of giving the government _____ demanding that the tax be repealed, Gandhi led a nonviolent protest.
    - (A) an inhibition
    - (B) a mannerism
    - (C) an ultimatum
    - (D) a protocol
    - (E) a mettle

24. No _____ held back Gandhi or his thousands of followers as they marched to the Arabian Sea to make their own salt.
    - (A) ultimatums
    - (B) submissions
    - (C) clemencies
    - (D) mannerisms
    - (E) inhibitions

25. The _____, or mildness, of the weather is evident in the pictures taken of Gandhi and his followers on the march.
    - (A) mannerism
    - (B) clemency
    - (C) mettle
    - (D) ultimatum
    - (E) submission

26. Gandhi probably expected British soldiers to make trouble and _____ the marchers, but he had confidence in the character, the _____, of his followers.
    - (A) harass . . . clemency
    - (B) purge . . . protocol
    - (C) censure . . . inhibition
    - (D) harass . . . mettle
    - (E) inhibit . . . submission

27. Obviously, soldiers were not meeting Gandhi in an official ceremony; therefore, procedures of _____ did not apply. _____ alone restrained soldiers from attacking.
    - (A) mettle . . . Mannerisms
    - (B) inhibition . . . Mettles
    - (C) protocol . . . Inhibitions
    - (D) mannerism . . . Clemencies
    - (E) mettle . . . Inhibitions

28. Making salt was not a _____ or painstaking job for the marchers. They simply needed to obtain the _____ sea water and let it evaporate, as the procedure required.
    - (A) meticulous . . . mandatory
    - (B) manneristic . . . mettlesome
    - (C) mandatory . . . meticulous
    - (D) mettlesome . . . mandatory
    - (E) submissive . . . meticulous

29. Gandhi's passive way of responding to arrests probably was a _____ that aggravated soldiers, especially if they were trying to give him _____ to stop making salt.
    - (A) protocol . . . a submission
    - (B) clemency . . . a mettle
    - (C) mettle . . . an inhibition
    - (D) submission . . . a clemency
    - (E) mannerism . . . an ultimatum

30. Once again, Gandhi was arrested, but jail never forced him into _____ to unfair British laws. He did not beg for _____ because he did not want mercy for himself—he wanted liberty for India.
    - (A) ultimatum . . . clemency
    - (B) clemency . . . submission
    - (C) inhibition . . . mettle
    - (D) submission . . . clemency
    - (E) protocol . . . mannerism

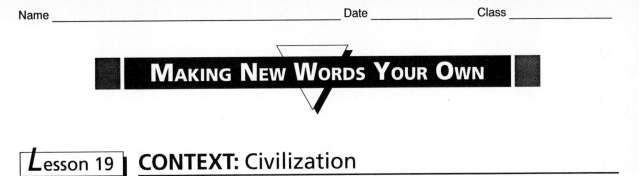

MAKING NEW WORDS YOUR OWN

Lesson 19 | **CONTEXT:** Civilization

Science Fiction: Into the Future

Science fiction often describes the development and achievements of newly imagined civilizations, but science fiction writing is often not taken very seriously. Many respected science fiction writers, such as Andre Norton, Robert Heinlein, Ursula K. LeGuin, and Ray Bradbury, have addressed problems of the modern world by placing them in futuristic settings or in worlds different from our own. In the nineteenth century, Mary Shelley's *Frankenstein* and Jules Verne's *Twenty Thousand Leagues Under the Sea* are early and now well-respected works of science fiction that speak to our desire for adventure and our need to remember that we are one small part of an enormous universe.

In the following exercises, you will have the opportunity to expand your vocabulary by reading about one student's obsession with science fiction. Below are ten vocabulary words that will be used in these exercises.

admirably	amnesty	censure	inalienable	rift
affidavit	bias	diminutive	mosque	timorous

EXERCISE 1   *Mapping*

Directions. In the item below, a vocabulary word is provided and used in a sentence. Take a guess at the word's meaning and write it in the box labeled **Your Guess**. Then look the word up in your dictionary and write the definition in the box labeled **Definition**. Finally, use your dictionary to find other forms of the word, such as adjective and noun forms. Write these words in the box labeled **Other Forms**.

Then, following the same procedure, draw your own map for each of the nine remaining vocabulary words. Use a separate sheet of paper.

1.

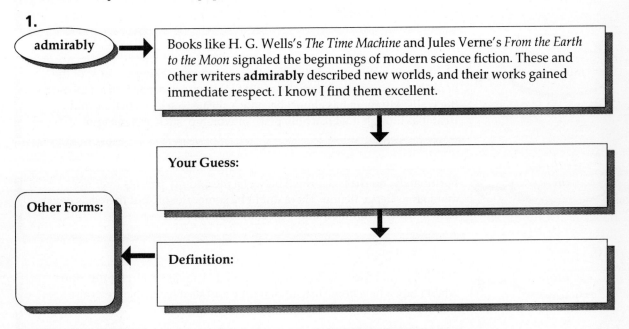

admirably →

Books like H. G. Wells's *The Time Machine* and Jules Verne's *From the Earth to the Moon* signaled the beginnings of modern science fiction. These and other writers **admirably** described new worlds, and their works gained immediate respect. I know I find them excellent.

Your Guess:

Other Forms:

Definition:

2.

affidavit →

Science fiction is as important to me as breathing, eating, and sleeping. My parents desperately want me to cut back on my reading. They would like me to sign an **affidavit** promising under oath that I will not buy more books for my collection.

3.

amnesty →

I think I should receive **amnesty** from my parents. They should pardon me for reading science fiction because some of it is considered great literature. One example is Mary Shelley's *Frankenstein,* the tale of a scientist's mad desire to create a living being.

4.

bias →

Everyone will tell you that I have a definite **bias** toward science fiction. Although I am not really prejudiced against other forms of literature, I hardly ever read anything but science fiction.

5.

censure →

Some of my teachers **censure** this habit of mine. They criticize the books I read and try endlessly to get me to read anything written about the earth under my feet.

6.

diminutive →

Evidently, some of my teachers think that science fiction holds a **diminutive** status in the world of literature. They feel that it is of small or no importance.

7.

inalienable →

I don't agree with them. I think I have an **inalienable** right to read what I choose. Of course, no one is taking away my right to read the books I want, but I wish they wouldn't be so judgmental.

8.

mosque →

My collection of science fiction books is enormous, taking up most of the bookshelves in my bedroom. In addition, I have science fiction art all over the walls. My room has almost become a shrine to science fiction, and I treat it as though it were a holy place of worship, such as a **mosque**.

9.

rift →

Fortunately, no **rift** has formed between me and my parents over my mania for science fiction. There might be some friction, but there has never been a break in our love and respect for one another.

10.

timorous →

Still, they want me to be less single-minded. I always feel a bit **timorous** when I buy a new book, fearful that they will start lecturing me again.

EXERCISE 2 *Context Clues* ✍

Directions. Scan the definitions in Column A. Then think about how the boldface words are used in the sentences in Column B. To complete the exercise, match each definition in Column A with the correct vocabulary word from Column B. Write the letter of your choice on the line provided; then write the vocabulary word on the line preceding the definition.

COLUMN A

_____ **11.** word: _____
v. to criticize or blame; *n.* a condemning judgment; a reprimand

_____ **12.** word: _____
n. a Muslim house of worship

_____ **13.** word: _____
n. a general pardon, especially for political prisoners

_____ **14.** word: _____
v. to break open; to split; *n.* a split; a break in friendly relations

_____ **15.** word: _____
adv. in a worthy manner; commendably; excellently

_____ **16.** word: _____
adj. not capable of being given or taken away

_____ **17.** word: _____
n. a line slanting diagonally across the weave of a fabric; a prejudice or personal tendency; *v.* to prejudice or influence

_____ **18.** word: _____
adj. easily frightened; fearful; timid; cowardly

_____ **19.** word: _____
n. a written statement made under oath

_____ **20.** word: _____
n. referring to suffixes or altered word forms that designate smallness, affection, or familiarity; a very small person or thing; *adj.* tiny; of small size

COLUMN B

(A) My English teacher, Mr. Widman, did not approve of my single-minded devotion to science fiction. I thought one way to bridge the **rift** between us was to organize a science fiction story-writing contest. It might mend the break in our relationship if we both served as judges.

(B) I thought I would be granted **amnesty** and forgiveness if I proved to him that science fiction stories could be interesting and literary.

(C) I was feeling a little **timorous** about asking Mr. Widman. Yet my desire to promote science fiction made me overcome my fear.

(D) Mr. Widman agreed to the idea—he didn't **censure** it—although at first he was not sure he wanted to read dozens of science fiction stories.

(E) In the end, he acted **admirably**—offering to make announcements in his classes, set the deadline date, and find prizes for the winners. He was truly worthy of a science fiction fan's respect.

(F) He suggested that I sign an oath, an **affidavit** of sorts, that promised I wouldn't let my involvement in the writing contest keep me from my other homework.

(G) He also asked that we judge each story separately, so that my comments would not **bias** or influence his decisions.

(H) He said, "I know that you love science fiction, that you read it with devotion, like a worshiper attending a service at a church or **mosque**, but I can't let your opinion interfere with mine."

(I) "I can't deprive you of your **inalienable** right to read what you like. No one can take that away."

(J) In a very short time, my small, even **diminutive**, request turned into a contest for the whole school. As a result, I got to read lots of science fiction stories—and many of them were pretty good.

EXERCISE 3 Sentence Completion ✍

Directions. For each of the following items, circle the letter of the choice that best completes the meaning of the sentence or sentences.

21. The students responded _____. More than a hundred stories came in—a sure sign that most everyone approved and felt no _____ against science fiction.
    (A) timorously . . . mosque
    (B) diminutively . . . censure
    (C) admirably . . . bias
    (D) inalienably . . . amnesty
    (E) admirably . . . affidavit

22. One story was about two warring planets. They had formerly been united under a single ruler, but a violent _____ between opposing factions had resulted in a split government.
    (A) bias
    (B) alienation
    (C) admire
    (D) affidavit
    (E) rift

23. Another story was about a mad scientist and his young daughter, whom he calls Natty, a _____ form of her name, Natalie.
    (A) bias
    (B) diminutive
    (C) mosque
    (D) affidavit
    (E) rift

24. The scientist invents a machine that makes decisions for people, thus depriving them of their _____ right to think for themselves.
    (A) timorous
    (B) inalienable
    (C) diminutive
    (D) biased
    (E) censured

25. The story focuses on how Natalie overcomes her shy and _____ nature and her small, _____ size in order to stand up against her twisted father.
    (A) timorous . . . diminutive
    (B) diminutive . . . timorous
    (C) inalienable . . . biased
    (D) biased . . . admirable
    (E) censured . . . inalienable

26. When Natalie _____ her father's actions, he is disgusted by her obvious _____, or favorable inclination, toward people, and he ignores her criticisms completely.
    (A) rifts . . . mosque
    (B) censures . . . bias
    (C) biases . . . rift
    (D) admires . . . amnesty
    (E) biases . . affidavit

27. Natalie secretly acts against her father, creating _____ between them.
    (A) a mosque
    (B) a bias
    (C) a censure
    (D) a rift
    (E) an affidavit

28. To put an end to her father's evil, Natalie publicly signs _____, an oath, stating that she has witnessed his abuses against people. In the end, Natalie becomes an important intergalactic diplomat. On some planets, her speeches are delivered in sacred places of worship much like ornate _____.
    (A) a censure . . . biases
    (B) a mosque . . . rifts
    (C) an affidavit . . . mosques
    (D) an admiration . . . censures
    (E) a rift . . . affidavits

29. Natalie refuses to grant her evil father _____, and he is forced to live alone and unforgiven, exiled on a distant planet.
    (A) bias
    (B) censure
    (C) amnesty
    (D) affidavit
    (E) rift

30. Obviously, I spent a lot of time on this story, but it didn't win the contest. Although it was _____ told and was worthy of a prize, the other judge, Mr. Widman, discovered that I had written it!
    (A) admirably
    (B) inalienably
    (C) timorously
    (D) diminutively
    (E) flagrantly

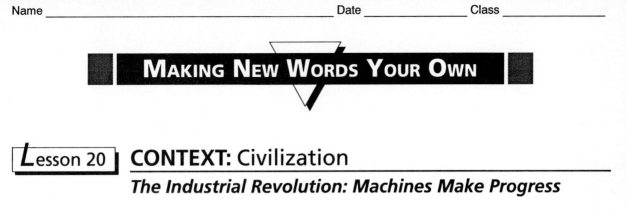

MAKING NEW WORDS YOUR OWN

Lesson 20 | CONTEXT: Civilization

The Industrial Revolution: Machines Make Progress

We take machines for granted most of the time because our lives are so filled with them. If it's difficult to picture life without computers, televisions, and cars, just try to imagine the world before the Industrial Revolution. There were catapults, water wheels, clocks, windmills, and printing presses, but machines that helped people pump water out of mine shafts, supply power to boats, or make textiles, did not yet exist. These were all developed during the late eighteenth and nineteenth centuries.

In the following exercises, you will have the opportunity to expand your vocabulary by reading about the changes machines brought about during the Industrial Revolution. Below are ten vocabulary words that will be used in these exercises.

bedlam	consolidate	curtail	emancipate	ornate
colloquial	constituent	destitute	exultant	prelude

EXERCISE 1 *Mapping*

Directions. In the item below, a vocabulary word is provided and used in a sentence. Take a guess at the word's meaning and write it in the box labeled **Your Guess**. Then look the word up in your dictionary and write the definition in the box labeled **Definition**. In the **Other Forms** box, write as many other forms of the word, such as adjective and noun forms, as you can think of or find in your dictionary.

Then, following the same procedure, draw your own map for each of the nine remaining vocabulary words. Use a seperate sheet of paper.

1.

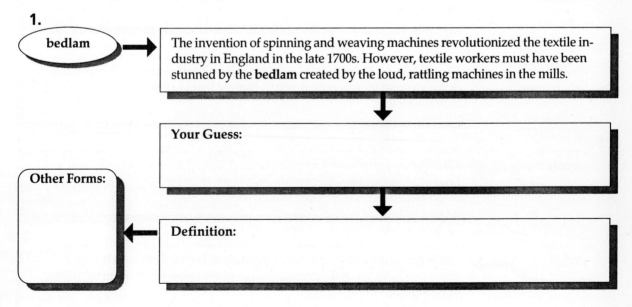

bedlam → The invention of spinning and weaving machines revolutionized the textile industry in England in the late 1700s. However, textile workers must have been stunned by the **bedlam** created by the loud, rattling machines in the mills.

Your Guess:

Other Forms:

Definition:

2.

colloquial →

Poor people came from rural areas to find jobs in the mills. They were accustomed to the **colloquial** speech used in the country and may have had a difficult time understanding the more formal speech of people in the cities.

3.

consolidate →

Mill owners expected their workers to produce enough textiles to meet world demand. As production increased, small mills were **consolidated**, or combined, to make larger ones.

4.

constituent →

The growth of the mills created new jobs. Machines had to be built, maintained, and repaired. Industries that produced machine **constituents** expanded so they could meet the demand for these important parts.

5.

curtail →

The development of the steam engine meant that manufacturers could expand, rather than **curtail**, production. Not only were steam engines used in manufacturing, but steam-driven trains could now carry all that was produced in the factories.

6.

destitute →

Cities were filled with **destitute** people who had moved from the country-side and could not find jobs or housing. Many of these poor people who found jobs were soon fired for not following the strict rules of the factories.

7.

emancipate →

In some ways, machines **emancipated** people by doing work for them. In other ways, however, machines imprisoned people by tying them to factory jobs.

8.

exultant →

Factory owners were **exultant** over the vast profits they made. They rejoiced in the accumulation of capital, which enabled them to live well and to expand their businesses.

9.

ornate →

Many of the factory owners who profited from the industrialization of England built and lived in **ornate** mansions; their employees, however, could not afford to live in such fancy homes.

10.

prelude →

The early textile mills were only a **prelude** to the vast changes brought about by the Industrial Revolution. As industrialization continued, working conditions grew worse.

EXERCISE 2 *Context Clues*

Directions. Scan the definitions in Column A. Then think about how the boldface words are used in the sentences in Column B. To complete the exercise, match each definition in Column A with the correct vocabulary word from Column B. Write the letter of your choice on the line provided; then write the vocabulary word on the line preceding the definition.

COLUMN A	COLUMN B

_____ **11.** word: _____
adj. elaborate; fancy; excessively adorned or ornamented

_____ **12.** word: _____
n. a necessary part or element; a voter represented by an elected official;
adj. necessary in making up a whole; component

_____ **13.** word: _____
adj. poverty-stricken; penniless; being without

_____ **14.** word: _____
n. anything serving as an introduction, such as an introductory section of a piece of music; an opening

_____ **15.** word: _____
adj. informal in language; conversational

_____ **16.** word: _____
adj. rejoicing greatly; jubilant; triumphant

_____ **17.** word: _____
n. a place or condition of uproar or confusion

_____ **18.** word: _____
v. to shorten; to reduce

_____ **19.** word: _____
v. to unite; to combine; to strengthen; to make solid or firmly established

_____ **20.** word: _____
v. to set free; to release from slavery or oppression

(A) Many workers who thought they would improve their lives by moving to the city found that their dreams were **curtailed**—reduced by poverty.

(B) The workers were **constituents** of the factory operation, which could not have produced goods without them.

(C) Full of uproar and confusion, the crowded streets of the cities must have been total **bedlam**.

(D) Sometimes it turned out that the poverty and hard work on the farms had just been a **prelude** to worse poverty and harder work in the factories.

(E) Once workers were employed by the factories, nothing except illness or death could **emancipate** them from their servitude.

(F) One way in which workers kept their spirits up was to talk among themselves in their **colloquial** language, which the factory owners probably did not understand.

(G) Meanwhile, landowners **consolidated** farms and put up fences in order to raise sheep for wool to supply the mills. Combining the farms in this way eliminated most traditional agricultural jobs.

(H) People who had moved to the cities and could not get or keep jobs had no farm jobs to return to. They remained **destitute** and hungry in the cities.

(I) The poor people must have resented the **ornate,** or fancy, homes of the wealthy mill owners.

(J) Most of the poor would have been happy just to have enough to eat. They would have been **exultant** to also have a warm place to sleep.

EXERCISE 3 Sentence Completion ✍

Directions. For each of the following items, circle the letter of the choice that best completes the meaning of the sentence or sentences.

21. Coal and steam were essential components of manufacturing. They became _____ of the Industrial Revolution, replacing water and wind as forms of energy.
    (A) bedlams
    (B) emancipations
    (C) constituents
    (D) colloquialisms
    (E) consolidations

22. Power machinery added to the _____ of crowded workplaces. Most of the machinery was very noisy.
    (A) prelude
    (B) constituent
    (C) consolidation
    (D) emancipation
    (E) bedlam

23. It took decades for the Industrial Revolution to spread widely. What happened in England was _____ to what would happen throughout the Western world.
    (A) a prelude
    (B) a bedlam
    (C) an exultation
    (D) a constituent
    (E) a colloquialism

24. Although workers did not receive adequate pay for the hours and working conditions they endured, those who kept their jobs were not _____ like the unemployed.
    (A) colloquial
    (B) destitute
    (C) exultant
    (D) ornate
    (E) constituent

25. In later years, workers _____ their scattered forces to gain enough power to demand better pay, shorter hours, and better working conditions.
    (A) curtailed
    (B) emancipated
    (C) exulted
    (D) consolidated
    (E) constituted

26. In the early years, workers made little effort to _____ themselves from their almost slavelike conditions. They feared being replaced by the _____ street people who desperately needed jobs.
    (A) consolidate . . . ornate
    (B) curtail . . . colloquial
    (C) emancipate . . . destitute
    (D) curtail . . . exultant
    (E) emancipate . . . ornate

27. The mill owners showed little interest in stopping or _____ their accumulation of wealth. They saw the success of the mills as a _____, or opening, to more profit.
    (A) consolidating . . . destitution
    (B) emancipating . . . curtailment
    (C) consolidating . . . constituent
    (D) curtailing . . . colloquialism
    (E) curtailing . . . prelude

28. England exported cloth to the Americas, Africa, and the Far East, where people were tired of paying high prices for luxurious, _____, handmade fabrics.
    (A) constituent
    (B) ornate
    (C) exultant
    (D) colloquial
    (E) destitute

29. The _____, everyday speech of the mill workers probably included plenty of colorful words to describe the noisy confusion, or _____, in which they worked.
    (A) exultant . . . emancipation
    (B) ornate . . . consolidation
    (C) constituent . . . ornateness
    (D) colloquial . . . bedlam
    (E) exultant . . . destitution

30. Better pay and working conditions made workers _____, rejoicing because they saw improvements as a _____ to a better life, an opening to greater opportunities.
    (A) colloquial . . . bedlam
    (B) ornate . . . constituent
    (C) exultant . . . prelude
    (D) destitute . . . bedlam
    (E) constituent . . . consolidation

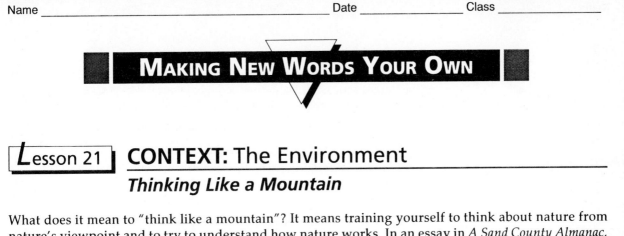

MAKING NEW WORDS YOUR OWN

Lesson 21 | **CONTEXT:** The Environment

Thinking Like a Mountain

What does it mean to "think like a mountain"? It means training yourself to think about nature from nature's viewpoint and to try to understand how nature works. In an essay in *A Sand County Almanac*, conservationist Aldo Leopold tells how he learned to do this. As a young forester, Leopold helped kill a wolf family. He thought the killings would increase the deer population. However, when he looked into a dying wolf's eyes, Leopold realized what the mountains already knew—that predators are important, too. From that day on, Leopold started learning how to think like a mountain—and you can, too.

In the following exercises, you will have the opportunity to expand your vocabulary by reading about Aldo Leopold and *A Sand County Almanac*. Below are ten vocabulary words that will be used in these exercises.

bestride	debut	fluctuate	reprieve	theoretical
casement	documentary	melancholy	requiem	vehement

EXERCISE 1   *Mapping* ✍

Directions. In the item below, a vocabulary word is provided and used in a sentence. Take a guess at the word's meaning and write it in the box labeled **Your Guess**. Then look the word up in your dictionary and write the definition in the box labeled **Definition**. In the **Other Forms** box, write as many other forms of the word, such as adjective and noun forms, as you can think of or find in your dictionary.

Then, following the same procedure, draw your own map and follow the same instructions for each of the nine remaining vocabulary words. Use a separate sheet of paper.

1.

(**bestride**) ➡ Dora, here I am **bestriding** the fence on my cousin's farm and anxious to share with you my opinions of Aldo Leopold's *A Sand County Almanac*. I find it difficult, however, to write a letter while straddling a fence!

⬇

Your Guess:

Other Forms:

⬇

Definition:

2.

casement ➡ I know that Aunt Diane is watching me from the **casement** because I heard the hinges squeak when she opened it to let air in. As you can tell, I'm trying to train my senses in the best Aldo Leopold manner.

3.

debut ➡ I'm sorry I missed your **debut** party. Was your formal entrance into society as wonderful as you had hoped?

4.

documentary ➡ After reading Leopold's classic book about his experiences in nature and with wildlife, I've decided on my career—to make **documentaries** about nature. Would you watch my fact-based films, even though they wouldn't have hot stars like Tom Cruise and Mel Gibson?

5.

fluctuate ➡ Leopold says there is a lot to learn in nature, and that's true. For example, the way the depth of the river has **fluctuated** this summer interests me. Why does the level rise and fall so frequently?

6.

melancholy ➡ Leopold didn't let himself become **melancholy** by thinking about the harm people have done to nature. He saw no reason for such sadness and gloom because he was confident that people could be taught to appreciate nature and to take care of it.

7.

reprieve ➡ If someone were sentenced to prison for harming the environment, I'll bet that Leopold would ask that a **reprieve** be granted so that he could teach the person about the environment before the sentence began. After all, he does feel strongly about education!

8.

requiem ➡ I hope that Leopold and his friends had a **requiem** for the wolf family they killed. In my opinion, animals, like people, should be honored by a funeral service after their death.

9.

theoretical ➡ One thing I like about Leopold's book is that the essays are not just **theoretical**. His essays are based on concrete observations and experiences, not just theory.

10.

vehement ➡ Leopold has definite, strong convictions about nature, but he expresses them in a calm rather than a **vehement** manner. I know that you would like his friendly style of writing.

EXERCISE 2 — *Context Clues* ✍

Directions. Scan the definitions in Column A. Then think about how the boldface words are used in the sentences in Column B. To complete the exercise, match each definition in Column A with the correct vocabulary word from Column B. Write the letter of your choice on the line provided; then write the vocabulary word on the line preceding the definition.

COLUMN A	COLUMN B

COLUMN A

_____ **11.** word: _____

adj. based on or consisting of documents; employing facts rather than fiction; *n.* a presentation (such as a film) built on factual conditions or historical events

_____ **12.** word: _____

n. a temporary relief (from pain or trouble); an order temporarily delaying punishment or the execution of a sentence

_____ **13.** word: _____

v. to rise and fall or move back and forth; to change irregularly

_____ **14.** word: _____

n. a window that opens on hinges along its side

_____ **15.** word: _____

adj. marked by great emotion, force, or conviction; intense; strong; violent

_____ **16.** word: _____

v. to present for the first time; to make a debut; *n.* a first public appearance, as of an actor; a formal entrance into society

_____ **17.** word: _____

adj. sad; depressed; causing or suggesting sadness; *n.* gloom; low spirits

_____ **18.** word: _____

n. music to honor the dead; a mass for the dead

_____ **19.** word: _____

adj. hypothetical; based on theory; unproved or uncertain

_____ **20.** word: _____

v. to sit on something with a leg on each side; to straddle

COLUMN B

(A) Didn't you say that your famous uncle **debuted** as an actor in 1949? *A Sand County Almanac* first appeared in that year, too.

(B) Maybe your uncle would star in my **documentary** film based on the facts of Aldo Leopold's interesting life.

(C) I am **vehement** about the project because I strongly admire Leopold as a forester, a conservationist, an educator, and a writer.

(D) I know your uncle has played mostly **melancholy** characters, but maybe he wouldn't mind being cheerful for once.

(E) Too bad I'm not filming now. He probably would appreciate a **reprieve** from that troublesome TV show for a month or so. The time out would probably be a relief to him.

(F) Anyway, my project is just a **theoretical** idea right now. Do you think your uncle would be interested now, or should I talk to him when the project is less hypothetical and more certain?

(G) I see him so clearly as Leopold, **bestriding** an old fence at the farm. It would be safer than straddling the backs of the horses he's used to!

(H) Maybe there would be a part for Aunt Diane, too. Believe it or not, she is still looking out the **casement** on the north side of the house!

(I) Maybe I could get your friend Dr. Webster to write a **requiem**. This funeral music could be played when the wolves die in the "Thinking Like a Mountain" segment.

(J) I'm sure my ideas will shift and **fluctuate** many times before I actually am able to make a film about Aldo Leopold's life.

EXERCISE 3   *Sentence Completion* 👉

Directions. For each of the following items, circle the letter of the choice that best completes the meaning of the sentence or sentences.

21. Of course, my _____ would be strictly factual and would include details of Leopold's pioneering work with the U. S. Forest Service. The film would not be unrealistic in any way.
    - (A) documentary
    - (B) requiem
    - (C) casement
    - (D) melancholy
    - (E) reprieve

22. While I was reading *A Sand County Almanac*, my feelings about Leopold never _____; I liked him from the first and kept liking him throughout the book.
    - (A) consolidated
    - (B) bestrode
    - (C) debuted
    - (D) fluctuated
    - (E) perceived

23. I reread parts of the book when I am _____ because Leopold's writing lifts my spirits and keeps me from feeling down.
    - (A) theoretical
    - (B) vehement
    - (C) melancholy
    - (D) documentary
    - (E) reprieved

24. Of course, this is only a _____ idea—I have no way of proving it—but I'd bet Leopold's ideas could change the whole world if everyone knew about them.
    - (A) fluctuating
    - (B) theoretical
    - (C) vehement
    - (D) melancholy
    - (E) debuting

25. Leopold is _____ in his call for people to accept more responsibility for the environment. That's a conviction I strongly share.
    - (A) theoretical
    - (B) melancholy
    - (C) fluctuating
    - (D) documentary
    - (E) vehement

26. Dora, would you believe that my aunt is still staring out the _____ ? She looks _____ and sad, as though she's lonely.
    - (A) debut . . . melancholy
    - (B) requiem . . . theoretical
    - (C) casement . . . melancholy
    - (D) melancholy . . . documentary
    - (E) documentary . . . vehement

27. Now Aunt Diane is actually _____ the window sill, as though she's sitting on a horse. I now have proof— _____ evidence—that she is distracted.
    - (A) bestriding . . . melancholy
    - (B) debuting . . . documentary
    - (C) besieging . . . vehement
    - (D) bestriding . . . documentary
    - (E) debuting . . . theoretical

28. Maybe she needs a _____ from her work—time out in order to relieve her stress.
    - (A) debut
    - (B) requiem
    - (C) casement
    - (D) melancholy
    - (E) reprieve

29. Whatever the reason, she looks depressed, as if she has been listening to a really bleak _____ at a funeral. Perhaps I should ask her to join me for a nature walk and talk to her about _____ topics, such as speculations about what really causes crop circles.
    - (A) requiem . . . theoretical
    - (B) reprieve . . . melancholy
    - (C) documentary . . . vehement
    - (D) casement . . . documentary
    - (E) melancholy . . . theoretical

30. I could offer her her first role in a film and she could _____ as Leopold's wife. I'll let you know if she _____ rejects the idea in her usual intense way.
    - (A) debut . . . theoretically
    - (B) bestride . . . vehemently
    - (C) debut . . . vehemently
    - (D) convene . . . theoretically
    - (E) bestride . . . theoretically

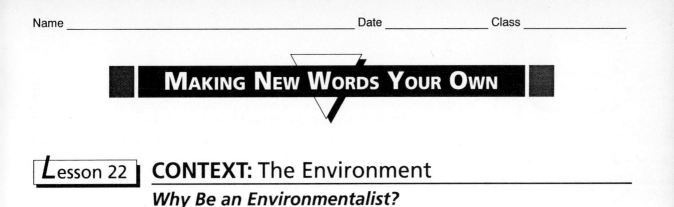

MAKING NEW WORDS YOUR OWN

Lesson 22 **CONTEXT:** The Environment

Why Be an Environmentalist?

A surprising letter for these environmentally aware times arrived recently at the newspaper's editorial office. A young woman asked, "Why should I be an environmentalist?" In thinking about how to respond to her question, our editorial writers recalled the start of the modern environmental movement. The publication in 1960 of Rachel Carson's book *Silent Spring* alerted society to the dangers of pesticides and the need to protect our environment. Our writers jotted down some thoughts about why it is still important to be an environmentalist today. Here are some of their thoughts.

In the following exercises, you will have the opportunity to expand your vocabulary by reading about the importance of being an environmentalist in today's society. Below are ten vocabulary words that will be used in these exercises.

| clangor | gloat | legacy | mortify | patriarch |
| enjoin | indict | livid | patent | wheedle |

EXERCISE 1 *Mapping*

Directions. In the item below, a vocabulary word is provided and used in a sentence. Take a guess at the word's meaning and write it in the box labeled **Your Guess**. Then look the word up in your dictionary and write the definition in the box labeled **Definition**. In the **Other Forms** box, write as many other forms of the word, such as adjective and noun forms, as you can think of or find in your dictionary.

Then, following the same procedure, draw your own map for each of the nine remaining vocabulary words. Use a separate sheet of paper.

1.

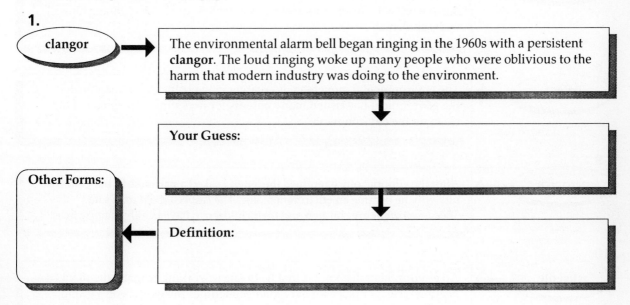

clangor

The environmental alarm bell began ringing in the 1960s with a persistent **clangor**. The loud ringing woke up many people who were oblivious to the harm that modern industry was doing to the environment.

Your Guess:

Other Forms:

Definition:

2.

enjoin → The governments of many countries have **enjoined** industries from polluting the environment with toxic chemicals. We all need to urge our government to continue to forbid industries from harming the earth.

3.

gloat → In the early years of America's expansion, settlers **gloated** over their mastery of nature. Now, however, nature is too precious and too endangered for anyone to regard it with greedy pleasure.

4.

indict → A man was **indicted** recently for dumping trash in a rural community. The local people approved of the charge because they want a clean environment that will fulfill the rights of "life, liberty, and the pursuit of happiness."

5.

legacy → I became active in environmental issues when I inherited my father's farm in Arkansas. In accepting this **legacy,** I learned the importance of being a caretaker of the land and not just someone who uses it.

6.

livid → Why should you be an environmentalist? Aren't you **livid** when you see and breathe pollution and when you view dirty, crowded cities? Aren't you furious when you read about the destruction of the rain forests and the damage to the earth's ozone layer?

7.

mortify → A friend became so upset over environmental issues that he **mortified** himself by fasting for a week. I think he would have accomplished more by volunteering to work with an environmental group than he did by disciplining himself with self-denial.

8.

patent → The environmental movement is creating new businesses. I imagine that the government has issued many **patents** for inventions designed to help clean up the environment.

9.

patriarch → After the editorial office received the letter, I asked a **patriarch** in our community why he became an environmentalist. The respected old man said, "Because I want my children and their children to have healthy, happy lives."

10.

wheedle → An environmentalist knows that he or she is working to make the planet a healthier, cleaner place for everyone. Sometimes the work is on a grand scale, and sometimes it is on a small scale, such as **wheedling,** or coaxing, a younger brother not to litter.

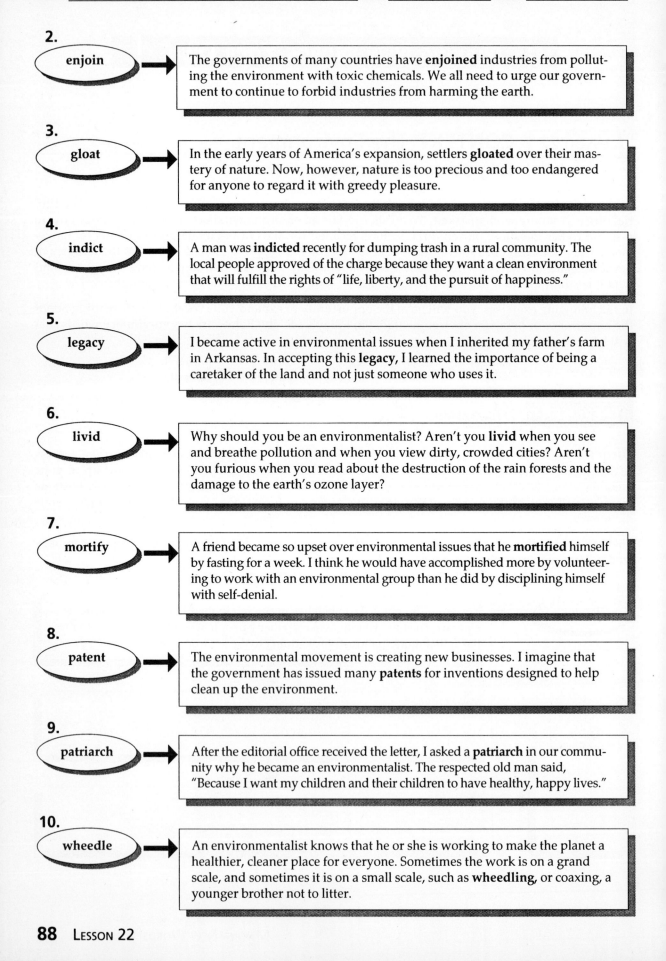

EXERCISE 2 Context Clues

Directions. Scan the definitions in Column A. Then think about how the boldface words are used in the sentences in Column B. To complete the exercise, match each definition in Column A with the correct vocabulary word from Column B. Write the letter of your choice on the line provided; then write the vocabulary word on the line preceding the definition.

COLUMN A

_____ **11.** word: _____

v. to regard with mean or greedy pleasure, greed, or exultation

_____ **12.** word: _____

n. something inherited or handed down; money or property left by a will

_____ **13.** word: _____

n. a continuous clanging; a loud ringing sound, as of metal being hit

_____ **14.** word: _____

v. to influence or persuade by using flattery or soothing, sweet words; to coax

_____ **15.** word: _____

n. a government document giving a person the right to profit from an invention; *v.* to acquire such a document; *adj.* evident; obvious

_____ **16.** word: _____

v. to charge with an offense or a crime; to make a formal accusation on the basis of legal evidence

_____ **17.** word: _____

n. a founder and leader of a tribe or family; a respected old man

_____ **18.** word: _____

v. to humiliate or shame; to discipline oneself by self-denial or punishment

_____ **19.** word: _____

v. to command, especially in law; to forbid or prohibit

_____ **20.** word: _____

adj. purplish or bluish from a bruise; pale, white, or red with anger or affliction; very angry or furious

COLUMN B

(A) Do we want our **legacy** to future generations to be a planet that is hopelessly spoiled and polluted?

(B) If you think of the earth as a living being, then you must realize that it is as **livid** as someone covered with purplish bruises from head to toe.

(C) Instead of just being **mortified** at what humanity has done to the environment, people should transform their shame into positive action.

(D) As an attorney, you could help collect evidence to **indict** an individual or a company polluting or harming the environment.

(E) You could work through legal channels to **enjoin** these companies, persuading them to follow government environmental regulations.

(F) If you were an inventor, your environmental concerns might lead you to develop and **patent** an invention to protect or clean up the environment.

(G) By using flattery and sweet words, I have successfully **wheedled** friends to recycle more.

(H) An environmentalist enjoys hearing the **clangor** of aluminum and tin cans being dumped into recycling barrels.

(I) Environmentalists must not **gloat** over their successes, but they gain pleasure in continued efforts to care for the planet.

(J) Every family member, from the leading **patriarch** on down, has a responsibility to do his or her share to keep the environment clean.

EXERCISE 3 *Sentence Completion* ✍

Directions. For each of the following items, circle the letter of the choice that best completes the meaning of the sentence or sentences.

21. Doesn't the _____ sound of the bell on the city's recycling truck remind you of your own recycling responsibilities?
  (A) livid
  (B) impartial
  (C) patent
  (D) gloating
  (E) clangorous

22. It is in everyone's best interests to be aware of people who break air and water pollution laws and to help _____ polluters.
  (A) gloat
  (B) patent
  (C) indict
  (D) quibble
  (E) wheedle

23. Much obvious, or _____, evidence exists to prove that environmental quality affects the quality of life.
  (A) clangorous
  (B) oblivious
  (C) livid
  (D) patent
  (E) mortifying

24. Naturalist Aldo Leopold, the _____ of the modern environmental family, says we have obligations to the natural world.
  (A) clangor
  (B) patriarch
  (C) legacy
  (D) patent
  (E) wheedler

25. I am _____ that all countries are not protecting endangered species and also angry that some people must be _____, or restrained, by law before they will stop polluting.
  (A) patent . . . indicted
  (B) clangorous . . . patented
  (C) livid . . . wheedled
  (D) patent . . . gloated
  (E) livid . . . enjoined

26. You may call me a _____, but I really would like to coax you to read Leopold's essays.
  (A) wheedler
  (B) patriarch
  (C) clangor
  (D) patent
  (E) legacy

27. Aren't you _____ and ashamed that you haven't joined our movement, especially since two of your friends received _____ for environment-saving inventions?
  (A) gloated . . . clangors
  (B) enjoined . . . patriarchs
  (C) indicted . . . legacies
  (D) patented . . . patriarchs
  (E) mortified . . . patents

28. I've gathered legal evidence to _____ one polluting company, but I don't _____ over my successes or take mean pleasure in them.
  (A) wheedle . . . patent
  (B) gloat . . . indict
  (C) patent . . . enjoin
  (D) indict . . . gloat
  (E) gloat . . . mortify

29. Sometimes I become _____ at companies that harm the environment. My anger motivates me to vote for elected officials who will pass laws _____ companies from harming the environment.
  (A) patent . . . gloating
  (B) clangorous . . . indicting
  (C) livid . . . enjoining
  (D) patent . . . wheedling
  (E) immaculate . . . patenting

30. It is very important to me that we leave our children the _____ of a healthy, clean, beautiful planet.
  (A) legacy
  (B) clangor
  (C) patriarch
  (D) patent
  (E) legacy

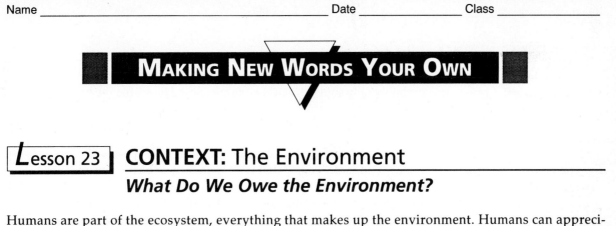

MAKING NEW WORDS YOUR OWN

Lesson 23 ## CONTEXT: The Environment
What Do We Owe the Environment?

Humans are part of the ecosystem, everything that makes up the environment. Humans can appreciate and understand nature and value nature for what it gives them. Does this mean that humans have special responsibilities and obligations toward nature? What ethics—moral standards and values—apply to people's responsibility to nature? These questions are explored in *Environmental Ethics—Duties to and Values in the Natural World* by Holmes Rolston III.

In the following exercises, you will have the opportunity to expand your vocabulary by reading about environmental ethics. Below are ten vocabulary words that will be used in these exercises.

botch	closure	convene	impartial	momentum
clientele	condole	crony	inertia	stipulate

EXERCISE 1 *Mapping*

Directions. In the item below, a vocabulary word is provided and used in a sentence. Take a guess at the word's meaning and write it in the box labeled **Your Guess**. Then look the word up in your dictionary and write the definition in the box labeled **Definition**. In the **Other Forms** box, write as many other forms of the word, such as adjective and noun forms, as you can think of or find in your dictionary.

Then, following the same procedure, draw your own map for each of the nine remaining vocabulary words. Use a separate sheet of paper.

1.

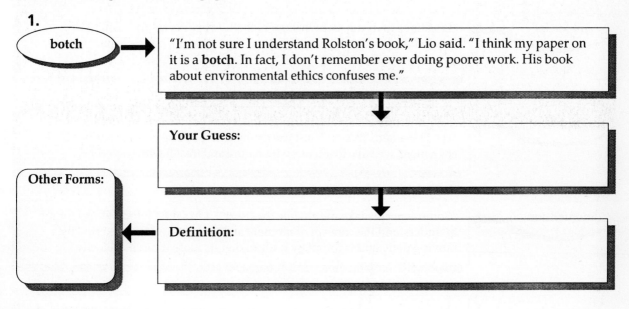

botch → "I'm not sure I understand Rolston's book," Lio said. "I think my paper on it is a **botch**. In fact, I don't remember ever doing poorer work. His book about environmental ethics confuses me."

Your Guess:

Other Forms:

Definition:

2.

clientele → "Well, *Environmental Ethics* isn't exactly a popular book," Hana said, "and it is probably only sold to a select **clientele**. Still, I like what the book says."

3.

closure → "I do, too," Van said. "I agree that we have a duty to be responsible to the environment. That may mean supporting the **closure** of some businesses that don't value the environment. They should go out of business."

4.

condole → "I **condole** with you about your paper, Lio, and I also have sympathy for the fact that Rolston's theories are confusing you," Hana said. "Don't you see that nature and culture go together and that we have to think about our responses to the environment?"

5.

convene → "I'm glad we're **convening** here today," Lio said. "Meeting together will give us a chance to discuss environmental ethics, and maybe I will understand the subject better than I did during class."

6.

crony → "One reason I understand it," Van said, "is that a **crony** of my father's is a philosophy professor, and he frequently talks about what Rolston calls 'values carried by nature.' My father's friend really helped me understand Rolston's theories."

7.

impartial → "Do I have to decide if environmental ethics are necessary? Can't I be **impartial** and not take sides?" Lio asked. "After all, nature is just there for us to enjoy and use."

8.

inertia → "The environmental movement will fail if people give in to **inertia** and don't act," Hana said. "We can't just use nature as if it's there only for our personal enjoyment; we have to interact with nature and treat it with respect."

9.

momentum → "Some concepts take me a while to absorb," Lio said. "It took weeks for me to understand the concept of **momentum,** which is the force exerted by a moving body and is found by multiplying its mass times its velocity."

10.

stipulate → "I think people should have to sign agreements with their local governments that **stipulate** that they will take care of the environment," Van said. "I would gladly make such a promise."

EXERCISE 2 *Context Clues* ✍

Directions. Scan the definitions in Column A. Then think about how the boldface words are used in the sentences in Column B. To complete the exercise, match each definition in Column A with the correct vocabulary word from Column B. Write the letter of your choice on the line provided; then write the vocabulary word on the line preceding the definition.

COLUMN A

_____ **11.** word: _____
n. the act of closing or condition of being closed; a conclusion or finish

_____ **12.** word: _____
n. a tendency not to move, act, or change

_____ **13.** word: _____
n. a close friend or companion; a buddy

_____ **14.** word: _____
v. to call, bring, or gather together; to assemble for a common purpose; to meet

_____ **15.** word: _____
v. to spoil by poor work or performance; *n.* a poor piece of work

_____ **16.** word: _____
adj. fair; just; showing no favoritism; without bias or prejudice

_____ **17.** word: _____
v. to express sympathy; to mourn in sympathy; to commiserate

_____ **18.** word: _____
v. to specify as a condition of an agreement; to guarantee in an agreement; to promise

_____ **19.** word: _____
n. customers or patrons collectively

_____ **20.** word: _____
n. the force exerted by a moving body, found by multiplying its mass times its speed; impetus; speed or force, usually growing in strength

COLUMN B

(A) "If you think of human responsibility to nature as being a job, then we've done poor work; we've **botched** it," Van said.

(B) "But it's too early to mourn nature and **condole** with one another about nature's end," Hana said. "There's still hope."

(C) "Books like *Environmental Ethics* have given impetus to a movement to care for nature, and the **momentum** is growing."

(D) "Yes, thank goodness **inertia** has failed to set in, and the movement is very active!" Van said.

(E) "The **clientele** at local stores are requesting products that don't harm the environment," Hana said.

(F) "I wonder if any employment contracts **stipulate** that employees must recycle and otherwise respect the environment."

(G) "Environmentalists from around the world have **convened** to discuss our duties to the natural world," Van said.

(H) "My parents went to an environmental convention as unbiased, **impartial** observers" said Hana, "but they came away loyal environmentalists."

(I) "A buddy of my father's and a few of his other **cronies** recently attended a local convention on environmental ethics," Van said.

(J) "I was going to join them on the last day, but there was an early **closure** of the convention because of bad weather."

EXERCISE 3 *Sentence Completion* ✍

Directions. For each of the following items, circle the letter of the choice that best completes the meaning of the sentence or sentences.

21. Is it right for a store owner to be forced out of business or for the _____ of his store to be required just because he did not re-spect nature?
(A) crony
(B) inertia
(C) momentum
(D) closure
(E) impartiality

22. Imagine that the previously loyal _____ of a store became upset with the owner's environmental record.
(A) botch
(B) momentum
(C) clientele
(D) closure
(E) inertia

23. The owner's lease contained the _____ that he could dump trash into a river. The guarantee was legal.
(A) momentum
(B) stipulation
(C) clientele
(D) condolence
(E) crony

24. The owner really _____ his reputation with the public when he polluted the river and spoiled the environment.
(A) stipulated
(B) condoled
(C) convened
(D) closed
(E) botched

25. Can you be _____ and unbiased and say whether or not the store owner violated his duty—his ethical responsibility to nature?
(A) condolatory
(B) inertial
(C) impartial
(D) imperceptible
(E) momentous

26. Should we _____ a group of people from the community to discuss the situation and invite all the store's regular _____?
(A) convene . . . clientele
(B) botch . . . inertia
(C) stipulate . . . momentums
(D) botch . . . closures
(E) condole . . . inertia

27. This is an ethical matter that should not be decided by the owner's _____ and close friends. You should urge people to be as _____, or unbiased, as possible.
(A) closures . . . inertial
(B) botches . . . stipulated
(C) momentums . . . condolatory
(D) cronies . . . impartial
(E) condolences . . . impartial

28. Do you think the sheer force, or _____, of the environmental movement will work against the store owner and that the public will sup-port the store's forced _____?
(A) crony . . . inertia
(B) botch . . . stipulation
(C) closure . . . crony
(D) inertia . . . momentum
(E) momentum . . . closure

29. Will the store owner's _____, his failure to change his ways, be a factor when the con-cerned citizens _____ to discuss the store owner's environmental record?
(A) momentum . . . stipulate
(B) inertia . . . convene
(C) closure . . . condole
(D) momentum . . . botch
(E) clientele . . . convene

30. Is your sympathy with the environment in this theoretical situation, or would you _____ with the store owner? Would you want to reopen the store or support its _____?
(A) convene . . . momentum
(B) botch . . . crony
(C) condole . . . closure
(D) gloat . . . botch
(E) stipulate . . . clientele

MAKING NEW WORDS YOUR OWN

Lesson 24 **CONTEXT:** The Environment

Laboratory Lakes for Acid Rain

In Canada, scientists have turned a group of forty-six remote lakes into a laboratory known as the Experimental Lakes Area. In 1976, scientists began experiments to determine the effects of adding acids to the lakes. Results have proven that acids—such as those found in acid rain caused by the burning of fossil fuels—do damage plant and animal life.

In the following exercises, you will have the opportunity to expand your vocabulary by reading about Canada's Experimental Lakes Area and acid rain. Below are ten vocabulary words that will be used in these exercises.

arbiter	cant	imperceptible	rectify	subsidiary
breach	equilibrium	oblivious	stratagem	substantially

EXERCISE 1 *Mapping*

Directions. In the item below, a vocabulary word is provided and used in a sentence. Take a guess at the word's meaning and write it in the box labeled **Your Guess**. Then look the word up in your dictionary and write the definition in the box labeled **Definition**. In the **Other Forms** box, write as many other forms of the word, such as adjective and noun forms, as you can think of or find in your dictionary.

Then, following the same procedure, draw your own map for each of the nine remaining vocabulary words. Use a separate sheet of paper.

1.

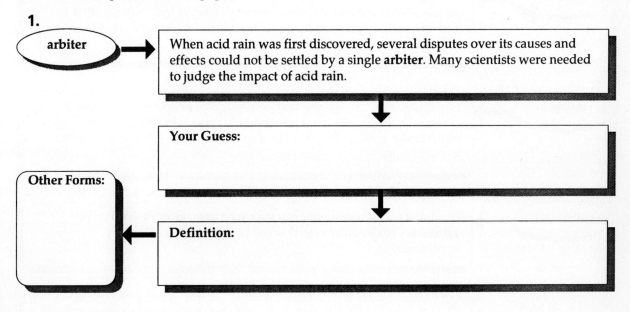

arbiter → When acid rain was first discovered, several disputes over its causes and effects could not be settled by a single **arbiter**. Many scientists were needed to judge the impact of acid rain.

Your Guess:

Other Forms:

Definition:

2.

breach

Along with gaps, or **breaches,** in the earth's ozone layer and the destruction of the earth's rain forests, acid rain has become a major environmental problem.

3.

cant

In the last several decades, enough research has been done to establish that acid rain is indeed a serious environmental problem. More than mere **cant** about the subject is necessary; sincere talk followed by action is needed.

4.

equilibrium

In Canada's laboratory lakes, acids destroyed the delicate **equilibrium** that existed among organisms. Scientists say it may take hundreds of years for the natural balance to be restored.

5.

imperceptible

Scientists began adding acid to Lake 223 in 1976. At first, the damage to the lake was **imperceptible,** but the damage became very noticeable by the third year.

6.

oblivious

Acidity increased in following years, as did damage to life in the lake. The effects on such creatures as freshwater shrimp and trout were so obvious that even a nonscientist could not be **oblivious** to them.

7.

rectify

Fish reproduction had stopped, and some species had vanished completely toward the end of the eighth year. To begin to **rectify** the situation, scientists reduced the amount of acid put into the lake, and conditions started improving.

8.

stratagem

From these experiments one may conclude that people need to think of clever schemes, or **stratagems,** to combat acid rain in lakes. Perhaps more importantly, though, they need to stop putting acids into the environment in the first place.

9.

subsidiary

In light of such experiments, can we afford to make our environment **subsidiary** to our other needs? Is our planet really of secondary importance?

10.

substantially

Tests at Lake 223 have shown that, soon after acid amounts are cut, the environment does recover somewhat. However, it may take hundreds of years for the lake to improve **substantially** and for a considerable amount of life to return.

EXERCISE 2 Context Clues ✍

Directions. Scan the definitions in Column A. Then think about how the boldface words are used in the sentences in Column B. To complete the exercise, match each definition in Column A with the correct vocabulary word from Column B. Write the letter of your choice on the line provided; then write the vocabulary word on the line preceding the definition.

COLUMN A

____ **11.** word: _____
adj. unmindful; forgetful

____ **12.** word: _____
n. a company controlled by another company; *adj.* subordinate; secondary

____ **13.** word: _____
n. insincere or almost meaningless talk; jargon; hypocritical talk; *v.* to speak insincerely or tritely

____ **14.** word: _____
n. a state of balance; mental or emotional poise or control

____ **15.** word: _____
v. to set right; to remedy; to adjust

____ **16.** word: _____
adv. largely; considerably; significantly

____ **17.** word: _____
n. a person chosen to decide a dispute; a judge

____ **18.** word: _____
n. a scheme or trick for achieving some purpose, such as to deceive a military enemy; a deception

____ **19.** word: _____
adj. too slight, subtle, or gradual to be noticed

____ **20.** word: _____
v. to break through; to violate; to leap clear of; *n.* a violation of a law, obligation, or standard; a gap or broken place

COLUMN B

(A) If the research findings are **substantially** true (and there's no reason for them not to be accurate), then acid rain is a problem.

(B) A friend's mother works for a **subsidiary** of a large company that has donated millions of dollars to research into acid rain.

(C) Don't be **oblivious** to the problem; be mindful of it. Read about acid rain and experiments like the ones conducted by Canada's Department of Fisheries and Oceans.

(D) Lake 223's conditions showed that large amounts of acid can cause biological destruction and upset nature's delicate balance, its **equilibrium**.

(E) Though **imperceptible** to human eyes, many of the lake's tiny animals, some of them microscopic, still absorbed large amounts of acid.

(F) What comes to mind is a cartoon of a clever trout that has developed a **stratagem** to escape the acid. In Lake 223, however, its scheme wouldn't work.

(G) You've probably seen pictures of whales **breaching**. In my cartoon the trout leaps out of the water like a whale and yells, "Help!"

(H) Unfortunately, people around the lake would be engaged in **cant** and wouldn't even look up from their meaningless talk.

(I) The image is fanciful, but it illustrates the situation of helpless animals that can't **rectify**, or remedy, the problems we cause them.

(J) Do you think the Experimental Lakes Area project is worthy? If we disagree, an **arbiter** may be needed to settle the argument.

EXERCISE 3 *Sentence Completion* ✍

Directions. For each of the following items, circle the letter of the choice that best completes the meaning of the sentence or sentences.

21. Ms. Simmons, our science teacher, is the final _____ on all arguments about science. Everyone trusts her judgment.
    (A) stratagem
    (B) breach
    (C) equilibrium
    (D) subsidiary
    (E) arbiter

22. Paul's uncle works for a small local _____ of a large corporation. The local company uses fossil fuels and may be polluting area lakes. It has been receiving a lot of complaints from environmentalists.
    (A) equilibrium
    (B) cant
    (C) subsidiary
    (D) breach
    (E) stratagem

23. Paul says the talk that the business is creating acid rain is just _____ from dissatisfied employees. He says that we shouldn't take their insincere, meaningless talk seriously.
    (A) cant
    (B) subsidiary
    (C) breach
    (D) equilibrium
    (E) arbiter

24. Lorna said that Paul and many others are _____ to what is really happening and need to become more aware.
    (A) imperceptible
    (B) impartial
    (C) oblivious
    (D) substantial
    (E) subsidiary

25. Ms. Simmons suggested that the class conduct its own experiments to determine if acid rain has _____ harmed area lakes, leaving observable evidence.
    (A) obliviously
    (B) subsidiarily
    (C) impartially
    (D) immaculately
    (E) substantially

26. "Has acid rain _____ hurt the lakes, or is it possible that the effect has been _____, or almost impossible to see?" Paul asked.
    (A) imperceptibly . . . oblivious
    (B) substantially . . . imperceptible
    (C) substantially . . . strategic
    (D) obliviously . . . subsidiary
    (E) imperceptibly . . . oblivious

27. "I don't know, but we'll find out if the _____ in the lakes has been disturbed. Unfortunately, once an imbalance occurs, it is sometimes difficult to _____, or remedy."
    (A) cant . . . breach
    (B) subsidiary . . . substantiate
    (C) breach . . . rectify
    (D) equilibrium . . . rectify
    (E) arbiter . . . breach

28. "Well," Lorna said, "my emotional _____ will be unbalanced and I will be upset if we find out that the _____ has ruined our lakes. Doesn't the parent company care?"
    (A) arbiter . . . stratagem
    (B) breach . . . cant
    (C) equilibrium . . . subsidiary
    (D) cant . . . breach
    (E) subsidiary . . . arbiter

29. Lorna added, "I just hope that the company doesn't think of some _____, or scheme, to stop us from experimenting. If there are problems, they need to be quickly _____, or taken care of."
    (A) breach . . . canted
    (B) equilibrium . . . rectified
    (C) subsidiary . . . canted
    (D) cant . . . breached
    (E) stratagem . . . rectified

30. "I know a working scientist who can be the _____ in this dispute," Ms. Simmons said. "It might be _____, or violation, of my contract for me to become involved."
    (A) arbiter . . . a breach
    (B) cant . . . an arbiter
    (C) subsidiary . . . a cant
    (D) breach . . . an equilibrium
    (E) equilibrium . . . a stratagem

MAKING NEW WORDS YOUR OWN

| Lesson 25 | **CONTEXT:** The Environment

Rinsing the Ketchup Bottle: Recycling

You've read about the different ages of humankind—the Stone Age, the Bronze Age, and so on. You could say that now we are passing from the Trash Age, or the Throwaway Age, to the Recycling Age. Recycling is considered the best solution to the waste-disposal crisis in the United States. The Environmental Protection Agency (EPA) says recycling is the best way to cope with our trash problems. Several states and communities nationwide now have recycling laws, and recycling has become big business.

In the following exercises, you will have the opportunity to expand your vocabulary by reading about recycling efforts in the United States. Below are ten vocabulary words that will be used in these exercises.

debase	explicate	imposition	quibble	sporadic
effervescent	immaculate	mull	resonant	synthesis

| **EXERCISE 1** | *Mapping*

Directions. In the item below, a vocabulary word is provided and used in a sentence. Take a guess at the word's meaning and write it in the box labeled **Your Guess**. Then look the word up in your dictionary and write the definition in the box labeled **Definition**. In the other forms box, write as many other forms of the word, such as adjective and noun forms, as you can think of or find in the dictionary.

Then, following the same procedure, draw your own map for each of the nine remaining vocabulary words. Use a separate sheet of paper.

1.

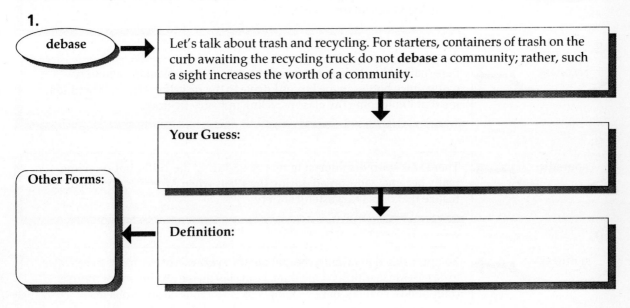

debase → Let's talk about trash and recycling. For starters, containers of trash on the curb awaiting the recycling truck do not **debase** a community; rather, such a sight increases the worth of a community.

Your Guess:

Other Forms:

Definition:

2.

effervescent →

We must all think about recycling and reusing containers. Don't throw away those glass bottles after the **effervescent** mineral water has bubbled out. Save them to be recycled into other glass products.

3.

explicate →

I'd like to give you a detailed explanation of why recycling is so important. Do we have enough time for me to **explicate** the terrible, overflowing conditions of the nation's landfills?

4.

immaculate →

Don't think that I'm a recycling saint who has never sinned by throwing away a recyclable glass bottle or plastic container. I am not **immaculate**, but I'm learning.

5.

imposition →

Now, it is true that some people consider recycling to be an **imposition**, something they are forced to do. Many others, however, feel good about recycling and enjoy doing it.

6.

mull →

If you are thinking our country recycles most of its waste, **mull** this over: The United States recycles only about 10 percent of its waste, including only 1 percent of its plastics, 8 to 10 percent of its metals, 10 percent of its glass, and 33 percent of its newsprint.

7.

quibble →

With figures like these, I don't want to hear any **quibbles** about having to recycle those newspapers and bottles. Any petty objections pale beside the great need to clean up our act.

8.

resonant →

Personally, I like to hear the **resonant,** resounding, clanking sound of empty juice bottles in the box as I drive to the recycling center. It reminds me that I'm helping the glass recycling industry to grow.

9.

sporadic →

There was **sporadic** interest in recycling during the 1970s, but recycling really became widespread during the 1980s when Americans began to realize that ours is a wasteful society.

10.

synthesis →

You probably don't want to hear about the **synthesis** of chemicals that creates toxic gases in landfills. I don't think I can explain the production of complex compounds, anyway, but I do know this is a serious health problem.

EXERCISE 2 *Context Clues* ✍

Directions. Scan the definitions in Column A. Then think about how the boldface words are used in the sentences in Column B. To complete the exercise, match each definition in Column A with the correct vocabulary word from Column B. Write the letter of your choice on the line provided; then write the vocabulary word on the line preceding the definition.

COLUMN A	COLUMN B

COLUMN A

_____ **11.** word: _____
v. to think about at length; to ponder

_____ **12.** word: _____
n. something forced on a person, such as a tax, an undue burden, or oneself

_____ **13.** word: _____
n. the combining of separate elements or substances to form a whole; the production of a complex compound by union of chemical elements

_____ **14.** word: _____
adj. high-spirited; lively; giving off many small bubbles of gas; foaming, bubbly

_____ **15.** word: _____
v. to lower the character or worth of something

_____ **16.** word: _____
adj. deep and rich in tone or sound; resounding or re-echoing

_____ **17.** word: _____
v. to explain in detail; to clarify the meaning of

_____ **18.** word: _____
adj. without stain or spot; free from error; innocent, without sin; pure

_____ **19.** word: _____
v. to find a minor fault with; *n.* a petty objection

_____ **20.** word: _____
adj. occurring at irregular intervals; occasional; not widespread

COLUMN B

(A) An **effervescent** woman at a recent party carried on a lively conversation about the great recycling program in New Jersey.

(B) She had a **resonant** voice that echoed throughout the room as she urged one and all to "reduce, reuse, and recycle."

(C) "You must **mull** this over: In 1991 New Jersey had a 51 percent recycling rate. Just think about it!" she exclaimed.

(D) She shared more details. "That was way ahead of the state goal, which is 60 percent for 1995," she **explicated**.

(E) "Some people could **quibble** with a few aspects of New Jersey's recycling laws, but why criticize minor details?"

(F) "The fact is that officials in New Jersey have combined many fine recycling ideas to form a highly workable **synthesis**."

(G) I was able to give only **sporadic** attention to the woman, Ms. Toranz, but my occasional chats with her were fascinating.

(H) "You know," she said, "I really hope you don't find my 'trash talk' an **imposition**. I try not to force myself on people."

(I) "Not at all," I assured her, bending down to wipe a spot off the otherwise **immaculate** dining room floor.

(J) "I think people **debase** themselves if they don't recycle," she said. "At least, their characters are lowered in my eyes."

EXERCISE 3 Sentence Completion ✍

Directions. For each of the following items, circle the letter of the choice that best completes the meaning of the sentence or sentences.

21. Ms. Toranz offered me _____ ginger ale that foamed and bubbled, and we talked more about recycling.
(A) an immaculate
(B) an effervescent
(C) a resonant
(D) a subsidiary
(E) a sporadic

22. "Of course, I don't even like dirt, much less trash," she said. "I keep my house looking _____, not a spot anywhere."
(A) effervescent
(B) sporadic
(C) explicative
(D) resonant
(E) immaculate

23. The doorbell, which was surprisingly _____ compared with the people's sometimes shrill and argumentative voices, startled us.
(A) resonant
(B) immaculate
(C) sporadic
(D) effervescent
(E) explicative

24. Other people were arriving at the party _____, so occasionally Ms. Toranz had new people with whom to share her recycling knowledge.
(A) effervescently
(B) theoretically
(C) immaculately
(D) sporadically
(E) resonantly

25. "Try taking some time to _____ over the remarkable statistics that the amount of glass we throw away every two weeks would fill the World Trade Center's twin towers. Those are statistics to ponder!"
(A) debase
(B) resonate
(C) mull
(D) impose
(E) explicate

26. Ms. Toranz _____ the topic of recycling. She explained that each year Americans produce over eleven billion tons of solid waste. She was lively and _____ as she listed more statistics.
(A) mulled . . . immaculate
(B) convened . . . resonant
(C) explicated . . . effervescent
(D) debased . . . sporadic
(E) imposed . . . resonant

27. " _____ with my ideas if you will," she said, "but no one can find fault with the hard facts. Do you need more _____?"
(A) Debase . . . resonance
(B) Quibble . . . explication
(C) Debase . . . imposition
(D) Mull . . . quibble
(E) Quibble . . . imposition

28. "We can put together all the statistics to form a true _____ that tells us much about our recycling habits. Are you still _____ over the World Trade Center figures?"
(A) quibble . . . mulling
(B) imposition . . . explicating
(C) resonance . . . debasing
(D) effervescence . . . quibbling
(E) synthesis . . . mulling

29. One _____ comment that I repeated now and then was that some companies think the quality of their products will be _____ if the packaging isn't catchy and durable.
(A) sporadic . . . debased
(B) effervescent . . . explicated
(C) resonant . . . mulled
(D) sporadic . . . explicated
(E) resonant . . . debased

30. "Well," she said, "it's a big _____ to remove the heavy packaging; I know I find it a burden. And what is the point of keeping a basketball _____ in a box, when it is supposed to be played with?"
(A) quibble . . . sporadic
(B) synthesis . . . resonant
(C) quibble . . . sporadic
(D) imposition . . . immaculate
(E) patriarch . . . effervescent

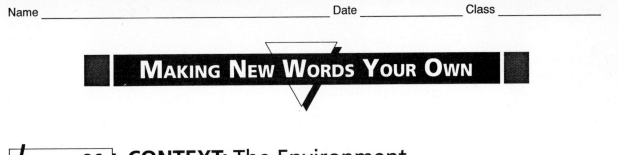

MAKING NEW WORDS YOUR OWN

| Lesson 26 | **CONTEXT:** The Environment

More Than Spilled Milk: 11 Million Gallons of Oil in the Sea

On the night of March 23, 1989, the *Exxon Valdez*, one of the largest ocean vessels in the world, hit Bligh Reef, off the coast of Alaska. This accident caused serious damage to the environment. The *Valdez* was carrying 53 million gallons of crude oil. When the bottom of the ship was ripped open by the reef, 11 million gallons spewed into Prince William Sound, a part of Alaska with a large wildlife population and beautiful scenery. This was just one of many severe oil tanker catastrophes that have occurred around the world.

In the following exercises, you will have the opportunity to expand your vocabulary by reading about the environmental damage from oil spills in the ocean. Below are ten vocabulary words that will be used in these exercises.

abdicate	inadvertent	itinerary	rankle	stimulant
episode	infallible	naive	sardonic	translucent

EXERCISE 1 *Mapping*

Directions. In the item below, a vocabulary word is provided and used in a sentence. Take a guess at the word's meaning and write it in the box labeled **Your Guess**. Then look the word up in your dictionary and write the definition in the box labeled **Definition**. In the **Other Forms** box, write as many other forms of the word, such as adjective and noun forms, as you can think of or find in your dictionary.

Then, following the same procedure, draw your own map for each of the nine remaining vocabulary words. Use a separate sheet of paper.

1.

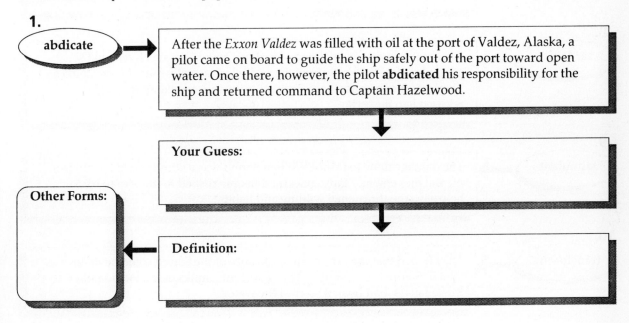

After the *Exxon Valdez* was filled with oil at the port of Valdez, Alaska, a pilot came on board to guide the ship safely out of the port toward open water. Once there, however, the pilot **abdicated** his responsibility for the ship and returned command to Captain Hazelwood.

2. episode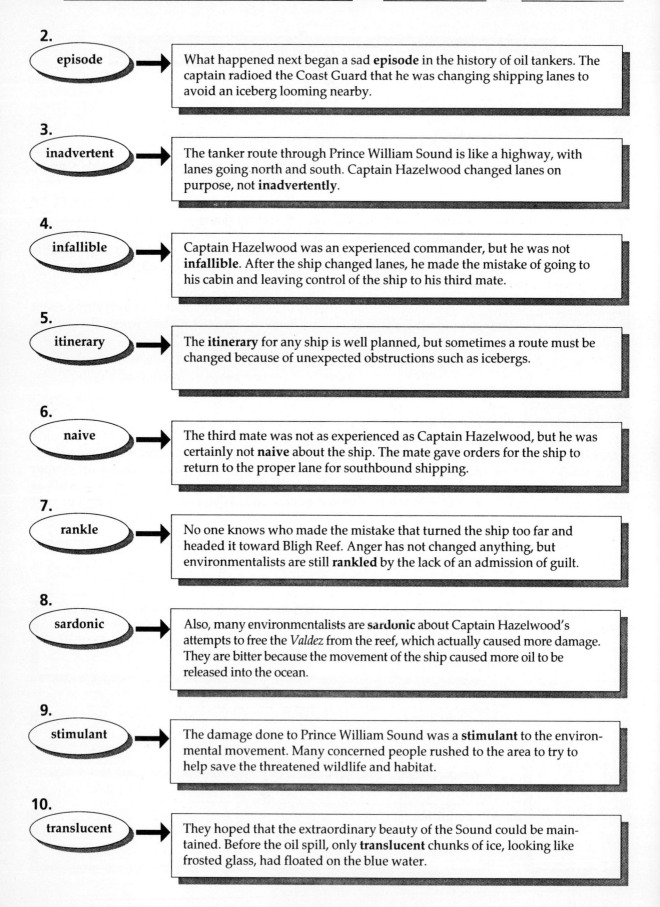

What happened next began a sad **episode** in the history of oil tankers. The captain radioed the Coast Guard that he was changing shipping lanes to avoid an iceberg looming nearby.

3. inadvertent

The tanker route through Prince William Sound is like a highway, with lanes going north and south. Captain Hazelwood changed lanes on purpose, not **inadvertently**.

4. infallible

Captain Hazelwood was an experienced commander, but he was not **infallible**. After the ship changed lanes, he made the mistake of going to his cabin and leaving control of the ship to his third mate.

5. itinerary

The **itinerary** for any ship is well planned, but sometimes a route must be changed because of unexpected obstructions such as icebergs.

6. naive

The third mate was not as experienced as Captain Hazelwood, but he was certainly not **naive** about the ship. The mate gave orders for the ship to return to the proper lane for southbound shipping.

7. rankle

No one knows who made the mistake that turned the ship too far and headed it toward Bligh Reef. Anger has not changed anything, but environmentalists are still **rankled** by the lack of an admission of guilt.

8. sardonic

Also, many environmentalists are **sardonic** about Captain Hazelwood's attempts to free the *Valdez* from the reef, which actually caused more damage. They are bitter because the movement of the ship caused more oil to be released into the ocean.

9. stimulant

The damage done to Prince William Sound was a **stimulant** to the environmental movement. Many concerned people rushed to the area to try to help save the threatened wildlife and habitat.

10. translucent

They hoped that the extraordinary beauty of the Sound could be maintained. Before the oil spill, only **translucent** chunks of ice, looking like frosted glass, had floated on the blue water.

EXERCISE 2 *Context Clues*

Directions. Scan the definitions in Column A. Then think about how the boldface words are used in the sentences in Column B. To complete the exercise, match each definition in Column A with the correct vocabulary word from Column B. Write the letter of your choice on the line provided; then write the vocabulary word on the line preceding the definition.

COLUMN A

_____ **11.** word: _____
adj. letting some light through without being completely transparent

_____ **12.** word: _____
n. a route, plan, or record of a trip

_____ **13.** word: _____
n. something that excites or activates; a substance or an agent that quickens body activity temporarily

_____ **14.** word: _____
adj. free from or incapable of error; absolutely reliable and dependable

_____ **15.** word: _____
adj. bitter; sarcastic; scornful

_____ **16.** word: _____
adj. not done on purpose; unintentional

_____ **17.** word: _____
adj. lacking in sophistication; simple; inexperienced; revealing a lack of subtlety and insight

_____ **18.** word: _____
v. to give up or renounce power

_____ **19.** word: _____
v. to cause continual irritation, anger, bitterness, or pain

_____ **20.** word: _____
n. an event or a series of events that is part of a larger continuing experience; an incident in a written work; an installment, as of a series of television programs

COLUMN B

(A) Exxon agreed to conduct a cleanup of the area, but the oil company was **naive**, revealing a lack of insight about the magnitude of the disaster.

(B) The **itinerary** of the ship had placed it in an area with salmon hatcheries and other wildlife habitats that could be destroyed by the spill.

(C) **Sardonic** onlookers criticized the way the cleanup was handled, but no one had all the answers.

(D) Experts admit that even the best cleanup techniques are far from **infallible**. Mistakes are made repeatedly.

(E) If the oil spills and resulting damage **rankle** enough people, maybe their bitterness will lead them to demand that better techniques be developed.

(F) The fact that oil spills are **inadvertent** does not relieve the people in charge of the tanker companies from responsibility.

(G) In 1978, the *Amoco Cadiz* spilled 68 million gallons of oil into the English Channel, causing widespread damage. How many **episodes** of this sort will it take before cleanup techniques are improved?

(H) Experts say that it is considered good when 10 to 20 percent of the oil can be recovered. These figures should be a **stimulant**, activating more research into ways to recover a greater percentage.

(I) Some people think that whoever is responsible for disasters such as the *Valdez* and the *Cadiz* should **abdicate** and let others who are more careful take control.

(J) Oil spills like that from the *Valdez* are thick and black and no light shines through them. They are not **translucent** on the water or on the wildlife they smother.

EXERCISE 3 *Sentence Completion* ✍

Directions. For each of the following items, circle the letter of the choice that best completes the meaning of the sentence or sentences.

21. Because oil spills are complex problems, _____ solutions will not work.
    (A) naive
    (B) inadvertent
    (C) sardonic
    (D) translucent
    (E) infallible

22. Each _____ in the history of oil spills requires different answers because of varying natural conditions.
    (A) itinerary
    (B) stimulant
    (C) inadvertence
    (D) episode
    (E) abdication

23. Often further damage occurs during cleanups. People often _____ cause this damage when the side effects of their cleanup efforts unexpectedly do more harm than good.
    (A) episodically
    (B) inadvertently
    (C) translucently
    (D) infallibly
    (E) sardonically

24. No one system of cleanup is _____, or free of problems. For instance, burning the oil off the water gets rid of some of the oil but causes air pollution.
    (A) sardonic
    (B) inadvertent
    (C) infallible
    (D) translucent
    (E) naive

25. People who are _____ about cleanup efforts should offer workable solutions instead of sarcasm.
    (A) inadvertent
    (B) infallible
    (C) translucent
    (D) episodic
    (E) sardonic

26. Perhaps the _____ of tankers should avoid areas like Prince William Sound. Is this idea a simplistic or _____ suggestion?
    (A) episodes . . . sardonic
    (B) stimulants . . . translucent
    (C) itineraries . . . naive
    (D) abdications . . . inadvertent
    (E) translucence . . . infallible

27. The _____ of many cruise ships include Prince William Sound. People who had expected to enjoy the beauty of the area were _____ by the change of scene after the oil spill. It's easy to understand their anger.
    (A) episodes . . . abdicated
    (B) stimulants . . . rankled
    (C) itineraries . . . abdicated
    (D) itineraries . . . rankled
    (E) abdications . . . rankled

28. The light filtering through the _____ icebergs has been known to charm even the most cynical, _____ person.
    (A) infallible . . . inadvertent
    (B) translucent . . . sardonic
    (C) inadvertent . . . naive
    (D) sardonic . . . translucent
    (E) episodic . . . infallible

29. The cold air probably acted as _____ to some cleanup workers, activating them to work quickly. Others were probably _____ by it, angry because of the discomfort.
    (A) a stimulant . . . rankled
    (B) an itinerary . . . abdicated
    (C) an episode . . . paraphrased
    (D) an inadvertence . . . perceived
    (E) a translucence . . . rankled

30. Competent leaders should not _____ responsibility and leave the power in the hands of _____ people who may mean well, but may not have the experience necessary to handle the situation. The cleanup of oil spills is a challenge for experts.
    (A) rankle . . . infallible
    (B) rankle . . . translucent
    (C) abdicate . . . naive
    (D) abdicate . . . infallible
    (E) abdicate . . . sardonic

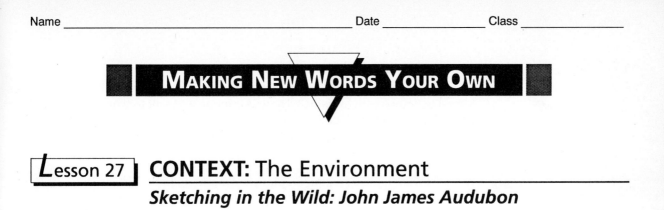

MAKING NEW WORDS YOUR OWN

Lesson 27 **CONTEXT: The Environment**

Sketching in the Wild: John James Audubon

There are fountains in the park near where we live, and birds gather around them to drink. I became curious about the different kinds of birds. When I asked a librarian where I could find information about birds, he recommended John James Audubon's *Birds of America*, first published in the 1830s in four large volumes. What a beautiful, ambitious work! From the books, I was able to identify all of the birds I'd been seeing. Then I began to wonder what sort of man Audubon was and what motivated him to paint pictures of so many birds.

In the following exercises, you will have the opportunity to expand your vocabulary by reading about John James Audubon and his life's work. Below are ten vocabulary words that will be used in these exercises.

demure	intermittent	irrelevant	redundant	sequel
edify	intuition	pallid	reminiscent	synopsis

EXERCISE 1 *Mapping*

Directions. In the item below, a vocabulary word is provided and used in a sentence. Take a guess at the word's meaning and write it in the box labeled **Your Guess**. Then look the word up in your dictionary and write the definition in the box labeled **Definition**. In the **Other Forms** box, write as many other forms of the word, such as adjective and noun forms, as you can think of or find in your dictionary.

Then, following the same procedure, draw your own map for each of the nine remaining vocabulary words. Use a separate sheet of paper.

1.

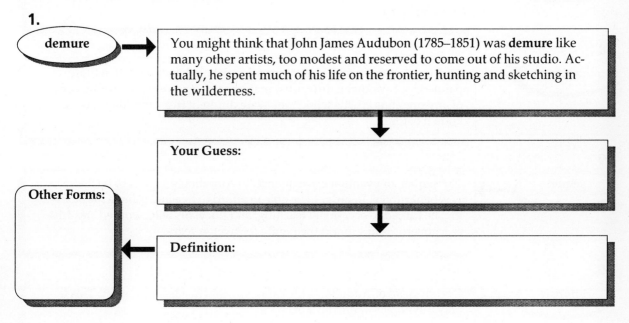

demure → You might think that John James Audubon (1785–1851) was **demure** like many other artists, too modest and reserved to come out of his studio. Actually, he spent much of his life on the frontier, hunting and sketching in the wilderness.

Your Guess:

Other Forms:

Definition:

2.

edify ➤ He was born on his father's plantation in Haiti, but at an early age he returned to France with his father. There, Audubon was sent to school to be **edified,** to be prepared for an upstanding adult life.

3.

intermittent ➤ When he was eighteen, Audubon came to America to find work, but his work was **intermittent**. He tried mining lead in Pennsylvania, operating a store in Kentucky, and pursuing other business ventures, all of which were short-lived.

4.

intuition ➤ His businesses failed because he spent most of his time exploring the wilderness. His **intuition** led him to concentrate on art and the outdoors, though logically he probably knew he should be working at his business.

5.

irrelevant ➤ Audubon found business **irrelevant**. It did not relate or apply to his primary interest and ambition—the completion of his collection of bird paintings for publication.

6.

pallid ➤ To Audubon, whatever else he saw or experienced in life seemed **pallid** compared with the exciting, colorful, vital world of birds.

7.

redundant ➤ He did not regard his repeated trips to the forests as **redundant**. He was always able to collect new specimens to add to his collection of stuffed and mounted birds.

8.

reminiscent ➤ Audubon's paintings of birds were more detailed and exact than those painted by any other nature artist in the past. They were not **reminiscent** of any previous artist's work; they were different from anything seen or known before.

9.

sequel ➤ The **sequel,** or eventual consequence, to Audubon's neglect of business was bankruptcy. In order to be able to afford to live and pursue his painting, he turned to occasional teaching; and Lucy, his wife, worked steadily as a governess to support the family for twelve years.

10.

synopsis ➤ Of course, all of Audubon's life cannot be told in a few sentences. This is only a **synopsis** of the full story.

EXERCISE 2 Context Clues ✍

Directions. Scan the definitions in Column A. Then think about how the boldface words are used in the sentences in Column B. To complete the exercise, match each definition in Column A with the correct vocabulary word from Column B. Write the letter of your choice on the line provided; then write the vocabulary word on the line preceding the definition.

COLUMN A	COLUMN B

COLUMN A

____ **11.** word: _____

adj. abnormally pale; lacking in color, vitality, or interest

____ **12.** word: _____

adj. stopping and starting with pauses between; occurring at irregular intervals; occasional

____ **13.** word: _____

adj. unnecessarily wordy or repetitive; superfluous

____ **14.** word: _____

n. a story complete in itself that continues an earlier one; continuation; a consequence

____ **15.** word: _____

adj. assuming an air of modesty or shyness; reserved

____ **16.** word: _____

adj. not applicable; not relevant; not related to the subject

____ **17.** word: _____

n. a brief review, outline, or condensation; a summary

____ **18.** word: _____

v. to instruct, especially morally or spiritually; to enlighten

____ **19.** word: _____

n. a knowing or becoming aware through an inner feeling rather than through reasoning; immediate understanding; sharp insight

____ **20.** word: _____

adj. thinking or telling about events of the past; suggestive of something seen or known before

COLUMN B

(A) I don't want to be **redundant** in telling about Audubon, but I have to repeat that his obsession with birds eventually did pay off.

(B) In Audubon's case, disregarding everything that he considered **irrelevant** to his artwork gave him time to concentrate on all that he thought related to it.

(C) He was not **demure** or modest about promoting his paintings. In fact, he was unreserved when he approached potential publishers.

(D) A **synopsis** of this period in Audubon's life would be a summary of his experiences of disappointment and rejection.

(E) Although American publishers told him his artwork was **edifying** or enlightening, they also said that publishing the paintings would require more skill than their engravers had.

(F) During this discouraging time, Audubon **intermittently** painted people's portraits. He knew that by occasionally painting portraits, he could earn a little money.

(G) But his **intuition** told him to continue with the bird studies and paintings, although his conscious reasoning told him that he would make no money with them.

(H) His struggles are **reminiscent** of those of many other artists who were not properly appreciated or supported during their lifetimes.

(I) But, whereas many of them became **pallid** and sick from living in unhealthful cities, Audubon stayed healthy by stalking specimens in the outdoors.

(J) And the **sequel** to this discouraging time in his life is better than what happened later to some other underappreciated artists.

EXERCISE 3 *Sentence Completion* ✍

Directions. For each of the following items, circle the letter of the choice that best completes the meaning of the sentence or sentences.

21. Audubon was certain that his paintings would _____ the world if they were published—that they would teach people about the wonders of nature.

(A) reminisce
(B) synopsize
(C) edify
(D) intermit
(E) intuit

22. He decided that he must not be _____ about seeking a publisher. He boldly went alone to England.

(A) irrelevant
(B) demure
(C) redundant
(D) reminiscent
(E) pallid

23. Audubon hoped that the lack of skilled engravers in America would be _____ to his success; surely there would be engravers available in England.

(A) pallid
(B) reminiscent
(C) intermittent
(D) demure
(E) irrelevant

24. Audubon and his paintings were well received in the British Isles. What a relief after his _____ reception in America, where it seemed that no one was excited about or interested in his work.

(A) pallid
(B) redundant
(C) irrelevant
(D) reminiscent
(E) synoptic

25. In a _____, or summary, of Audubon's life, I read that in 1827 he was elected to the Royal Society of Edinburgh.

(A) sequel
(B) redundancy
(C) synopsis
(D) stratagem
(E) pallidness

26. It is probably _____ to say that an offer from a publisher elated and overjoyed Audubon, but the fact bears repeating.

(A) demure
(B) reminiscent
(C) intermittent
(D) redundant
(E) pallid

27. His _____ had been right. He had always felt that the work he found _____ would someday be enlightening to others.

(A) demureness . . . irrelevant
(B) intermittence . . . pallid
(C) redundancy . . . reminiscent
(D) synopsis . . . intermittent
(E) intuition . . . edifying

28. The engraver Robert Havell offered Audubon steady, not _____, financial support. Havell's work was certainly not _____ to the project, either. He contributed the necessary engraving skills.

(A) redundant . . . pallid
(B) demure . . . reminiscent
(C) intermittent . . . irrelevant
(D) pallid . . . redundant
(E) synoptic . . . edifying

29. Audubon's success enabled him to live a life of luxury _____ of his privileged childhood. He continued to write and paint, but birds had become _____ to him; he did not want to repeat himself.

(A) intermittent . . . pallid
(B) reminiscent . . . redundant
(C) irrelevant . . . demure
(D) pallid . . . intermittent
(E) redundant . . . synoptic

30. A _____ of the early part of Audubon's professional life would be a summary of the ups and downs of his career. But the _____ to the story is all good: Audubon went on to become famous.

(A) synopsis . . . sequel
(B) pallidness . . . synopsis
(C) redundancy . . . pallidness
(D) demureness . . . intuition
(E) reminiscence . . . demureness

Name _____ Date _____ Class _____

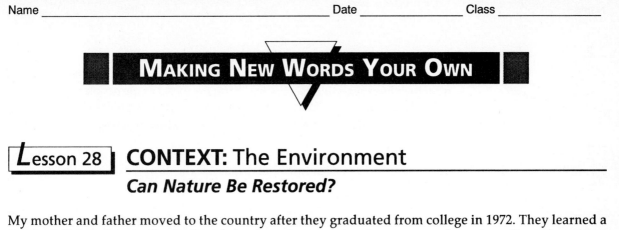

MAKING NEW WORDS YOUR OWN

Lesson 28 | **CONTEXT:** The Environment

Can Nature Be Restored?

My mother and father moved to the country after they graduated from college in 1972. They learned a lot about living close to the earth and developed a respect and a reverence for nature. Even though we live in a city now and don't have a large garden or keep chickens anymore, we continue to be concerned about the way nature is treated. My parents have taught me to respect and protect the wonder and diversity of our environment.

In the following exercises, you will have the opportunity to expand your vocabulary by reading about the concern one family has for the environment. Below are ten vocabulary words that will be used in these exercises.

detonate	irrational	lexicon	potency	seethe
eject	jostle	merge	rendezvous	simulate

EXERCISE 1

Directions. In the item below, a vocabulary word is provided and used in a sentence. Take a guess at the word's meaning and write it in the box labeled **Your Guess**. Then look the word up in your dictionary and write the definition in the box labeled **Definition**. In the **Other Forms** box, write as many other forms of the word, such as adjective and noun forms, as you can think of or find in your dictionary.

Then, following the same procedure, draw your own map for each of the nine remaining vocabulary words. Use a separate sheet of paper.

1.

(detonate) → There were times, my father said, when he was afraid that the nuclear arms race would **detonate** the world. What good would the world be, if it were blown to bits and pieces?

↓

Your Guess:

Other Forms:

↓

Definition:

2.

eject → He and my mother decided to work toward a more peaceful world and **eject** from their lives everything that would harm the world or the people in it. One of the things they expelled from their lives was nonorganic produce.

3.

irrational → With the world's resources in short supply, it seemed **irrational** to them to waste anything. It was much more reasonable to try to conserve these resources.

4.

jostle → They saw that the world's population was increasing and its resources decreasing. News stories showed starving people in poor countries **jostling** and pushing each other as riots nearly broke out when food was distributed.

5.

lexicon → New words entered the **lexicon** of my parents' generation: Spaceship Earth, global warming, environmental concerns, endangered species, back-to-the-land movement, recycle, organic farming, and counterculture.

6.

merge → Individual concerns about polluted air and water, overuse of pesticides, and industrial pollution **merged** into one global concern: doing what was best for the earth.

7.

potency → The **potency** of the movement was seen when people got together to protest wasteful or dangerous practices and got results. The environmental movement became stronger during the seventies and eighties.

8.

rendezvous → Often groups would decide on a **rendezvous**, and everyone would meet at one place with signs and banners that stated the reason for the protest.

9.

seethe → My mother says that it does no good just to **seethe** with anger over the abuse suffered by the earth. What is needed is consistent, daily action to restore health to the natural world.

10.

simulate → And she said that some people **simulate** interest but actually do not care enough to help. They don't recycle or stop using products that harm the environment.

EXERCISE 2 *Context Clues* ✍

Directions. Scan the definitions in Column A. Then think about how the boldface words are used in the sentences in Column B. To complete the exercise, match each definition in Column A with the correct vocabulary word from Column B. Write the letter of your choice on the line provided; then write the vocabulary word on the line preceding the definition.

<table>
<tr><td>COLUMN A</td><td>COLUMN B</td></tr>
</table>

COLUMN A

_____ **11.** word: _____

n. a dictionary; the vocabulary of a particular trade, group of people, or the like

_____ **12.** word: _____

v. to look or act like; to pretend to be like; to imitate

_____ **13.** word: _____

v. to throw out forcefully; to expel; to evict or drive out

_____ **14.** word: _____

n. a designated meeting place; a place where people habitually meet; a pre-arranged meeting; *v.* to meet or bring together at a certain place and time

_____ **15.** word: _____

v. to blow up; to explode; to cause to explode; *n.* an explosion

_____ **16.** word: _____

n. strength; power; a capacity for development

_____ **17.** word: _____

adj. illogical; senseless; not reasonable

_____ **18.** word: _____

v. to boil; to saturate; to be highly agitated

_____ **19.** word: _____

v. to shove or push rudely; to come into close contact with; to collide

_____ **20.** word: _____

v. to blend or combine in a way that results in the loss of separate identity; to unite

COLUMN B

(A) One of the things we do at home is **merge** our shopping lists into one so that we make fewer trips to the store.

(B) We also try to avoid rush hours when people are **jostling** one another and intersections are so busy that our car has to idle for long periods of time.

(C) Some of the kids at school **seethe** with resentment if they have to walk home from a neighbor's house. Most can't wait until they have their own cars.

(D) We need to **eject** the dependence on personal motorized vehicles from our lives. What's wrong with walking, riding bikes, or using public transportation?

(E) Simple ideas like using cloth lunch sacks and napkins that can be washed and reused are not **irrational** or unreasonable.

(F) We need to be "green consumers" (another expression in some environmentalists' **lexicon**). That is, we need to be people who purchase only goods that don't harm the environment.

(G) We can replace cleaning agents of harmful **potency** with unharmful but effective agents such as white vinegar.

(H) In order to work, cleansers don't have to appear to **detonate** or explode when they are added to water. Remember that whatever goes down a drain ends up in the earth.

(I) I suppose we could think of the earth as a **rendez-vous** point for everything that is thrown away. It's pretty scary to think of all the junk in existence coming to meet in one place!

(J) Maybe in real life we shouldn't **simulate** the waste we see on TV, where just about everything that is advertised seems to be disposable.

EXERCISE 3   *Sentence Completion* ✍

Directions. For each of the following items, circle the letter of the choice that best completes the meaning of the sentence or sentences.

21. Three words that all environmentalists have in their _____ are *reuse, recycle,* and *reject.*
   (A) detonation
   (B) ejection
   (C) potency
   (D) lexicon
   (E) rendezvous

22. In many landfills that contain harmful compounds, the earth _____ when it rains, becoming saturated with vile bubbling fluids.
   (A) jostles
   (B) seethes
   (C) ejects
   (D) simulates
   (E) detonates

23. Some people have to have their memories _____ or shaken continually to remember not to be wasteful.
   (A) jostled
   (B) ejected
   (C) detonated
   (D) merged
   (E) seethed

24. We should _____ from our minds the notion that the earth is doomed. If we all work together, nature can be restored.
   (A) detonate
   (B) merge
   (C) simulate
   (D) eject
   (E) rendezvous

25. Animals, plants, and people need hospitable environments. Our _____ abuses of nature, which contradict common sense, have threatened habitats everywhere.
   (A) simulated
   (B) ejectable
   (C) irrational
   (D) detonating
   (E) merging

26. It shouldn't take _____ or other violent human-caused catastrophe to make people realize that we must _____, or unite, our needs with the needs of nature.
   (A) an ejection . . . jostle
   (B) a simulation . . . merge
   (C) a lexicon . . . detonate
   (D) an irrationalism . . . seethe
   (E) a detonation . . . merge

27. People should stop _____ and colliding with nature. They should stop behaving in _____, unreasonable manner.
   (A) detonating . . . a simulated
   (B) jostling . . . an irrational
   (C) ejecting . . . a detonating
   (D) jostling . . . a merging
   (E) ejecting . . . a seething

28. The public pressure has had enough _____ to force companies to seek new, safer technologies. Some companies have _____ outdated equipment and replaced it with equipment that is nonpolluting.
   (A) ejection . . . jostled
   (B) simulation . . . merged
   (C) potency . . . ejected
   (D) rendezvous . . . detonated
   (E) lexicons . . . simulated

29. Nature cannot be imitated; if it is destroyed, it cannot be _____ for future generations. We need to make sure we do not behave in a senseless, _____ way.
   (A) ejected . . . simulated
   (B) merged . . . jostling
   (C) jostled . . . merging
   (D) simulated . . . irrational
   (E) seethed . . . seething

30. There is strength and _____ to my mother's argument that either we must stop being inconsiderate of Mother Nature or we will all face a _____ with disaster—a meeting we won't look forward to.
   (A) detonation . . . lexicon
   (B) simulation . . . potency
   (C) ejection . . . detonation
   (D) irrationality . . . lexicon
   (E) potency . . . rendezvous

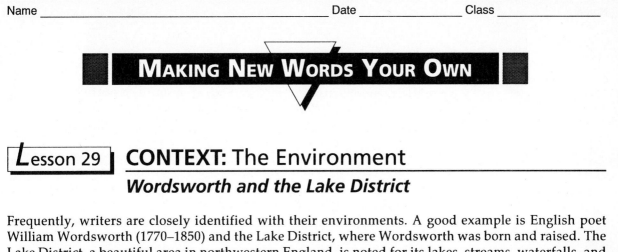

MAKING NEW WORDS YOUR OWN

Lesson 29 | **CONTEXT:** The Environment

Wordsworth and the Lake District

Frequently, writers are closely identified with their environments. A good example is English poet William Wordsworth (1770–1850) and the Lake District, where Wordsworth was born and raised. The Lake District, a beautiful area in northwestern England, is noted for its lakes, streams, waterfalls, and mountains. In 1799, Wordsworth made the Lake District his permanent home. The area filled Wordsworth with inspiration and the appreciation of nature, which is reflected in much of his poetry.

In the following exercises, you will have the opportunity to expand your vocabulary by reading about William Wordsworth and his beloved Lake District. Below are ten vocabulary words that will be used in these exercises.

| decrepit | inconsistent | jargon | obligatory | pertinent |
| farce | irksome | malignant | parody | rebuke |

EXERCISE 1 | *Mapping*

Directions. In the item below, a vocabulary word is provided and used in a sentence. Take a guess at the word's meaning and write it in the box labeled **Your Guess**. Then look the word up in your dictionary and write the definition in the box labeled **Definition**. In the **Other Forms** box, write as many other forms of the word, such as adjective and noun forms, as you can think of or find in your dictionary.

Then, following the same procedure, draw your own map for each of the nine remaining vocabulary words. Use a separate sheet of paper.

1.

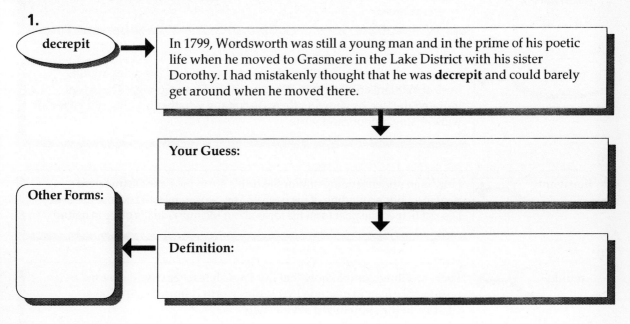

decrepit → In 1799, Wordsworth was still a young man and in the prime of his poetic life when he moved to Grasmere in the Lake District with his sister Dorothy. I had mistakenly thought that he was **decrepit** and could barely get around when he moved there.

Your Guess:

Other Forms:

Definition:

2.

farce

→ It would be a **farce** to think of Wordsworth living in the Lake District and completely ignoring his surroundings. Such an absurdity is not in keeping with what we know of Wordsworth's interests and habits.

3.

inconsistent

→ Wordsworth certainly was not **inconsistent** in his love for the Lake District. His decision to live there as an adult was in complete harmony with his early love of his "dear native regions."

4.

irksome

→ When reading about Wordsworth, you might find constant references to the Lake District **irksome**. You may not be annoyed by the references, however, if you understand the district's impact on his life and poetry.

5.

jargon

→ Our teacher rented a videotape about Wordsworth and the Lake District, but something was wrong with the tape. The faulty tape made it sound like the narrator was speaking **jargon,** gibberish that none of us could understand.

6.

malignant

→ After seeing the video, I cannot imagine any **malignant** influences ever having settled on Dove Cottage, Wordsworth's home in Grasmere. Surely no evil would touch such a peaceful, enchanting home.

7.

obligatory

→ There was no **obligatory** reason that Wordsworth decided to move to the Lake District. He moved there totally of his own choice because he truly loved the area.

8.

parody

→ I once saw a humorous skit in which actors **parodied** the quiet, routine lives of William and Dorothy Wordsworth at Dove Cottage. The actors imitated the two by showing them discussing whether they should go for a walk or stay indoors and write.

9.

pertinent

→ How is an understanding of Wordsworth's life in the Lake District **pertinent** to an understanding of his poetry? The two are related because the Lake District helped the poet form his ideas about the individual's place in nature.

10.

rebuke

→ I hate scoldings, and I know that my English teacher would give me a **rebuke** if I failed to mention that Wordsworth is buried in the Lake District, in the churchyard at Grasmere.

EXERCISE 2   *Context Clues* 👈

Directions. Scan the definitions in Column A. Then think about how the boldface words are used in the sentences in Column B. To complete the exercise, match each definition in Column A with the correct vocabulary word from Column B. Write the letter of your choice on the line provided; then write the vocabulary word on the line preceding the definition.

COLUMN A

_____ **11.** word: _____
adj. annoying; irritating; tiresome

_____ **12.** word: _____
adj. actively evil; having an evil influence; tending to do great harm; life-threatening

_____ **13.** word: _____
n. a broad comedy using exaggeration and ridiculous action; an absurdity; mockery; empty pretense

_____ **14.** word: _____
n. an imitation (usually of a serious literary or artistic work) that ridicules the original; *v.* to imitate in order to ridicule; to mimic

_____ **15.** word: _____
n. the specialized language of a trade or profession; nonsensical speech; gibberish

_____ **16.** word: _____
v. to blame or scold sharply; *n.* a scolding; a sharp reprimand

_____ **17.** word: _____
adj. worn out or broken down by old age, illness, or long use; feeble; weak

_____ **18.** word: _____
adj. related to the matter at hand; to the point; appropriate

_____ **19.** word: _____
adj. not in harmony or agreement; containing elements that contradict one another; changeable

_____ **20.** word: _____
adj. required; compulsory; legally binding

COLUMN B

(A) My mother found out that her tumor is not **malignant,** so we don't have to worry anymore.

(B) To celebrate before she gets "old and **decrepit,**" as she puts it, Mother took us on vacation to England's Lake District.

(C) Some people find traveling **irksome,** but I never tire of traveling.

(D) On the plane to London, I listened to the flight attendants, trying to understand the **jargon** they used to communicate with each other.

(E) I promised that I would go with Mother to Wordsworth's Dove Cottage. We made the **obligatory** trip late one afternoon.

(F) Unfortunately, the cottage and Wordsworth Museum were closed, and Mother **rebuked** me. "I'm not to blame," I said.

(G) "This whole trip is turning into some kind of ridiculous comedy, a **farce,** because we don't check the times," she said.

(H) She was right, and I thought about writing a **parody** of our adventures. I could accompany an imitation of a famous Wordsworth ballad on my guitar!

(I) Mother's moods were **inconsistent**. She soon changed her attitude and said, "Well, we'll come back tomorrow."

(J) "Let's find a schedule for tourist sights," I said. "That would be something **pertinent** we could do to help ourselves."

EXERCISE 3 *Sentence Completion* ✍

Directions. For each of the following items, circle the letter of the choice that best completes the meaning of the sentence or sentences.

21. In the _____ of old-time jazz musicians, Mother and I had a "groovy," or great, time in the Lake District.
(A) rebuke
(B) parody
(C) jargon
(D) farce
(E) irksomeness

22. In our "city clothes," we probably looked silly, even _____, hiking around the lakes and mountains.
(A) consistent
(B) malignant
(C) obligatory
(D) pertinent
(E) farcical

23. I tried to _____ Wordsworth creating poetry as he hiked, but Mother said it wasn't polite to mimic such a great poet.
(A) seethe
(B) rebuke
(C) malign
(D) parody
(E) irk

24. She _____ me in a gently scolding way and told me about Wordsworth's visit to Tintern Abbey and the resulting poem.
(A) simulated
(B) rebuked
(C) protruded
(D) parodied
(E) irked

25. "That poem isn't about this area," she said, "but it is _____ because it relates to Wordsworth's appreciation of his surroundings."
(A) malignant
(B) decrepit
(C) pertinent
(D) obligatory
(E) inconsistent

26. "He could have found beauty in _____ chair that was ready for the dump," I said, thinking the comment _____, or to the point.
(A) a decrepit . . . pertinent
(B) an inconsistent . . . malignant
(C) a pertinent . . . decrepit
(D) an irksome . . . inconsistent
(E) a malignant . . . irksome

27. "The Lake District is so peaceful, far away from all talk about tumors and _____," Mother said. "Isn't it wonderful not to have to listen to any more medical _____? I'm glad to be away from that technical talk."
(A) farce . . . parody
(B) inconsistency . . . rebuke
(C) jargon . . . farce
(D) malignancy . . . jargon
(E) parody . . . rebuke

28. "Modern life can be _____," I said. "There's little that is annoying here. I feel that life can go on here forever and that nothing can ever be harmful or _____."
(A) pertinent . . . decrepit
(B) decrepit . . . inconsistent
(C) obligatory . . . malignant
(D) inconsistent . . . pertinent
(E) irksome . . . malignant

29. "Your going with me to Lake District National Park is _____, not optional," Mother said. I felt tired, worn, and _____ after vigorously hiking the day before.
(A) farcical . . . malignant
(B) irksome . . . obligatory
(C) obligatory . . . decrepit
(D) irksome . . . pertinent
(E) malignant . . . inconsistent

30. I thought the park might be _____ with the rest of the area, but it was in harmony. I didn't find the boat ride at all _____ or tiresome.
(A) decrepit . . . malignant
(B) inconsistent . . . irksome
(C) obligatory . . . decrepit
(D) pertinent . . . obligatory
(E) irksome . . . inconsistent

MAKING NEW WORDS YOUR OWN

Lesson 30 **CONTEXT: The Environment**

Moving Continents, If You Get My Drift

When you look at a globe, you see that the continents look like pieces of a jigsaw puzzle. It is easy to imagine that they could fit together. Many geologists believe that they once formed a single huge continent, which they call Pangea. According to those scientists, Pangea broke apart about 200 million years ago. The continents are still drifting today, thanks to constantly shifting tectonic plates, or large crustal slabs. Although we can't see or feel the movement—except, of course, during earthquakes—the continents are in motion. Where will they be in another 200 million years?

In the following exercises, you will have the opportunity to expand your vocabulary by reading about students in a geology class who are learning about continental drift. Below are ten vocabulary words that will be used in these exercises.

carp	coincidental	negligible	protrude	sordid
caustic	incendiary	odious	scenario	transition

EXERCISE 1 *Mapping*

Directions. In the item below, a vocabulary word is provided and used in a sentence. Take a guess at the word's meaning and write it in the box labeled **Your Guess**. Then look the word up in your dictionary and write the definition in the box labeled **Definition**. In the **Other Forms** box, write as many other forms of the word, such as adjective and noun forms, as you can think of or find in your dictionary.

Then, following the same procedure, draw your own map for each of the nine remaining vocabulary words. Use a separate sheet of paper.

1.

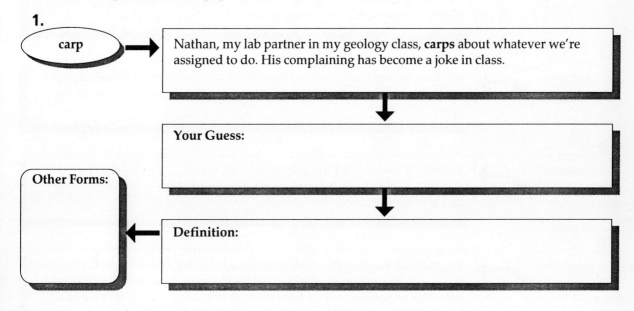

carp → Nathan, my lab partner in my geology class, **carps** about whatever we're assigned to do. His complaining has become a joke in class.

Your Guess:

Other Forms:

Definition:

2.

caustic → Our teacher tends to be rather **caustic,** so between his sarcasm and Nathan's comments, I often feel as if I were in a war zone.

3.

coincidental → Nathan and I are friends, so it's not **coincidental** that we are lab partners. We planned it that way. Besides, no one else wants to listen to him.

4.

incendiary → We took chemistry together, too. Now, Nathan isn't an **incendiary** who sets fire to property, but it seems as if every time he gets into a chemistry lab, something bursts into flames.

5.

negligible → Our chemistry teacher didn't consider the damage **negligible,** and he was right. By the end of the semester, it added up to quite a lot.

6.

odious → Anyway, we switched to geology because it seemed safer. Nathan actually likes science, but he regards all the assignments as **odious,** or disgusting.

7.

protrude → We're learning about how the continents broke apart and drifted away from one another millions of years ago. It's easy to see how they could have fitted together because wherever the Americas **protrude,** there is a matching indentation in Europe or Africa.

8.

scenario → Mr. Simons, our teacher, asked the class to write a **scenario** for a documentary film about what took place when Pangea, the single continent, broke apart.

9.

sordid → Nathan, of course, said it was a **sordid** assignment, too degrading for scientific-minded people, but he pitched in and helped with the planning and writing.

10.

transition → We discussed setting the scene on Pangea, focusing on the physical characteristics in documentary style, but before we knew it, we had changed subjects. The **transition** took us from geology to zoology, as we speculated on the effect the continental breakup had had on dinosaurs.

EXERCISE 2 *Context Clues* ✍

Directions. Scan the definitions in Column A. Then think about how the boldface words are used in the sentences in Column B. To complete the exercise, match each definition in Column A with the correct vocabulary word from Column B. Write the letter of your choice on the line provided; then write the vocabulary word on the line preceding the definition.

<table>
<tr><td>COLUMN A</td><td>COLUMN B</td></tr>
</table>

COLUMN A

_____ **11.** word: _____
adj. too small or unimportant to bother with; insignificant

_____ **12.** word: _____
adj. dirty; degrading; ignoble; squalid; greedy and selfish

_____ **13.** word: _____
v. to thrust forth; to project or stick out

_____ **14.** word: _____
v. to find fault in an unpleasant or nagging way; to complain, especially about a minor grievance

_____ **15.** word: _____
adj. capable of causing fire; stirring up discord or rebellion; *n.* a person who sets fire to property; a person who stirs up discord or rebellion

_____ **16.** word: _____
n. a substance that burns or corrodes; *adj.* corrosive; marked by sharp and biting wit; sarcastic

_____ **17.** word: _____
n. a brief summary of a play or opera; a script of a motion picture; an outline of proposed events, real or imagined

_____ **18.** word: _____
n. a changing from one form, state, or place to another; a passing from one subject to another

_____ **19.** word: _____
adj. hateful; disgusting; detestable

_____ **20.** word: _____
adj. occurring together by accident; existing or happening at the same time

COLUMN B

(A) My contribution to the assignment was **negligible**. Right after we started working on it, I got sick and had to miss school.

(B) I had an **odious** illness with hateful symptoms. It lasted a whole week.

(C) When I came back to school, the class had already written an outline, or **scenario**, and plans were being made to make models of Pangea and the continents that formed when Pangea broke up.

(D) We built Pangea and the smaller continents out of plaster so that we could form mountains that would **protrude** above the surface.

(E) Some people wanted to use real sedimentary rocks for some landforms and **carped** about the plaster, which they complained didn't look real.

(F) Such complaints seemed **incendiary**, but after a while people cooled down and compromised. Some real rocks, both sedimentary and igneous, were combined with the plaster.

(G) We talked to Mr. Simons about the best way to show the **transition** from one continent to several continents.

(H) He said that the changes occurred over millions of years and that it could not be known exactly which ones were **coincidental**.

(I) Nathan offered to go to the chemistry lab and get a **caustic** that would burn through the plaster, thus separating the continents. We immediately vetoed that idea.

(J) To get Nathan's mind off the chemistry lab, Mr. Simons gave him what Nathan called a **sordid** job: cleaning some rocks we had recently collected on a field trip.

EXERCISE 3 *Sentence Completion* ✍

Directions. For each of the following items, circle the letter of the choice that best completes the meaning of the sentence or sentences.

21. It's interesting to think that the land at the poles today may once have been near the equator. Continents move so slowly that the change or _____ must have taken eons.
    (A) caustic
    (B) scenario
    (C) transition
    (D) incendiary
    (E) coincidence

22. Continental drift, which goes on all of the time, is so slow that it seems _____ to us. In geologic terms, however, significant changes are taking place.
    (A) odious
    (B) caustic
    (C) incendiary
    (D) negligible
    (E) sordid

23. As the molten rock from within the earth _____ through the ocean floor, the ocean floor spreads and moves the continents.
    (A) protrudes
    (B) carps
    (C) condoles
    (D) debases
    (E) rankles

24. One possible outline, or _____, of geologic change shows the Pacific Ocean getting smaller and the Red Sea getting larger.
    (A) incendiary
    (B) protrusion
    (C) reprieve
    (D) caustic
    (E) scenario

25. These changes may seem _____ to some people, but actually there is no need to think of them as hateful. The change takes place too slowly to affect us.
    (A) caustic
    (B) odious
    (C) incendiary
    (D) negligible
    (E) transitional

26. Sometimes, as the plates that make up the earth's crust move against each other, there are _____, or simultaneous, occurrences such as volcanic eruptions and earthquakes. Lava flows often _____ from the ocean floor, forming new land masses.
    (A) caustic . . . carp
    (B) coincidental . . . protrude
    (C) sordid . . . incendiary
    (D) negligible . . . enjoin
    (E) sordid . . . protrude

27. People who live near fault lines have a right to _____ and complain when shifts in the earth's crust cause _____ happenings.
    (A) protrude . . . caustic
    (B) carp . . . negligible
    (C) protrude . . . coincidental
    (D) carp . . . odious
    (E) debut . . . incendiary

28. Flowing lava is _____: The intense heat often causes wooden structures many feet away to burst into flames. Damage from lava flows varies from _____ to excessive.
    (A) coincidental . . . sordid
    (B) caustic . . . coincidental
    (C) incendiary . . . negligible
    (D) odious . . . incendiary
    (E) carping . . . transitional

29. We made a videotape of the breakup of Pangea as we imagined it had happened. Of course, among us there was some _____ and complaining, but no one we showed it to made any _____ or sarcastic comments.
    (A) protruding . . . sordid
    (B) carping . . . transitional
    (C) edifying . . . incendiary
    (D) protruding . . . coincidental
    (E) carping . . . caustic

30. We had really made a mess of the lab, but since we had had fun we didn't mind the _____, distasteful task of cleaning things up.
    (A) negligible
    (B) sordid
    (C) transitional
    (D) odious
    (E) caustic

CONNECTING NEW WORDS AND PATTERNS

Why We Practice Analogies

Practice with analogies develops proficiency in logic. To answer analogy questions correctly, you analyze two words and identify the relationship between them; then you identify another pair of words that has the same relationship. In addition, when you study analogies, you think about the precise meanings of words and fix these definitions in your memory. Finally, studying word analogies will help you to gain higher scores on national tests that include multiple-choice analogy questions. The new Scholastic Aptitude Test-I Verbal Reasoning Test, for example, includes analogy questions.

Understanding Word Analogies

A word analogy is a comparison between two pairs of words. Here's how word analogies are written:

EXAMPLE 1   FIND : LOCATE :: lose : misplace

The colon (:) stands for the phrase "is related to." Here's how to read the relationships in Example 1:

> FIND [is related to] LOCATE
> lose [is related to] misplace

The double colon [::] between the two pairs of words stands for the phrase "in the same way that." Here's how to read the complete analogy:

> FIND [is related to] LOCATE
> [in the same way that]
> lose [is related to] misplace

Here's another way:

> FIND is to LOCATE as lose is to misplace.

A properly constructed analogy, then, tells us that the relationship between the first pair of words is the same as the relationship between the second pair of words. In Example 1, *find* and *locate* are synonyms, just as *lose* and *misplace* are synonyms.

Let's look at another example:

EXAMPLE 2   GIFT : JOY :: grief : tears

What's the relationship here? A *gift* causes *joy*, just as *grief* causes *tears*. A cause-and-effect relationship links the two pairs of words in Example 2. To help you identify the relationships expressed in analogies, we have designed the chart on page 124. No chart, of course, could include all possible relationships between words, but these twelve relationships are frequently presented. You should familiarize yourself with these relationships.

TYPES OF ANALOGIES		
RELATIONSHIP	**EXAMPLE**	**EXPLANATION**
Synonym	DRY : ARID :: lost : mislaid	*Dry* is similar in meaning to *arid*, just as *lost* is similar in meaning to *mislaid*.
Antonym	KIND : CRUEL :: happy : sad	*Kind* is the opposite of *cruel*, just as *happy* is the opposite of *sad*.
Part and Whole	CHAPTER : BOOK :: fender : automobile	A *chapter* is a part of a *book*, just as a *fender* is a part of an *automobile*.
	POEM : STANZAS :: play : acts	A *poem* is composed of *stanzas*, just as a *play* is composed of *acts*.
Characteristic Quality	MIRROR : SMOOTH :: sandpaper : rough	*Mirrors* are characteristically smooth, just as *sandpaper* is characteristically rough.
Classification	POLKA : DANCE :: frog : amphibian	A *polka* may be classified as a *dance*, just as a *frog* may be classified as an *amphibian*.
	BIRD : CARDINAL :: house : igloo	A *cardinal* is classified as a *bird*, just as an *igloo* is classified as a *house*.
Cause and Effect	GIFT : JOY :: rain : flood	A *gift* can cause *joy*, just as *rain* can cause a *flood*.
	TEARS : SADNESS :: smiles : joy	*Tears* are an effect of *sadness*, just as *smiles* are an effect of *joy*.
Function	KNIFE : CUT :: shovel : dig	The function of a *knife* is to *cut*, just as the function of a *shovel* is to *dig*.
Location	FISH : SEA :: moose : forest	A *fish* can be found in the *sea*, just as a *moose* can be found in a *forest*.
Degree	CHUCKLE : LAUGH :: whimper : cry	*Chuckle* and *laugh* have similar meanings, but differ in degree in the same way that *whimper* and *cry* have similar meanings but differ in degree.
Performer and Related Object	CASHIER : CASH :: plumber : pipe	A *cashier* works with *cash*, just as a *plumber* works with *pipe*.
Performer and Related Action	AUTHOR : WRITE :: chef : cook	You expect an *author* to *write*, just as you expect a *chef* to *cook*.
Action and Related Object	BOIL : EGG :: throw : ball	You *boil* an *egg*, just as you *throw* a *ball*. (In these items, the object always receives the action.)

A Process for Solving Analogies

Your job in solving multiple-choice analogy questions is to identify the relationship between the first two words and then to find the pair of words that has the most similar relationship. Here are four hints to help you:

Hint #1. Eliminate choices that represent relationships that do not match the relationship between the capitalized words.

Hint #2. Eliminate choices that have vague relationships. Remember, the original relationship will always be clear. So, too, will the answer's relationship.

Hint #3. Eliminate word pairs that express the same relationship as the capitalized pair, but appear in the opposite word order.

Hint #4. If you can't determine the relationship between two words, try reading them backward. Remember that a cause-and-effect relationship, for example, exists whether the pair is written *Cause* : *Effect* or *Effect* : *Cause*.

Here's a process that will help you with analogy questions:

Answering Analogy Questions: A 3-Step Method
1. Identify the relationship between the capitalized pair of words.
2. Look for that relationship in the pairs of words in the answer choices. Eliminate those that do not have that relationship.
3. Choose the pair of words whose relationship and word order match those of the capitalized pair.

Let's apply this pattern to a sample question in Example 3.

EXAMPLE 3   FISH : SEA ::

    (A) sun : star
    (B) hero : villain
    (C) moose : forest
    (D) rocket : astronaut
    (E) garage : car

1. *Identify the relationship.* It's location; a *fish* can be found in the *sea*.
2. *Eliminate choices.* Choice A has a relationship of classification; the *sun* is a *star*. Choice B has two opposites; *hero* is an antonym for *villain*. Choice D consists of a performer (*astronaut*) and a related object (*rocket*). None of these choices match.
3. *Choose the correct answer.* Choices C and E both have location relationships: A *moose* can be found in a *forest,* and a *car* can be found in a *garage.* But Choice E could only be correct if the words appeared in the opposite order— *car* : *garage.* So Choice C must be correct.

A Final Word

Analogies are easier to tackle if you approach them with flexibility. Allow yourself to discover the relationship between the first pair of words and to explore the relationships between the words in the answer choices. Keep in mind that some words can represent more than one part of speech and that most words have multiple meanings. Remember, these little verbal puzzles are a test of your ability to demonstrate flexibility as well as logic.

Name _____ Date _____ Class _____

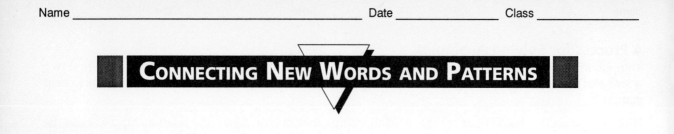

Lesson 1 | ANALOGIES

Directions. For each of the following items, choose the lettered pair of words that expresses a relationship that is most similar to the relationship between the pair of capitalized words. Write the letter of your answer on the line provided before the number of the item.

_____ **1.** CONDESCEND : SNOB ::
    (A) offend : manner
    (B) pluck : string
    (C) eat : food
    (D) help : assistant
    (E) march : ballerina

_____ **2.** CONTEMPTUOUS : SCORNFUL ::
    (A) careful : cautious
    (B) brotherly : fatherly
    (C) majestic : maternal
    (D) awkward : spry
    (E) confused : changed

_____ **3.** ELITE : SUPERIOR ::
    (A) pedestrians : few
    (B) inferiors : proud
    (C) heroes : brave
    (D) poor : wealthy
    (E) fantasy : real

_____ **4.** EVOLVE : CHANGE ::
    (A) swing : slide
    (B) spin : twirl
    (C) slip : rise
    (D) read : lecture
    (E) recall : forget

_____ **5.** EXCERPT : SELECTED ::
    (A) poem : hummed
    (B) symphony : run
    (C) quotation : heard
    (D) play : performed
    (E) creation : destroyed

_____ **6.** FORTITUDE : WEAKNESS ::
    (A) forgetfulness : memories
    (B) anxiety : calm
    (C) relaxation : rest
    (D) tension : strain
    (E) forethought : meditation

_____ **7.** MENTOR : ADVISE ::
    (A) physician : strike
    (B) map : travel
    (C) employer : argue
    (D) critic : review
    (E) chord : strike

_____ **8.** NOTORIETY : FAME ::
    (A) expense : money
    (B) song : singer
    (C) merit : worth
    (D) celebrity : celebration
    (E) fortune : publicity

_____ **9.** PAUPER : BEG ::
    (A) bag : rip
    (B) orphan : adopt
    (C) waiter : serve
    (D) convict : imprison
    (E) hostage : capture

_____ **10.** PROPHETIC : PREDICTIVE ::
    (A) prosperous : poor
    (B) propelled : poured
    (C) remarkable : outstanding
    (D) remote : remodeled
    (E) dangerous : scared

CONNECTING NEW WORDS AND PATTERNS

Lesson 2 | ANALOGIES

Directions. For each of the following items, choose the lettered pair of words that expresses a relationship that is most similar to the relationship between the pair of capitalized words. Write the letter of your answer on the line provided before the number of the item.

_____ 1. AMIABLE : PLEASANT ::
(A) tearful : soaked
(B) rapid : confusing
(C) mild : rough
(D) inviting : appealing
(E) infinite : short

_____ 2. APPREHENSIVE : CALM ::
(A) nervous : nervy
(B) apparent : obvious
(C) cool : cold
(D) tranquil : stormy
(E) withdrawn : quiet

_____ 3. BAYOU : LOUISIANA ::
(A) swamp : desert
(B) glacier : Alaska
(C) skyscraper : building
(D) pasture : city
(E) ocean : New Mexico

_____ 4. CALLOUS : DICTATOR ::
(A) magical : mother
(B) appropriate : answer
(C) greedy : glutton
(D) dishonest : police officer
(E) cowardly : boxer

_____ 5. COMMENDABLE : PRAISEWORTHY ::
(A) commanding : worthwhile
(B) horrible : awful
(C) critical : excellent
(D) repairable : fixed
(E) plain : desirable

_____ 6. GRIMACE : PAIN ::
(A) riddle : puzzle
(B) freckle : skin
(C) laughter : joke
(D) foolishness : fear
(E) sun : warmth

_____ 7. MALLEABLE : CLAY ::
(A) flexible : rubber
(B) slight : heavyweight
(C) light : iron
(D) bright : darkness
(E) soft : marble

_____ 8. MELODRAMATIC : SOAP OPERA ::
(A) melodious : rhythm
(B) necessary : schedule
(C) gentleness : cruelty
(D) funny : comedy
(E) mysterious : movie

_____ 9. SUCCUMB : PATIENT ::
(A) rip : scissors
(B) jog : driver
(C) threaten : terrorist
(D) assign : student
(E) plan : date

_____ 10. WHIMSICAL : FANCIFUL ::
(A) wild : tame
(B) approachable : shy
(C) odd : normal
(D) hysterical : mythical
(E) tired : weary

CONNECTING NEW WORDS AND PATTERNS

Lesson 3 | ANALOGIES

Directions. For each of the following items, choose the lettered pair of words that expresses a relationship that is most similar to the relationship between the pair of capitalized words. Write the letter of your answer on the line provided before the number of the item.

_____ **1.** ATROCIOUS : BAD ::
- (A) nice : clean
- (B) gradual : changeable
- (C) honest : selfish
- (D) wonderful : good
- (E) strange : average

_____ **2.** COMPASSION : SUFFERING ::
- (A) outrage : crime
- (B) justice : knowledge
- (C) court : defendant
- (D) injury : pain
- (E) twins : family

_____ **3.** DETERIORATE : IMPROVE ::
- (A) banish : expel
- (B) succeed : fail
- (C) devise : instruct
- (D) organize : classify
- (E) teethe : bite

_____ **4.** ECSTATIC : GLAD ::
- (A) temperamental : calm
- (B) pleased : disappointed
- (C) terrified : afraid
- (D) bendable : flexible
- (E) frozen : solid

_____ **5.** INSIPID : FLAVORLESS ::
- (A) active : listless
- (B) countless : worthless
- (C) amazing : astonishing
- (D) similar : different
- (E) lofty : aloft

_____ **6.** LOATHE : DISLIKE ::
- (A) invigorate : invest
- (B) love : learn
- (C) desire : pursue
- (D) disturb : divorce
- (E) adore : like

_____ **7.** PAINSTAKING : EMBROIDERING ::
- (A) tedious : breathing
- (B) tense : relaxing
- (C) thrilling : parachuting
- (D) threadbare : sewing
- (E) painful : swinging

_____ **8.** POMPOUS : HUMBLE ::
- (A) biased : basic
- (B) aggressive : forceful
- (C) acute : keen
- (D) knowledgeable : ignorant
- (E) troubled : terrible

_____ **9.** PORTLY : STOUT ::
- (A) single : multiple
- (B) striped : designed
- (C) whimpering : laughing
- (D) rigid : stiff
- (E) solemn : solitary

_____ **10.** REJUVENATE : FACE LIFT ::
- (A) age : wrinkle
- (B) revise : book
- (C) protect : armor
- (D) file : fingernail
- (E) grasps : eagle

CONNECTING NEW WORDS AND PATTERNS

Lesson 4 | ANALOGIES

Directions. For each of the following items, choose the lettered pair of words that expresses a relationship that is most similar to the relationship between the pair of capitalized words. Write the letter of your answer on the line provided before the number of the item.

_____ **1.** EMPHATICALLY : FORCEFULLY ::
(A) sweetly : bitterly
(B) quietly : violently
(C) severely : sternly
(D) softly : loudly
(E) strangely : familiarly

_____ **2.** FABRICATE : EXCUSE ::
(A) sew : needle
(B) interview : reporter
(C) tell : story
(D) puncture : hole
(E) witness : material

_____ **3.** IMPEDIMENT : OBSTACLE ::
(A) foot : tie
(B) peddler : ware
(C) device : machine
(D) hunch : observation
(E) conservation : energy

_____ **4.** MARTIAL : WEAPONRY ::
(A) spacious : astronauts
(B) annoyed : animals
(C) sold : salesperson
(D) soft : wool
(E) married : state

_____ **5.** MEDIOCRE : GOOD ::
(A) major : minor
(B) fine : superb
(C) tasty : sour
(D) fashionable : tasteless
(E) melodious : rhythmic

_____ **6.** QUALM : DOUBT ::
(A) ducking : quacking
(B) question : answer
(C) trembling : quaking
(D) theory : solution
(E) quantity : quality

_____ **7.** RECIPIENT : DONOR ::
(A) rug : carpet
(B) receipt : purchase
(C) buyer : seller
(D) broker : stock
(E) recess : judge

_____ **8.** STAMINA : EXERCISE ::
(A) stress : difficulty
(B) pulse : heart attack
(C) gymnasium : athlete
(D) basketball : sport
(E) anxiety : vacation

_____ **9.** ZEALOUS : UNENTHUSIASTIC ::
(A) crazed : insane
(B) taxed : wealthy
(C) strong : mighty
(D) old : dull
(E) timid : courageous

_____ **10.** ZEPHYR : GENTLE ::
(A) breeze : harsh
(B) sea : boiling
(C) cloud : solid
(D) bird : feathered
(E) kite : bulky

CONNECTING NEW WORDS AND PATTERNS

Lesson 5 ANALOGIES

Directions. For each of the following items, choose the lettered pair of words that expresses a relationship that is most similar to the relationship between the pair of capitalized words. Write the letter of your answer on the line provided before the number of the item.

_____ 1. COMPATIBLE : FRIENDS ::
  (A) bitter : companions
  (B) hostile : enemies
  (C) political : company
  (D) rude : host
  (E) unfriendly : invitation

_____ 2. ENCOMPASS : INCLUDE ::
  (A) yield : command
  (B) aim : shield
  (C) gather : collect
  (D) sleep : camp
  (E) scout : hike

_____ 3. INANIMATE : ROCK ::
  (A) lively : stone
  (B) tame : shark
  (C) wet : water
  (D) free : inmate
  (E) ferocious : pet

_____ 4. INCENTIVE : MOTIVE ::
  (A) fee : payment
  (B) book : page
  (C) money : employment
  (D) friend : rival
  (E) competition : trophy

_____ 5. INDESTRUCTIBLE : FRAGILE ::
  (A) delicate : dainty
  (B) harmful : hateful
  (C) quarrelsome : agreeable
  (D) destructive : impulsive
  (E) constructive : helpful

_____ 6. MILITANT : SOLDIER ::
  (A) merry : prisoner
  (B) charitable : volunteer
  (C) peaceful : warrior
  (D) forceful : florist
  (E) grateful : doctor

_____ 7. PREVALENT : WIDESPREAD ::
  (A) unusual : expected
  (B) narrow : broad
  (C) ordinary : usual
  (D) common : rare
  (E) valiant : cowardly

_____ 8. RETRIBUTION : WRONGDOING ::
  (A) patience : virtue
  (B) wages : work
  (C) sympathy : villain
  (D) unhappiness : kindness
  (E) reward : sheriff

_____ 9. STRINGENT : LAX ::
  (A) retired : relaxed
  (B) thin : slim
  (C) frequent : rare
  (D) required : necessary
  (E) responsible : punctual

_____ 10. TRANSCEND : SURPASS ::
  (A) transfer : translate
  (B) overcome : sink
  (C) sing : hum
  (D) transport : store
  (E) recall : recollect

CONNECTING NEW WORDS AND PATTERNS

Lesson 6   ANALOGIES

Directions. For each of the following items, choose the lettered pair of words that expresses a relationship that is most similar to the relationship between the pair of capitalized words. Write the letter of your answer on the line provided before the number of the item.

_____ **1.** APPEASE : HUNGER ::
   (A) sell : merchant
   (B) bake : baker
   (C) strike : egg
   (D) cook : pot
   (E) toss : coin

_____ **2.** ARCHAIC : ARMOR ::
   (A) modern : castle
   (B) creative : artist
   (C) antique : computer
   (D) inventive : habit
   (E) hectic : arrangement

_____ **3.** BALMY : BREEZE ::
   (A) crazy : palm trees
   (B) windy : kite
   (C) hot : pepper
   (D) irritating : blanket
   (E) soothing : confusion

_____ **4.** COMMENCE : FINISH ::
   (A) communicate : talk
   (B) start : begin
   (C) celebrate : honor
   (D) waste : save
   (E) mention : maintain

_____ **5.** DEVASTATION : DAMAGE ::
   (A) design : plan
   (B) danger : health
   (C) vegetation : rose
   (D) desert : oasis
   (E) luxury : comfort

_____ **6.** ESPIONAGE : SPY ::
   (A) law : nurse
   (B) plumbing : waiter
   (C) preaching : minister
   (D) sales : professor
   (E) masonry : manager

_____ **7.** INCLEMENT : STORMY ::
   (A) clever : considerate
   (B) insincere : honest
   (C) earnest : wealthy
   (D) remarkable : noteworthy
   (E) tender : tough

_____ **8.** INVINCIBLE : SUPERHERO ::
   (A) victorious : loser
   (B) lovely : scoundrel
   (C) heroic : coward
   (D) invigorating : exercise
   (E) boring : magician

_____ **9.** VIGILANT : WATCHFUL ::
   (A) distant : close
   (B) gallant : tall
   (C) gigantic : small
   (D) varied : similar
   (E) observant : attentive

_____ **10.** VULNERABLE : STRONG ::
   (A) guilty : responsible
   (B) shocking : startling
   (C) rough : smooth
   (D) useful : purposeful
   (E) temporary : timid

CONNECTING NEW WORDS AND PATTERNS

Lesson 7 | ANALOGIES

Directions. For each of the following items, choose the lettered pair of words that expresses a relationship that is most similar to the relationship between the pair of capitalized words. Write the letter of your answer on the line provided before the number of the item.

_____ **1.** CANINE : WOLF ::
   (A) neck : giraffe
   (B) bass : fish
   (C) turtle : stream
   (D) plant : leaf
   (E) feline : leopard

_____ **2.** DEFUNCT : EXTINCT ::
   (A) useful : useless
   (B) dead : dying
   (C) active : lively
   (D) existing : exciting
   (E) fun : risky

_____ **3.** HIEROGLYPHIC : EGYPT ::
   (A) handle : shovel
   (B) cactus : desert
   (C) pattern : design
   (D) archaeologist : scientist
   (E) alphabet : student

_____ **4.** INNOVATION : NEW ::
   (A) renovation : odd
   (B) utensil : unusual
   (C) antique : old
   (D) applause : unenthusiastic
   (E) rest : exhausting

_____ **5.** MEAGER : ABUNDANT ::
   (A) plentiful : grateful
   (B) modest : shy
   (C) awkward : graceful
   (D) eager : anxious
   (E) angry : furious

_____ **6.** OBLITERATE : CREATE ::
   (A) read : study
   (B) invent : devise
   (C) demolish : construct
   (D) tolerate : endure
   (E) think : ponder

_____ **7.** RAVAGE : LOCUSTS ::
   (A) pluck : feathers
   (B) pollinate : bees
   (C) climb : trees
   (D) hunch : shoulders
   (E) milk : cows

_____ **8.** RIVULET : RIVER ::
   (A) canoe : rapids
   (B) valley : mountain
   (C) footpath : road
   (D) brook : brink
   (E) roadway : waterway

_____ **9.** SUBSIDIZE : GRANT ::
   (A) lend : check
   (B) mortgage : dollar
   (C) divide : cent
   (D) buy : money
   (E) borrow : fund

_____ **10.** TAWNY : TAN ::
   (A) misty : hazy
   (B) colorful : drab
   (C) green : red
   (D) rapid : slow
   (E) pale : bright

CONNECTING NEW WORDS AND PATTERNS

Lesson 8 | ANALOGIES

Directions. For each of the following items, choose the lettered pair of words that expresses a relationship that is most similar to the relationship between the pair of capitalized words. Write the letter of your answer on the line provided before the number of the item.

____ **1.** APTITUDE : ABILITY ::
(A) talent : gift
(B) piano : music
(C) altitude : mountain
(D) arrangement : symphony
(E) attitude : reason

____ **2.** ASTUTE : KEEN ::
(A) dedicated : indecisive
(B) persuasive : convincing
(C) sharp : sensible
(D) stern : smart
(E) asleep : observant

____ **3.** BUFFET : DINING ROOM ::
(A) sedan : automobile
(B) newspaper : cartoons
(C) bed : closet
(D) sink : kitchen
(E) living room : bathtub

____ **4.** DELECTABLE : DISPLEASING ::
(A) boring : yawning
(B) delicate : hidden
(C) brittle : broken
(D) fragile : frightened
(E) delightful : disgusting

____ **5.** HORS D'OEUVRE : MEAL ::
(A) juice : thirst
(B) vineyard : grapes
(C) hunger : breakfast
(D) overture : opera
(E) chef : water

____ **6.** PALATABLE : FOOD ::
(A) fragrant : perfume
(B) spicy : eggs
(C) sweet : lemon
(D) crunchy : oranges
(E) messy : meal

____ **7.** PASTORAL : URBAN ::
(A) pasteurized : green
(B) leafy : fertile
(C) private : public
(D) smooth : soft
(E) editorial : opinionated

____ **8.** QUANTITATIVE : ECONOMICS ::
(A) genuine : imitation
(B) flexible : cash
(C) questionable : cause
(D) frustrating : wealth
(E) adventurous : safari

____ **9.** SUCCULENT : PLANT LIFE ::
(A) stem : flower
(B) granite : rock
(C) apples : orchard
(D) roof : greenhouse
(E) gem : pearl

____ **10.** ZENITH : PEAK ::
(A) zebra : animal
(B) violin : fiddle
(C) call : answer
(D) dock : canal
(E) point : pen

CONNECTING NEW WORDS AND PATTERNS

Lesson 9 | ANALOGIES

Directions. For each of the following items, choose the lettered pair of words that expresses a relationship that is most similar to the relationship between the pair of capitalized words. Write the letter of your answer on the line provided before the number of the item.

_____ **1.** ANNIHILATE : DEFEAT ::
- (A) thin : thicken
- (B) torment : bother
- (C) wander : direct
- (D) eliminate : add
- (E) multiply : divide

_____ **2.** DIVERSION : GOLF ::
- (A) food : cafeteria
- (B) talent : piano
- (C) occupation : carpentry
- (D) verification : proof
- (E) director : script

_____ **3.** HARASS : IRRITATION ::
- (A) hug : anxiety
- (B) hush : anger
- (C) praise : pride
- (D) argue : agreement
- (E) annoy : closeness

_____ **4.** INSOLENCE : DISRESPECTFUL ::
- (A) happiness : meaningless
- (B) energy : tiresome
- (C) celebration : joyous
- (D) consideration : thoughtless
- (E) sleep : exhausting

_____ **5.** MANDATORY : OPTIONAL ::
- (A) fixed : repaired
- (B) hesitant : certain
- (C) broken : cracked
- (D) lost : hunted
- (E) worthless : stolen

_____ **6.** METICULOUS : CAREFUL ::
- (A) observant : noticeable
- (B) destructive : determined
- (C) fatal : harmful
- (D) relieved : anxious
- (E) cheap : expensive

_____ **7.** METTLE : COURAGE ::
- (A) lock : safe
- (B) strength : exercise
- (C) metal : gold
- (D) curiosity : inquisitiveness
- (E) need : wish

_____ **8.** PURGE : RID ::
- (A) imprison : kill
- (B) hold : release
- (C) notify : notice
- (D) change : improve
- (E) show : display

_____ **9.** SADISTIC : KIND ::
- (A) mournful : sad
- (B) natural : normal
- (C) mature : childish
- (D) developed : ripe
- (E) good : saintly

_____ **10.** ULTIMATUM : DIPLOMAT ::
- (A) theater : actress
- (B) geranium : plant
- (C) cross-examination : lawyer
- (D) survey : voter
- (E) auditorium : stage

CONNECTING NEW WORDS AND PATTERNS

Lesson 10 ANALOGIES

Directions. For each of the following items, choose the lettered pair of words that expresses a relationship that is most similar to the relationship between the pair of capitalized words. Write the letter of your answer on the line provided before the number of the item.

_____ **1.** AFFIDAVIT : WITNESS ::
    (A) hospital : patient
    (B) sofa : cushion
    (C) furniture : chair
    (D) law : legislator
    (E) mason : stone

_____ **2.** BEDLAM : CONFUSED ::
    (A) peace : upsetting
    (B) food : quenching
    (C) puzzle : solved
    (D) riot : violent
    (E) exercise : amusing

_____ **3.** DESTITUTE : WEALTHY ::
    (A) depressed : pushed
    (B) homely : familiar
    (C) shy : bold
    (D) comfortable : comprehensive
    (E) elegant : sophisticated

_____ **4.** DIMINUTIVE : TINY ::
    (A) miniature : gigantic
    (B) ragged : tattered
    (C) formal : casual
    (D) sent : received
    (E) small : weak

_____ **5.** EXULTANT : PLEASED ::
    (A) metallic : ironed
    (B) sick : well
    (C) shocked : surprised
    (D) uttered : spoken
    (E) lovable : pretty

_____ **6.** MOSQUE : WORSHIPERS ::
    (A) church : cheerleaders
    (B) house : lawn
    (C) aquarium : fish
    (D) prayer book : minister
    (E) lobster : boat

_____ **7.** ORNATE : FANCY ::
    (A) organic : ornamental
    (B) fine : thick
    (C) foreign : native
    (D) natural : artificial
    (E) organized : orderly

_____ **8.** PRELUDE : INTRODUCE ::
    (A) piece : cut
    (B) preparation : confuse
    (C) ruler : measure
    (D) conclusion : create
    (E) lock : open

_____ **9.** RIFT : DISAGREEMENT ::
    (A) suffering : war
    (B) float : raft
    (C) rafter : roof
    (D) success : discouragement
    (E) recess : argument

_____ **10.** TIMOROUS : COURAGEOUS ::
    (A) timid : fearful
    (B) courtly : just
    (C) trembling : quaking
    (D) elderly : youthful
    (E) cordial : polite

CONNECTING NEW WORDS AND PATTERNS

Lesson 11 | ANALOGIES

Directions. For each of the following items, choose the lettered pair of words that expresses a relationship that is most similar to the relationship between the pair of capitalized words. Write the letter of your answer on the line provided before the number of the item.

____ **1.** CLANGOR : SOUND ::
  (A) onion : odor
  (B) vision : virtue
  (C) smell : fragrance
  (D) bitterness : disappointment
  (E) tongue : bell

____ **2.** DEBUT : ACTRESS ::
  (A) transport : highway
  (B) fall : singer
  (C) amuse : comedian
  (D) wind : film
  (E) invest : investigator

____ **3.** DOCUMENTARY : FILM ::
  (A) instrument : cello
  (B) biography : library
  (C) document : will
  (D) director : script
  (E) ballet : dance

____ **4.** GLOAT : ENJOY ::
  (A) acknowledge : ignore
  (B) glare : look
  (C) slip : skip
  (D) give : take
  (E) travel : ride

____ **5.** INDICT : GRAND JURY ::
  (A) rule : monarch
  (B) vote : laws
  (C) graduate : diplomats
  (D) argue : agreement
  (E) waver : decision

____ **6.** MELANCHOLY : GLOOM ::
  (A) merchant : buyer
  (B) tradition : custom
  (C) sadness : recollection
  (D) joy : tears
  (E) mood : caution

____ **7.** PATENT : INVENTION ::
  (A) patrol : security guard
  (B) lock : key
  (C) keep : vault
  (D) insure : valuables
  (E) create : inventor

____ **8.** PATRIARCH : LEAD ::
  (A) romance : roam
  (B) president : elect
  (C) patron : support
  (D) meeting : discuss
  (E) product : buy

____ **9.** REQUIEM : FUNERAL SERVICE ::
  (A) novel : literature
  (B) solo : flight
  (C) ceremony : graduation
  (D) oboe : bassoon
  (E) cemetery : tombstone

____ **10.** VEHEMENT : PASSIONATE ::
  (A) intense : calm
  (B) concerned : indifferent
  (C) earnest : sincere
  (D) violent : strict
  (E) romantic : sullen

CONNECTING NEW WORDS AND PATTERNS

Lesson 12 ANALOGIES

Directions. For each of the following items, choose the lettered pair of words that expresses a relationship that is most similar to the relationship between the pair of capitalized words. Write the letter of your answer on the line provided before the number of the item.

_____ **1.** ARBITER : DECIDE ::
(A) crane : hoist
(B) advisor : advance
(C) architect : design
(D) bell : ring
(E) crop : harvest

_____ **2.** BOTCH : SPOIL ::
(A) soil : clean
(B) burn : blush
(C) neglect : ignore
(D) improve : improvise
(E) chew : swallow

_____ **3.** CANT : TRITE ::
(A) attitude : meaningless
(B) conjunctions : connective
(C) babble : meaningful
(D) bubble : tough
(E) speech : silent

_____ **4.** CLIENTELE : CUSTOMERS ::
(A) class : teachers
(B) congregation : churches
(C) physician : patients
(D) spring : flowers
(E) replacements : substitutes

_____ **5.** CONVENE : MEMBERS ::
(A) join : club
(B) confide : confederacy
(C) sleep : protestors
(D) vote : citizens
(E) consent : conferences

_____ **6.** CRONY : BUDDY ::
(A) motive : crime
(B) complaint : compliment
(C) duty : obligation
(D) proof : dispute
(E) acquaintance : introduction

_____ **7.** IMPERCEPTIBLE : OBVIOUS ::
(A) perfect : excellent
(B) funny : hilarious
(C) serious : stubborn
(D) vague : clear
(E) imperial : royal

_____ **8.** OBLIVIOUS : SLEEPER ::
(A) alert : allergist
(B) lost : researcher
(C) watchful : guard
(D) delicate : detective
(E) thrifty : spendthrift

_____ **9.** RECTIFY : UPSET ::
(A) redeem : find
(B) nourish : starve
(C) retrieve : catch
(D) support : uphold
(E) retreat : withdraw

_____ **10.** STRATAGEM : DECEIVE ::
(A) joke : renew
(B) outline : organize
(C) strap : stride
(D) locomotive : locate
(E) fate : liberate

CONNECTING NEW WORDS AND PATTERNS

Lesson 13 ANALOGIES

Directions. For each of the following items, choose the lettered pair of words that expresses a relationship that is most similar to the relationship between the pair of capitalized words. Write the letter of your answer on the line provided before the number of the item.

_____ **1.** ABDICATE : THRONE ::
  (A) rule : king
  (B) veto : president
  (C) pass : law
  (D) decide : committee
  (E) determine : trial

_____ **2.** EFFERVESCENT : LISTLESS ::
  (A) brilliant : dull
  (B) persuasive : influential
  (C) engaging : unmarried
  (D) true : factual
  (E) feverish : restless

_____ **3.** IMMACULATE : PURE ::
  (A) precise : careless
  (B) simple : original
  (C) prior : religious
  (D) convinced : certain
  (E) coarse : refined

_____ **4.** INADVERTENT : INTENTIONAL ::
  (A) international : cosmic
  (B) advertised : verified
  (C) purposeful : forceful
  (D) unconcerned : worried
  (E) accidental : harmful

_____ **5.** INFALLIBLE : UNRELIABLE ::
  (A) truthful : trustworthy
  (B) ferocious : gentle
  (C) intriguing : unexplained
  (D) frequent : common
  (E) false : incorrect

_____ **6.** ITINERARY : TRAVELER ::
  (A) destination : journey
  (B) Vatican : Rome
  (C) case : camera
  (D) suitcase : luggage
  (E) whistle : referee

_____ **7.** NAIVE : SOPHISTICATED ::
  (A) jagged : notched
  (B) dreary : gloomy
  (C) perfect : flawed
  (D) sensible : correct
  (E) natural : whole

_____ **8.** RESONANT : CELLO ::
  (A) crunchy : milk
  (B) gentle : breeze
  (C) frowning : smile
  (D) elderly : children
  (E) purple : lemon

_____ **9.** STIMULANT : ACTIVATE ::
  (A) coach : exercise
  (B) dreams : interpret
  (C) actor : award
  (D) meditation : relax
  (E) clock : confuse

_____ **10.** TRANSLUCENT : FROSTED GLASS ::
  (A) unbreakable : glass
  (B) transparent : metal
  (C) white : frost
  (D) melted : mud
  (E) warm : winter

CONNECTING NEW WORDS AND PATTERNS

Lesson 14 | ANALOGIES

Directions. For each of the following items, choose the lettered pair of words that expresses a relationship that is most similar to the relationship between the pair of capitalized words. Write the letter of your answer on the line provided before the number of the item.

_____ 1. DEMURE : FLASHY ::
  (A) capable : competent
  (B) plain : fancy
  (C) frazzled : worn
  (D) delicate : frail
  (E) bright : brilliant

_____ 2. DETONATE : EXPLOSIVE ::
  (A) prosecute : attorney
  (B) attract : trap
  (C) leak : battery
  (D) strike : match
  (E) disguise : costume

_____ 3. JOSTLE : BUMP ::
  (A) polish : tarnish
  (B) hustle : bustle
  (C) beg : ask
  (D) wince : wink
  (E) skip : skimp

_____ 4. LEXICON : REFERENCE BOOK ::
  (A) understanding : explanation
  (B) matador : Spain
  (C) chapter : book
  (D) Judaism : religion
  (E) church : steeple

_____ 5. PALLID : PALE ::
  (A) pure : polluted
  (B) quiet : hushed
  (C) imprisoned : freed
  (D) masterful : mean
  (E) vicious : virtuous

_____ 6. REDUNDANT : REPETITIVE ::
  (A) spacious : crazy
  (B) drained : damp
  (C) expensive : quality
  (D) basic : elementary
  (E) excessive : simple

_____ 7. RENDEZVOUS : TROOPS ::
  (A) sign : contracts
  (B) betray : friends
  (C) congregate : members
  (D) join : churches
  (E) attend : tenants

_____ 8. SEETHE : FREEZE ::
  (A) stretch : bind
  (B) eat : fast
  (C) clutch : cling
  (D) invite : welcome
  (E) bury : cover

_____ 9. SEQUEL : CONTINUE ::
  (A) poem : alphabetize
  (B) writer : erase
  (C) foreword : introduce
  (D) note : notice
  (E) index : insure

_____ 10. SYNOPSIS : SUMMARIZE ::
  (A) manuscript : proofread
  (B) introduction : conclude
  (C) script : write
  (D) videotape : record
  (E) text : review

CONNECTING NEW WORDS AND PATTERNS

Lesson 15   ANALOGIES

Directions. For each of the following items, choose the lettered pair of words that expresses a relationship that is most similar to the relationship between the pair of capitalized words. Write the letter of your answer on the line provided before the number of the item.

_____ **1.** CARP : NAG ::
   (A) carpet : cover
   (B) knit : sew
   (C) march : stroll
   (D) offend : insult
   (E) bother : flatter

_____ **2.** CAUSTIC : SARCASM ::
   (A) frightening : comedy
   (B) formal : sweater
   (C) hollow : cavity
   (D) baked : recipe
   (E) anxious : joke

_____ **3.** DECREPIT : WORN ::
   (A) empty : crowded
   (B) solitary : lonely
   (C) slippery : cold
   (D) decent : evil
   (E) eager : willing

_____ **4.** FARCE : COMEDY ::
   (A) appetizer : meal
   (B) stag : theater
   (C) tragedy : drama
   (D) audience : auditorium
   (E) conductor : baton

_____ **5.** JARGON : UNINTELLIGIBLE ::
   (A) plateau : elevated
   (B) ball : square
   (C) whistle : silent
   (D) treat : ordinary
   (E) fabric : wooden

_____ **6.** MALIGNANT : HARMFUL ::
   (A) thoughtful : inconsiderate
   (B) shallow : deep
   (C) evil : mischievous
   (D) hidden : lost
   (E) charted : graphed

_____ **7.** NEGLIGIBLE : INSIGNIFICANT ::
   (A) negligent : dutiful
   (B) critical : crucial
   (C) important : severe
   (D) contrary : agreeable
   (E) authoritative : written

_____ **8.** ODIOUS : APPEALING ::
   (A) smelly : fishy
   (B) preferred : desired
   (C) realistic : fantastic
   (D) idolized : worshiped
   (E) adorable : cute

_____ **9.** PERTINENT : APPROPRIATE ::
   (A) prevented : allowed
   (B) swollen : shrunken
   (C) tiresome : annoying
   (D) sharp : salty
   (E) taxing : easy

_____ **10.** REBUKE : PRAISE ::
   (A) conclude : finalize
   (B) hamper : help
   (C) punish : penalize
   (D) assign : expect
   (E) call : persuade

Name _____ Date _____ Class _____

READING NEW WORDS IN CONTEXT

Why We Read Strategically

Reading is active. As you read, you step into the writer's world. When you come across a new idea, you usually look for a clue to help you determine the writer's meaning. You move ahead to see if the idea is explained, or you retrace your steps to look for any signs you missed.

You can use these same strategies to build your vocabulary. If you don't know the meaning of a word, you should look in the passage surrounding the word for hints. These hints are called context clues. The more you practice hunting for context clues, the better you can teach yourself new words, and the greater your vocabulary will grow. And strengthening your vocabulary skills will help you to score higher on standardized vocabulary tests.

The following example shows the kinds of context clues you will find in Reading New Words in Context lessons.

Strategic Reading: An Example

The state of Oklahoma is a state of nations. Although many people are aware that large numbers of Native Americans such as the Choctaw and the Chickasaw live in Oklahoma, they are not aware that the Indian nations of Oklahoma are **sovereign** peoples with their own constitutional governments. *In other words, like any other nation, they have the right to manage their own affairs.* However, because the tribes are nations within a nation, the United States government does have some **jurisdiction** over them. *For example, the federal government has the authority to govern its own activities when they take place on Native American land.* Even in these cases, though, the federal government's authority is limited.

In this case, the writer uses *restatement* to provide a clue to the meaning of the word **sovereign**.

Here, an *example* is used to provide a clue to the meaning of **jurisdiction**.

The ancestors of large numbers of Native Americans living in Oklahoma today came to Oklahoma on the **infamous** Trail of Tears. *In the 1830s, the United States government began to remove tribes of the Southeastern United States from their homelands. The government pushed these tribes on a forced march to the west that resulted in the death of up to one half of the members of some nations.* At the time, many Americans did not seem to recognize the inhumanity of this action. Today, *however*, almost everyone **acknowledges** the tragedy of the Indian Removal. It remains a *barbaric*, **hideous**, *and shameful* blot on the pages of United States history.

A *summary* of the events concerning the Trail of Tears provides a clue to the meaning of **infamous**.

Here, the writer makes the meaning of **acknowledges** clear though *contrast*.
The use of *items in a series* clarifies the meaning of **hideous**.

Many people who live in states without large American Indian populations mistakenly believe that the tribes in Oklahoma live on large federal reservations. *This* **fallacy** may result from the assumption that American Indians have been unable *either* to accommodate modern society *or* to **reconcile** ancient ways with the modern world. The fact is that Native Americans in Oklahoma own their own tribal lands and are not tenants on government-owned property.

Today, the Choctaw, the Chickasaw, the Creek, the Seminole, and the Cherokee—as well as the other tribes in Oklahoma—are involved in modern occupations. Native Americans are employed in the fields of education, civil service, law, medicine, computer technology, and so on. But maintaining the traditional cultures remains a **priority**, *the number-one concern,* of many tribal elders.

In many cases, the younger tribal members in Oklahoma are most **reluctant** to abandon the values of their traditional culture *because they find those values important in their own lives.* They are also learning the old arts and crafts. A young Choctaw might learn to create the jewelry, headpieces, shawls, or leggings that *are* the traditional **garb** of the tribe. Others concentrate on preserving the stories and the language. Some research and write about the history of their people so that the events of the past will not be **irretrievably** lost.

As a poet who writes a verse in the sand watches the tide erase it forever, Native Americans have watched the dreams and traditions of their grandparents fade into distant memories. Today, however, the Indian nations of Oklahoma struggle to regain their traditions and to make them meaningful in the present.

A *pronoun reference* is used here to provide a clue to the meaning of **fallacy**.

Note that a *coordinate* conjunction helps clarify the meaning of **reconcile**.

An *appositive* provides a clue to the meaning of **priority**.

The writer indicates the meaning of **reluctant** through a *cause-and-effect relationship*.

Note that a form of the verb *to be (are)* provides a clue to the meaning of **garb**.

Figurative language is the key understanding the meaning of **irretrievably**.

A Final Note

How can you learn strategic reading? Practice is a great way to improve your ability. The following lessons will help you recognize the different context clues a writer uses. As you complete each lesson, you will become a more effective reader.

READING NEW WORDS IN CONTEXT

Lesson 1 | CONTEXT: Expression

The passage gives you an opportunity to expand your vocabulary. Below are twenty vocabulary words that are used in the passage and in the exercises that follow it.

acquittal	contemptuous	excerpt	notoriety
analogy	electorate	fortitude	paternal
antiquity	elite	heresy	pauper
assert	ethical	inarticulate	posthumous
condescend	evolve	mentor	prophetic

Why Socrates Died

Socrates (c. 470–399 B.C.) is considered one of the greatest philosophers of **antiquity** (1). However, was this philosopher of ancient times as intelligent and wise as most people think he was? At his trial in Athens in 399 B.C., Socrates presented a defense that resulted in his being sentenced to death. Was this the outcome he wanted? Was his death necessary? An examination of his life, beliefs, and trial suggests that Socrates knew exactly what he was doing: By accepting death, he was remaining true to his principles.

Socrates' Goals and Methods

Socrates was born around 470 B.C. into a middle-class Athenian family. His father was a stone-cutter; his mother was a midwife. He followed his father's profession for a time but then decided to devote his life to teaching philosophy. Socrates did not charge his students for his teaching. He and his wife and three sons evidently lived on a modest **paternal** (2) inheritance made possible through his father's success as a stonecutter. However, Socrates apparently lived in near poverty much of the time. Compared to most of his students, who were from wealthy families, he was a **pauper** (3).

Teaching independent thinking was one of Socrates' primary goals. His method of teaching, the now-famous Socratic method, was to ask questions. By pretending ignorance of a subject, he would draw answers from his students. The students already knew the answers, he said; they just had to think clearly and formulate their thoughts. Socrates maintained that virtue is knowledge and that ignorance causes wickedness. He said people should concentrate on distinguishing between right and wrong. Such **ethical** (4) matters were of great concern to him.

Much of Socrates' thinking went against the accepted doctrines of his society, and his **heresy** (5) angered many prominent people. The sons of some of these people were Socrates' students, and these students considered the philosopher their **mentor** (6)—a wise and trusted advisor. Although Socrates achieved a good reputation among his students, their high regard was by no means shared by everyone: Socrates gained **notoriety** (7) throughout Athens. At the age of seventy, Socrates was brought to trial on charges of not believing in the state's gods and of "corrupting" the youth of Athens.

Socrates wrote nothing himself, but we know much about his life from the writing of two of his students, Plato and Xenophon. In the *Apology,* Plato, Socrates' most famous student, reenacts Socrates' defense at his trial. Speaking confidently to the jury, Socrates **asserts** (8) that there is "nothing real of which to accuse me." He also firmly declares that he will not submit to any compromise that will go against his beliefs. He clearly explains his life's work, as this **excerpt** (9) from the *Apology* shows: "I do nothing but go about persuading you all, old and young alike, not to take thought for your persons or your properties, but first and chiefly to care about the greatest improvement of the soul. . . . This is my teaching, and if this is the doctrine which corrupts the youth, I am a mischievous person." He describes his role as that of a "gadfly which God has attached to the state." These clearly formulated statements show that Socrates was far from an **inarticulate** (10) speaker.

Was Socrates Undemocratic?

That Socrates was tried in a democratic society for charges involving freedom of speech puzzles some people. Weren't the Athenians being undemocratic by denying Socrates free speech? In his book *The Trial of Socrates,* I. F. Stone declares that it was Socrates, not the Athenians, who was undemocratic. Stone says that Socrates was **contemptuous** (11) of the democratic form of government and frequently demonstrated scorn and disdain toward Athenian society. According to Stone, Socrates did not think that people should be self-governing; he rejected the power of the **electorate** (12). He believed, instead, that people should be governed by an absolute, knowledgeable ruler. Socrates used several **analogies** (13) to support his view. For example, he compared a country to a ship. Aboard a ship, Socrates pointed out, all obey one ruler, "the one who knows."

Stone also says that Socrates did not use the issue of free speech in his defense because he did not believe in free speech for everyone. He believed in free speech only for an **elite** (14) group, not for the masses. According to Stone, Socrates would not have stooped to do anything beneath his dignity; he would not have **condescended** (15) to defend himself with a principle that he did not actually believe in.

Socrates calmly accepted the guilty verdict—he had not expected an **acquittal** (16) anyway—and his punishment to die by drinking hemlock, a poison. Friends offered to help him escape, but Socrates refused to break the law. He did not fear death, as he believed that "no evil can happen to a good man, either in life or after death." He obviously had much **fortitude** (17), or moral strength.

After the sentencing, Socrates predicted that many others would soon come forth to condemn evil ways and to urge people to improve themselves. Socrates proved, indeed, to have **prophetic** (18) powers, for various schools of philosophy gradually developed, or **evolved** (19), from his teachings. In fact, Socrates' **posthumous** (20) influence became greater than the influence he had while he was alive. Stone says Socrates' death was a triumph for the philosopher's mission.

EXERCISE 1 *Finding Synonyms*

Directions. Reread the preceding passage. Then write on the line provided a synonym for each of the words in boldface. If you cannot think of an exact synonym, you may write a brief definition of the word.

1. antiquity _____

2. paternal _____

3. pauper _____

4. ethical _____

5. heresy _____

6. mentor _____

7. notoriety _____

8. asserts _____

9. excerpt _____

10. inarticulate _____

11. contemptuous _____

12. electorate _____

13. analogies _____

14. elite _____

15. condescended _____

16. acquittal _____

17. fortitude _____

18. prophetic _____

19. evolved _____

20. posthumous _____

EXERCISE 2 Reading Strategically

Directions. Now that you have read the passage and thought about the words in boldface, circle the letter of the correct answer to each of the following items. The numbers of the items are the same as the numbers of the boldface vocabulary words in the passage.

1. In the passage, **antiquity** means
  (A) modern times
  (B) the future
  (C) ancient times
  (D) great philosopher
  (E) Athenian trial

2. In the passage, why did Socrates have a modest **paternal** inheritance?
  (A) He was a teacher and philosopher and made a great amount of money.
  (B) His father was successful enough to leave him a little money.
  (C) He and his wife and children lived far below the poverty level.
  (D) Socrates' work as a stonecutter enabled him to support his family.
  (E) His mother made a lot of money, but she spent it before she died.

3. How does the writer provide a clue to the meaning of **pauper**?
   (A) The writer relates being a **pauper** to teaching.
   (B) The writer gives a synonym for **pauper**.
   (C) The writer provides examples of **paupers**.
   (D) The writer contrasts being a **pauper** with being wealthy.
   (E) The writer defines **pauper**.

4. We can infer from the passage that **ethical** matters are concerned with
   (A) distinguishing right from wrong
   (B) recognizing ignorance and stupidity
   (C) providing questions and answers
   (D) distinguishing faith from reason
   (E) maintaining students' interests

5. What strategy does the writer use to tell us that **heresy** is defined as a controversial or unorthodox opinion?
   (A) The writer explains that Socrates could not get along with most people in Athens.
   (B) The writer defines **heresy** along with other words in the sentence.
   (C) The writer describes Socrates' thinking as being similar to that of others in Athens.
   (D) The writer uses figurative language to illustrate the meaning of **heresy**.
   (E) The writer states that Socrates' thinking went against accepted doctrines.

6. In the passage, a **mentor** is a
   (A) revolutionary student
   (B) mentally unstable teacher
   (C) wise and trusted advisor
   (D) person of good reputation
   (E) person who gives poor advice

7. When we read in the passage that Socrates gained **notoriety**, we should realize that
   (A) **notoriety** is a good reputation
   (B) Socrates was virtually unknown
   (C) Socrates gained many followers
   (D) Socrates wrote several books
   (E) **notoriety** is a poor reputation

8. In the passage, when Socrates **asserts**, he _____ declares.
   (A) firmly
   (B) quietly
   (C) timidly
   (D) angrily
   (E) wrongly

9. What strategy does the writer use to tell us that **excerpt** is defined as a passage or scene from a speech or a book?
   (A) The writer uses a synonym for **excerpt**.
   (B) The writer uses an example of an **excerpt**.
   (C) The writer defines **excerpt**.
   (D) The writer describes ways to use **excerpt**.
   (E) The writer contrasts **excerpt** with an antonym.

10. In the passage, what does **inarticulate** mean?

    (A) It means clearly understandable.
    (B) It means glad to speak in public.
    (C) It means able to quote literature.
    (D) It means guilty of serious crimes.
    (E) It means unable to speak clearly.

11. The writer provides a clue to the meaning of **contemptuous** by

    (A) referring to the word undemocratic
    (B) linking **contemptuous** with the words scorn and disdain
    (C) relating **contemptuous** to a democratic government
    (D) implying that **contemptuous** means self-governing
    (E) explaining freedom of speech

12. We can infer from the passage that if the **electorate** has power, then

    (A) the society does not govern itself
    (B) the society is not democratic
    (C) no one in the society is allowed to vote
    (D) the society is self-governing
    (E) an absolute ruler governs the society

13. To illustrate Socrates' use of **analogies,** the writer cites Socrates' comparison of a

    (A) ruler to a country
    (B) ship to a ruler
    (C) country to a ship
    (D) leader to a country
    (E) country to a view

14. When we read in the passage that Socrates believed in free speech only for an **elite** group, we should realize that

    (A) he wanted everyone to have the right of free speech
    (B) he was totally committed to a democratic government
    (C) he thought free speech should be defined by voters
    (D) he believed in free speech for only selected people
    (E) he thought only he was worthy of the right to free speech

15. The writer provides a clue to the meaning of **condescended** by

    (A) earlier using the words "stooped to do anything beneath his dignity"
    (B) saying "to argue for a principle that he did not believe in"
    (C) relating **condescended** to the principle of free speech
    (D) implying that **condescended** means presented arguments about
    (E) saying that Socrates would stoop to anything to save himself

16. According to the passage, what does it mean to have an **acquittal**?

    (A) It means to defend yourself before a judge.
    (B) It means to receive a verdict of not guilty.
    (C) It means to be sentenced to life in prison.
    (D) It means to receive a verdict of guilty.
    (E) It means to accept a verdict without complaining.

17. In the passage, why is Socrates described as having much **fortitude**?

    (A) He wanted to escape from prison.
    (B) He always planned ahead.
    (C) He possessed great physical strength.
    (D) He was sentenced to die by poison.
    (E) He exhibited much moral strength and courage.

18. In the passage, Socrates' **prophetic** powers were proven by his ability to

    (A) help people improve themselves
    (B) predict what would happen
    (C) understand new philosophies
    (D) condemn evil ways of doing things
    (E) die without being critical

19. In the passage, **evolved** means

    (A) quickly developed
    (B) suspiciously appeared
    (C) gradually developed
    (D) was prophesied
    (E) disappeared suddenly

20. How does the writer provide a clue to the meaning of **posthumous**?

    (A) The writer relates **posthumous** to the word influence.
    (B) The writer defines **posthumous** as lively.
    (C) The writer implies that **posthumous** means great.
    (D) The writer contrasts **posthumous** with the word alive.
    (E) The writer refers to **posthumous** as a triumph.

READING NEW WORDS IN CONTEXT

| Lesson 2 | **CONTEXT:** Expression

The passage gives you an opportunity to expand your vocabulary. Below are twenty vocabulary words that are used in the passage and in the exercises that follow it.

amiable	commendable	judicious	personification
anthropology	grimace	malleable	succumb
apprehensive	indignant	melodramatic	verbatim
bayou	indomitable	mystic	visage
callous	ineffectual	paraphrase	whimsical

The World Beyond: Native American Tales

The evening light possessed a **mystic** (1) quality that made the Spanish moss hanging from the cypress trees look mysterious. We were camped near a **bayou** (2), a marshy inlet, on Caddo Lake in East Texas. My students gathered around the fire.

A few days before our camp-out, I had asked the campers to go to the library and read about Native American beliefs and legends. **Indignant** (3) or angry at what they thought was the unfairness of an "assignment" for a camp-out, some of the students **grimaced** (4). I ignored their disapproving faces. Later, when the group assembled around the campfire, I asked them to share the stories they had discovered. Now I saw only eager **visages** (5) illuminated in the firelight.

About the Stories

Telling these stories, rather than reading them, was important because the stories were originally spoken, not written, and they have come to us through the oral tradition. Many were collected from original Native American sources by people working in the field of **anthropology** (6)—the study of physical, cultural, and social development and behavior of humanity.

The stories from the different nations of native North Americans contain many similarities. Appearing in stories from nearly every tribe are recurring types of characters—most notably the Creator, the Hero, the Trickster, Grandmother Spider, and the War Twins (one good and one evil). Many stories involve **personification** (7), so inanimate objects with human qualities—the ability to speak, for example—are common.

A Story of the World's Creation

Eric told the first story, a typical Native American creation story from the Cheyenne. I will **paraphrase** (8) his story and a few others in my own words rather than repeat the tales **verbatim** (9).

Here is Eric's story: The Creator, Maheo, brings into being water, light, sky air, water creatures, and birds. When a type of bird called a loon asks Maheo to make a dry, solid place, the Creator is **amiable** (10). Although he good-naturedly agrees to the loon's request, Maheo says that he can make only four things by himself. He asks the water and sky creatures to help him by trying to find land. Several creatures fail, but finally a little coot swims to the bottom of the water and returns with mud. Maheo presses the **malleable** (11) mud between the palms of his hands. The mud becomes larger and Maheo places it on the back of Grandmother Turtle, forming the Earth. Maheo then creates many things and forms man and woman out of his own ribs. Finally, he creates the buffalo. The Cheyenne thought that creating the buffalo was a wise act because they depended on the buffalo for their livelihood. The Cheyenne praised the **judicious** (12) Maheo for his wisdom and care.

The Quest for Light

Sheila offered a "sun-catcher" story that is a favorite of many tribes. It's an example of a story that attempts to explain certain facts about the natural world. This Cherokee story is **whimsical** (13) rather than factual.

According to the story, long ago, animals in one part of the world had no light. They decide to take light from people on the opposite side of the world. An opossum makes the journey, snatches a piece of sun, and puts it on his bushy tail. When he returns, all the hair is burned off his tail. (This is the Cherokee explanation for why opossums' tails are mostly bare.) Because he doesn't achieve the desired results, the opossum's actions are considered **ineffectual** (14). Next, a buzzard volunteers, and he carries a portion of the sun back on his head, which explains why buzzards' heads are bald. Finally, the **indomitable** (15) Grandmother Spider says she will go. She may be quiet and small, but she's not easily overcome. She makes a clay bowl to take with her. As she journeys to the place of the sun, she spins a thread behind her so she can find her way home. When she sees the sun, she takes a small piece of it and puts it in the clay bowl. Carrying the bowl of sun, she travels back along the thread she has spun. This is why today all spiders' webs are shaped like the sun's disk and rays.

Stories of Dangerous Travels

As the evening progressed, the stories naturally became more unsettling, even spooky. Webster told one of my favorite stories, a Hopi tale sometimes called "The World Beyond."

The story features the kachinas, spirits that live within the San Francisco Peaks of the Hopi land in Arizona. When Hopi who are kind, generous, and tenderhearted die, they join the kachinas; **callous** (16) and cruel Hopi, on the other hand, end up in the country of the Two Hearts, the land of wicked, evil people. In this story, a young man discovers that his mother-in-law has become a Two Heart and is living with the Hopi tribe. Another Two Heart tries to capture the young man and take him to Two Heart country, but the young man refuses to **succumb** (17) to the evil force. Instead of giving in to the Two Heart, he prays to the Sun God, a kachina, who saves him. The evil mother-in-law soon wastes away and dies as a result of prayers to the kachinas.

The tale reminded Shanna of a Hopi story that cautions non-Hopi from walking down a sacred path on the Hopi land. The War Twins guard the path. The older, good twin tries to warn the non-Hopi away, but the younger, evil twin coaxes the unsuspecting traveler to Grandmother Spider. Grandmother Spider takes the person down under the rocks, into the womb of the Earth from which there is no escape. Shanna exhibited much emotion as she recounted the tale, telling the story in a lively, **melodramatic** (18) way.

After these scary tales, the young campers became **apprehensive** (19). In fact, they were so anxious that they kept the fire going until morning. I praised them for becoming so involved in the tales. I was especially pleased to note that they seemed to have felt a kinship with the original tellers. Their research and storytelling were most **commendable** (20).

EXERCISE 1   *Finding Synonyms*

Directions. Reread the preceding passage. Then write on the line provided a synonym for each of the words in boldface. If you cannot think of an exact synonym, you may write a brief definition of the word.

1. mystic _____

2. bayou _____

3. **indignant** _____

4. **grimaced** _____

5. **visages** _____

6. **anthropology** _____

7. **personification** _____

8. **paraphrase** _____

9. **verbatim** _____

10. **amiable** _____

11. **malleable** _____

12. **judicious** _____

13. **whimsical** _____

14. **ineffectual** _____

15. **indomitable** _____

16. **callous** _____

17. **succumb** _____

18. **melodramatic** _____

19. **apprehensive** _____

20. **commendable** _____

EXERCISE 2   *Reading Strategically* 👉

Directions. Now that you have read the passage and thought about the words in boldface, circle the letter of the correct answer to each of the following items. The numbers of the items are the same as the numbers of the boldface vocabulary words in the passage.

1. In the passage, **mystic** means
   (A) mysterious
   (B) serious
   (C) happy
   (D) similar
   (E) bright

2. How does the writer provide a clue to the meaning of **bayou**?

(A) The writer relates a **bayou** to a camp-out.
(B) The writer gives the synonym Spanish moss for **bayou**.
(C) The writer links **bayou** to cypress tree.
(D) The writer defines **bayou** as a marshy inlet.
(E) The writer implies that a **bayou** is dry and sandy.

3. In the passage, **indignant** means

(A) interested
(B) thoughtful
(C) happy
(D) ignorant
(E) angry

4. According to the passage, when the students **grimaced**, they had _____ looks on their faces.

(A) happy
(B) peaceful
(C) disapproving
(D) excited
(E) eager

5. What strategy does the writer use to tell us that **visage** is defined as a facial expression?

(A) The writer explains the many different uses of the word **visage**.
(B) The writer contrasts eager **visages** with disapproving faces.
(C) The writer provides a definition of **visages**.
(D) The writer uses figurative language to illustrate the meaning of **visage**.
(E) The writer states that the campers remained resentful when they told stories.

6. According to the passage, what do people who work in the field of **anthropology** do?

(A) They study volcanic eruptions, hurricanes, and other disasters.
(B) They study dinosaurs and other prehistoric creatures.
(C) They study the effects of weather on humans.
(D) They study the behavior and development of humanity.
(E) They study the relationship between humans and insects.

7. When we read in the passage that many Native American stories involve **personification**, we should realize that

(A) **personification** means having people with quality
(B) **personification** means giving inanimate objects human qualities
(C) **personification** means stories with personality
(D) the stories include different humans and animals
(E) **personification** is giving animal qualities to humans

8. When you **paraphrase** a story that you have heard, you

(A) tell the same story in your own words
(B) repeat the story using the speaker's exact words
(C) tell the same plot with a new ending
(D) use only direct quotations in the story
(E) tell a story that is difficult to understand

9. How does the writer provide a clue to the meaning of **verbatim**?

    (A) The writer uses an antonym for **verbatim**.

    (B) The writer uses an example of **verbatim**.

    (C) The writer defines **verbatim** as **paraphrase** and contrasts **verbatim** with **personification**.

    (D) The writer relates **verbatim** to the word repeat and contrasts **verbatim** with **paraphrase**.

    (E) The writer contrasts **verbatim** with the word story and relates **verbatim** to **paraphrase**.

10. In the passage, what does it mean to be **amiable**?

    (A) It means to be critical.

    (B) It means to have values.

    (C) It means to be good-natured.

    (D) It means to be creative.

    (E) It means to be solid and dry.

11. The writer provides a clue to the meaning of **malleable** by

    (A) linking it to the phrase "returns with mud"

    (B) referring to buffalo, spiders, ribs, and people

    (C) saying Maheo could press the mud between his hands

    (D) implying that **malleable** relates to pond water

    (E) saying it means something that cannot be shaped

12. We can infer from the passage that someone who is **judicious** is

    (A) serious

    (B) unfair

    (C) lively

    (D) judgmental

    (E) wise

13. The writer provides a clue to the meaning of **whimsical** by

    (A) comparing **whimsical** with natural

    (B) contrasting **whimsical** with factual

    (C) including a series of synonyms

    (D) giving an example of a depressing story

    (E) including **whimsical** in a story

14. According to the passage, something is **ineffectual** if it does not produce the _____ results.

    (A) worst

    (B) desired

    (C) related

    (D) considered

    (E) unwanted

15. In the passage, Grandmother Spider is **indomitable** because she is

    (A) not easily overcome

    (B) very large and noisy

    (C) argumentative

    (D) easily able to spin

    (E) easily overcome

16. When we read in the passage that **callous** Hopi end up in the country of the Two Hearts, we should realize that **callous** people
(A) are not kind and generous
(B) have supernatural powers
(C) are shy and gentle
(D) protect the kachinas
(E) walk barefoot

17. In the passage, if the young man in "The World Beyond" did **succumb** to the evil force, he would
(A) fight with it
(B) send it away
(C) give in to it
(D) be better off
(E) argue with it

18. We can infer that if Shanna tells the story in a **melodramatic** way, then she must tell the story
(A) with little interest
(B) with much emotion
(C) in a calm, easygoing manner
(D) shyly
(E) with illustrations

19. What strategy does the writer use to tell us that **apprehensive** is defined as fearful?
(A) The writer relates **apprehensive** to camping.
(B) The writer uses **apprehensive** in a question.
(C) The writer uses antonyms for **apprehensive**.
(D) The writer relates **apprehensive** to storytelling.
(E) The writer links **apprehensive** to the synonym anxious.

20. In the passage, the leader _____ the campers because their storytelling was **commendable**.
(A) punished
(B) questioned
(C) angered
(D) praised
(E) involved

READING NEW WORDS IN CONTEXT

Lesson 3 | CONTEXT: Expression

The passage gives you an opportunity to expand your vocabulary. Below are twenty vocabulary words that are used in the passage and in the exercises that follow it.

affiliate	deteriorate	lament	portly
ascertain	ecstatic	loathe	proximity
atrocious	encumber	painstaking	rejuvenate
compassion	insipid	plausible	repress
composure	invariably	pompous	unprecedented

Franz Kafka's Bug

Franz Kafka's (1883–1924) bug, the subject of the 1915 novella *The Metamorphosis,* is certainly the most famous insect in literature. In recent years, Kafka's bug even crawled to Broadway in a play starring ballet superstar Mikhail Baryshnikov (b. 1948). Just who or what is this bug? How much of the bug's life and personality mirror Kafka's? These are questions that **invariably** (1) challenge scholars. Such questions also constantly "bug" students throughout the world.

At Home, Sick with a Bug

The bug in *The Metamorphosis* is Gregor Samsa, a traveling salesman who lives with his parents and sister. Gregor has supported the family since his father's business collapsed five years earlier. Gregor **loathes** (2), or detests, his lonely, tiring job, but it is his life; he seems to have no other interests and finds little personal amusement. One morning Gregor awakes and finds that he has turned into a huge insect. He immediately **ascertains** (3) that he is not dreaming. This discovery doesn't seem to shock Gregor too much; he rationally analyzes his new situation. He realizes that he will lose his job unless he gets out of bed and opens the door to his room. But these formerly simple tasks must now be undertaken with **painstaking** (4) effort. Gregor has to move very carefully because he is now **encumbered** (5), or burdened, with a stiff, segmented body.

As you might expect, Gregor's family is not as matter-of-fact about the transformation as Gregor is. They realize that the bizarre metamorphosis is **unprecedented** (6), for nothing like this has happened before, at least not to any of their relatives or friends. His mother collapses in sorrow as she **laments** (7) the sickness that has befallen her son. His **portly** (8) father, grown fat from inactivity, shows no **compassion** (9). On the contrary, he is completely unsympathetic, threatening Gregor's life and hitting him with an apple. Gregor's young sister, Grete, copes the best. She mostly keeps her **composure** (10), like a nurse calmly caring for a patient, as she feeds and cleans up after Gregor each day. The family keeps the door to Gregor's room shut, for his very **proximity** (11) unnerves them. They do not want to be near him.

The story describes how Gregor **deteriorates** (12), his condition growing worse and worse. Readers also see the parallel breakdown of Gregor's family. His parents and sister are forced to get jobs and to take in boarders. The boarders are three **pompous** (13) men whose self-importance makes them the center of the household. It is they, in fact, who make a terrible fuss when they see Gregor for the first time. They hastily leave the Samsa house and refuse to pay rent after seeing the **atrocious** (14), appalling creature Gregor has become. Gregor finally understands that he is making life miserable for everyone, and he stops eating and sadly dies. After his death, his parents and sister are **ecstatic** (15) with relief, and they take a holiday to celebrate their delight. For the first time in years, they feel good about themselves, their jobs, and their future prospects.

Kafka's Bugging Device

What does this nightmarish story mean? What does it suggest about Gregor and his family? Most critics consider Gregor's metamorphosis a metaphor for his wasted life. It is clear that Gregor is a weak, passive person who lets his family use him and step on him—in effect, to treat him like a bug. Gregor's change is actually an outcome of his **insipid** (16) life—his dull, spiritless existence. As for Gregor's family, they are able to cope quite well without him. Gregor's father didn't tell Gregor that he had some business investments that were still good. This concealment is typical of the family's lack of communication and trust. As a result of Gregor's tragedy, the father **rejuvenates** (17) and vigorously assumes again the responsibility of head of the family.

Much has been written about the parallels between Gregor Samsa's personality and life and those of Franz Kafka. That the two are closely connected seems **plausible** (18), for there are reasonable parallels between them. Kafka was born in 1883 in Prague and was raised there in the German-Jewish section. Like Gregor, Kafka lived most of his life with his parents—a domineering father and an unaffectionate mother. A sensitive, private person, Kafka wrote letters about his inability to love. He earned a law degree and for many years was a successful attorney **affiliated** (19) with an accident-insurance corporation. However, Kafka's association with the company made him feel trapped, just as he felt trapped at home.

Publicly, Kafka **repressed** (20) his feelings. When he wrote his stories, however, he did not hold back how he felt. Kafka's fictional creations, such as Gregor, reflect his struggles to cope with the anxieties of modern life. Kafka died in 1924 of tuberculosis.

EXERCISE 1   *Finding Synonyms*

Directions. Reread the preceding passage. Then write on the line provided a synonym for each of the words in boldface. If you cannot think of an exact synonym, you may write a brief definition of the word.

1. invariably   _____

2. loathes   _____

3. ascertains   _____

4. painstaking   _____

5. encumbered   _____

6. unprecedented   _____

7. laments   _____

8. portly   _____

9. compassion   _____

10. composure   _____

11. proximity   _____

12. deteriorates _____

13. pompous _____

14. atrocious _____

15. ecstatic _____

16. insipid _____

17. rejuvenates _____

18. plausible _____

19. affiliated _____

20. repressed _____

EXERCISE 2 *Reading Strategically*

Directions. Now that you have read the passage and thought about the words in boldface, circle the letter of the correct answer to each of the following items. The numbers of the items are the same as the numbers of the boldface vocabulary words in the passage.

1. In the passage, **invariably** means
   (A) occasionally
   (B) constantly
   (C) never
   (D) sometimes
   (E) changeably

2. How does the writer provide a clue to the meaning of **loathes**?
   (A) The writer relates **loathes** to a business collapse.
   (B) The writer relates **loathes** to the words lonely and tiring.
   (C) The writer links **loathes** to the phrase "little personal amusement."
   (D) The writer defines **loathes** as appreciates.
   (E) The writer restates **loathes** with the synonym detests.

3. In the passage, Gregor **ascertains**, or _____, that he has turned into an insect.
   (A) denies with force
   (B) discovers with certainty
   (C) rejoices with discovery
   (D) analyzes with logic
   (E) rationalizes with excuses

4. In the passage, why are the tasks of getting out of bed and opening the door **painstaking**?

    (A) The tasks are easy because Gregor has many arms and legs.

    (B) The tasks are the same, but Gregor doesn't know where he is.

    (C) The tasks have always been difficult because Gregor is clumsy.

    (D) The tasks require great care and effort because Gregor's body is no longer human.

    (E) The tasks are different because Gregor's parents have moved the bed.

5. The writer provides a clue to the meaning of **encumbered** by

    (A) restating **encumbered** as the word burdened

    (B) contrasting **encumbered** with the words move carefully

    (C) relating **encumbered** to the word painstaking

    (D) referring to the word shock

    (E) implying that **encumbered** means without

6. When we read in the passage that the occurrence was **unprecedented,** we should realize that

    (A) the occurrence was an everyday happening

    (B) the occurrence happened occasionally

    (C) such an occurrence had never happened before

    (D) the family had heard stories of such occurrences

    (E) the occurrence was the beginning of a trend

7. We can infer from the passage that someone who is **lamenting** is

    (A) rejoicing

    (B) questioning

    (C) grieving

    (D) studying

    (E) lingering over

8. In the passage, Gregor's father is **portly** because he has not been _____.

    (A) reading

    (B) eating

    (C) talking

    (D) awake

    (E) active

9. In the passage, what does it mean to show **compassion**?

    (A) It means to be sympathetic.

    (B) It means to threaten.

    (C) It means to throw things at someone.

    (D) It means to show no support.

    (E) It means to express anger.

10. Because Grete keeps her **composure,** the writer compares her by simile to

    (A) Gregor's father

    (B) a patient

    (C) a younger person

    (D) a nurse

    (E) a bug

11. In the passage, **proximity** means

(A) distance
(B) nearness
(C) odor
(D) occupation
(E) helplessness

12. When we read in the passage that Gregor **deteriorates,** we should realize that he

(A) gets better
(B) dies
(C) gets worse
(D) is human again
(E) is healthier

13. We can infer from the passage that someone who is **pompous** is

(A) friendly, kind, and helpful
(B) filled with self-importance
(C) visiting for a short time
(D) quiet and formally polite
(E) overweight

14. What strategy does the writer use to tell us that **atrocious** is defined as horrifying?

(A) The writer contrasts **atrocious** with an antonym.
(B) The writer links **atrocious** to the word appalling.
(C) The writer relates **atrocious** to the word fuss.
(D) The writer describes the boarders as **atrocious**.
(E) The writer links **atrocious** to the word hastily.

15. In the passage, what does it mean to be **ecstatic**?

(A) It means to be sorrowful.
(B) It means to be miserable.
(C) It means to be understanding.
(D) It means to travel.
(E) It means to be delighted.

16. If Gregor's life was **insipid,** as the passage suggests, we may understand that Gregor

(A) was violent
(B) enjoyed being a bug
(C) was energetic
(D) was dull and lacked vigor
(E) felt excited

17. What strategy does the writer use to tell us that **rejuvenates** is defined as made young or vigorous again?

(A) The writer describes a positive change in Gregor's father.
(B) The writer describes Gregor's father as old and incapable.
(C) The writer surrounds **rejuvenates** with words that rhyme.
(D) The writer contrasts Gregor's father with Gregor's mother.
(E) The writer describes Gregor's father by using metaphors.

18. In the passage, something that is **plausible** is _____.

    (A) unlikely

    (B) reasonable

    (C) unbelievable

    (D) suspect

    (E) astounding

19. In the passage, when Kafka was **affiliated** with the insurance corporation, he was

    (A) fighting against it

    (B) corresponding with it

    (C) associated with it

    (D) hoping to work for it

    (E) president of it

20. In the passage, Kafka **repressed** his feelings except in his

    (A) social life

    (B) anguish

    (C) talking

    (D) stories

    (E) workplace

READING NEW WORDS IN CONTEXT

Lesson 4 | CONTEXT: Expression

The passage gives you an opportunity to expand your vocabulary. Below are twenty vocabulary words that are used in the passage and in the exercises that follow it.

aesthetic	fabricate	opportune	recipient
charisma	impediment	paradox	stamina
cliché	martial	prolific	wan
conceive	mediocre	qualm	zealous
emphatically	mien	reactionary	zephyr

Yukio Mishima: Japan's Literary Warrior

The life of Yukio Mishima (1925–1970), one of Japan's greatest modern novelists, was not a mere **zephyr** (1), or gentle breeze—it was a raging whirlwind. His career was a stormy blend of **aesthetic** (2), or artistic, and political projects. His personal activities were as headline-making as his literary works.

An Unpromising Beginning

Mishima, whose real name was Kimitake Hiraoka, was born in Tokyo in 1925. An unusual childhood paved the way for an unusual adult life. His father was a civil servant, and his mother was the daughter of a scholar. Mishima was the first of the couple's three children. His father's parents lived with the couple. Mishima's grandmother, who was sick and mentally unstable, took over as his caretaker and raised him. As a young child, Mishima rarely left his grandmother's dark room; as a result, he became weak and **wan** (3). His sickly paleness was evident when he began school and was around other children. By comparison with them, he was frail. Fears for his health resulted in his being forbidden to participate in activities outside the classroom.

Success as a Writer—and More

In middle school, however, Mishima finally asserted himself. He was a **zealous** (4) student, eager about writing in particular. He began to receive special recognition for his writing abilities. However, Mishima's assertive father **emphatically** (5) expressed his disapproval of his son's writing by tearing up any manuscripts he found. This forceful behavior led Mishima to hide his work with friends.

A turning point in Mishima's life came when a teacher asked Mishima to publish a story in *Art and Culture,* a literary magazine. The story, "A Forest in Full Bloom," shows Mishima's ability to **fabricate** (6) tales about ancestors and Japan's samurai, or warrior, past. He also made up strange stories involving themes of beauty and death. His early years were shaped by the Japanese Romantic School, a movement that emphasized nationalism, worship of the emperor, delight in beauty, and obsession with death. Soon after Mishima graduated at the top of his class in 1944, he found a publisher for his first book, entitled *The Forest in Full Bloom.*

However, the year 1944 was not an **opportune** (7) time to begin a literary career. Because of World War II, Mishima's ambitions were not well-timed. The war was an unavoidable **impediment** (8), or obstruction, to normal life in Japan. Mishima was diverted from his writing and forced to work in an airplane factory and then at a navy arsenal. He was eventually drafted but didn't pass the medical exam.

After the war, Mishima obtained a law degree and worked briefly for the Finance Ministry. Then, in 1948, Mishima turned to writing full time. He was a **prolific** (9) author who constantly turned out new works. Among his many works are the novels *Confessions of a Mask, The Temple of the Golden Pavilion,* and *The Sailor Who Fell from Grace with the Sea;* an autobiographical essay, *Sun and Steel;* short stories; and plays based on or inspired by the traditional Japanese Noh plays, in which four or five actors recite and dance to tell a story. Critics regard some of Mishima's work as merely **mediocre** (10), but they rate some of his novels and plays well above average, even excellent. In fact, Mishima was the **recipient** (11) of several awards for novels and plays, prizes given to him in recognition of the high quality of his work.

Writing was by no means Mishima's only activity. He also was an actor, a director of both plays and motion pictures, a singer, and a lecturer. Because of his interest in Japan's military tradition and history of war, Mishima admired the **martial** (12) arts. He took up kendo, fencing with wooden swords. Unlike his childhood self, his adult self obviously had much **stamina** (13)—that is, he possessed much vigor and strength. He admired physical abilities and worked hard to make himself superior in strength and endurance.

It would be a **cliché** (14) to say that Mishima was a man who wore many hats, but such a stale, overused saying is true in this case: Mishima had many interests and skills, both intellectual and physical. Above all, he possessed that special charm or magnetic appeal known as **charisma** (15), which made him and his works extremely popular with Japanese readers.

A Violent End

It is the **paradox** (16) of Mishima's character that at the same time he was full of life, he was also drawn to death. Many of his stories concern heroic deaths and suicides. His characters sacrifice themselves for Japan's traditional ideals by committing such ritual acts of suicide as hara-kiri, also called seppuku. Mishima's obsession with such topics arose from his idealization of the heroic aspects of Japan's past and his regret over the reduced position of the emperor, who had given up his divine, or godlike, status after the war.

Mishima **conceived** (17) the idea of creating his own private army to defend the emperor. In 1968, this newly formed idea became a reality in the form of the Shield Society. Through this army, Mishima hoped to revive the samurai tradition in Japan. Mishima, therefore, was considered a **reactionary** (18) because he cherished and wished to return to the prewar ways. In 1970, Mishima and four other Shield Society members entered the Self-Defense Headquarters in Tokyo by force. They took the commander hostage and ordered soldiers to assemble. Mishima, assuming the **mien** (19), or appearance and bearing, of a soldier, spoke to the group and urged them to overthrow Japan's constitution. The soldiers were not receptive. Mishima yelled, "Long live the Emperor!" and then followed the samurai warrior's form of ritual suicide known as seppuku.

In a letter written shortly before his death, Mishima said he wanted to sacrifice himself for the tradition of Japan that he admired and that was quickly disappearing. He apparently had no **qualms** (20) about his beliefs nor any doubts about his actions. Although his death was violent and sudden, he died at peace with himself and his philosophy.

EXERCISE 1 *Finding Synonyms*

Directions. Reread the preceding passage. Then write on the line provided a synonym for each of the words in boldface. If you cannot think of an exact synonym, you may write a brief definition of the word.

1. zephyr _____

2. aesthetic _____

3. wan _____

4. zealous _____

5. emphatically _____

6. fabricate _____

7. opportune _____

8. impediment _____

9. prolific _____

10. mediocre _____

11. recipient _____

12. martial _____

13. stamina _____

14. cliché _____

15. charisma _____

16. paradox _____

17. conceived _____

18. reactionary _____

19. mien _____

20. qualms _____

EXERCISE 2 — Reading Strategically ✍

Directions. Now that you have read the passage and thought about the words in boldface, circle the letter of the correct answer to each of the following items. The numbers of the items are the same as the numbers of the boldface vocabulary words in the passage.

1. In the passage, the writer contrasts Yukio Mishima's life with a **zephyr**. This metaphor compares his life to a

(A) novelist
(B) great wave
(C) falling star
(D) whirlwind
(E) headline

2. We can infer from the passage that **aesthetic** means
- (A) personal
- (B) without feeling
- (C) artistic
- (D) whirlwind
- (E) pathetic

3. In the passage, to be **wan** is to be _____.
- (A) alone and afraid
- (B) sad and depressed
- (C) dark and handsome
- (D) strong and energetic
- (E) pale and sickly

4. In the passage, when Mishima was **zealous** he was _____.
- (A) eager
- (B) timid
- (C) jealous
- (D) bored
- (E) recognized

5. What strategy does the writer use to tell us that **emphatically** is defined as forcefully?
- (A) The writer relates **emphatically** to Mishima's friends.
- (B) The writer contrasts **emphatically** with the words assertive and disapproval.
- (C) The writer refers to Mishima's father as supportive and interested in his son's work.
- (D) The writer explains the behavior of Mishima's father and describes it as forceful.
- (E) The writer relates **emphatically** to parental approval.

6. When we read in the passage of Mishima's ability to **fabricate** tales of Japan's past, we should realize that Mishima
- (A) liked to recite old stories
- (B) had a talent for making up stories
- (C) had no regard for the past
- (D) was not very original
- (E) faithfully worshiped ancestors

7. In the passage, why was 1944 not an **opportune** time to begin a literary career?
- (A) Mishima was in law school at the time.
- (B) Books were not popular in Japan.
- (C) Mishima could not write well.
- (D) Paper was not available.
- (E) World War II was being fought.

8. In the passage, an **impediment** is a(n)
- (A) moral support
- (B) military threat
- (C) arsenal
- (D) obstruction
- (E) driving force

9. In the passage, Mishima was a **prolific** writer because he wrote _____ books, short stories, and plays.

    (A) many
    (B) few
    (C) popular
    (D) simple
    (E) only

10. The writer provides a clue to the meaning of **mediocre** by

    (A) comparing Mishima's work to literature
    (B) explaining what a Noh play is
    (C) contrasting **mediocre** with the words well above average
    (D) implying that **mediocre** means well above average
    (E) relating **mediocre** to awards and prizes

11. When we read in the passage that Mishima was the **recipient** of many prizes, we should realize that

    (A) he refused many prizes
    (B) he received many prizes
    (C) he never was given prizes
    (D) his work was not well received
    (E) awards are not given for plays

12. We can infer from the passage that **martial** arts are related to

    (A) writing
    (B) acting
    (C) singing
    (D) law enforcement
    (E) war and the military

13. How does the writer provide a clue to the meaning of **stamina**?

    (A) The writer contrasts **stamina** with the word wooden.
    (B) The writer links **stamina** to the words vigor and strength.
    (C) The writer relates **stamina** to the words social activities.
    (D) The writer describes Mishima as basically inactive.
    (E) The writer links **stamina** to the words obviously had.

14. In the passage, a **cliché** is a

    (A) new thought
    (B) written opinion
    (C) type of hat
    (D) stale, overused saying
    (E) Japanese tradition

15. In the passage, Mishima's **charisma** resulted in his being

    (A) rude to friends and family
    (B) very popular with Japanese readers
    (C) always misunderstood
    (D) increasingly unpopular
    (E) rejected and unhappy

16. What strategy does the writer use to tell us that **paradox** is defined as a seemingly contradictory statement that is true?
  (A) The writer says that though Mishima was full of life, he was also drawn to death.
  (B) The writer describes Mishima as a reactionary who wanted to preserve traditional Japanese ways.
  (C) The writer follows **paradox** with descriptions of Mishima in old age.
  (D) The writer describes the Japanese emperor's loss of status.
  (E) The writer says Mishima wanted to be emperor.

17. In the passage, when Mishima **conceived** the idea to create a private army, he
  (A) publicized the idea
  (B) refused to consider the idea
  (C) formed the idea
  (D) gave up the idea
  (E) hoped to meet the emperor

18. When we read in the passage that Mishima was a **reactionary,** we should realize that
  (A) he wanted Japan to take new directions
  (B) he wished to rid Japan of the emperor
  (C) he rejected all ancient practices
  (D) he wanted to revive old traditions
  (E) he hoped to learn from the future

19. We can infer from the passage that when Mishima took on the **mien** of a soldier, he
  (A) tried to pretend that he was not a soldier
  (B) had the appearance and bearing of a soldier
  (C) argued with the emperor's guard
  (D) showed his hatred of soldiers and the military
  (E) did not look or act like a soldier

20. The writer provides a clue to the meaning of **qualms** by
  (A) relating **qualms** to the words quickly disappearing
  (B) saying that **qualms** are always apparent
  (C) relating **qualms** to ritual suicide
  (D) saying that Mishima's death was violent and sudden
  (E) linking **qualms** to the word doubts

READING NEW WORDS IN CONTEXT

Lesson 5 | CONTEXT: Expression

The passage gives you an opportunity to expand your vocabulary. Below are twenty vocabulary words that are used in the passage and in the exercises that follow it.

axiom	inanimate	mutable	recourse
compatible	incentive	percerption	retribution
compliance	indestructible	pivotal	stringent
encompass	innate	postulate	transcend
implacable	militant	prevalent	transitory

India's Three Great Beliefs

India's three major religions—Hinduism, Jainism, and Buddhism—first became **prevalent** (1) in the sixth and fifth centuries B.C. These widespread beliefs share a cultural and religious heritage, but each developed its own distinct **postulates** (2), or basic principles.

The Ancient Roots of Hinduism

Hinduism, one of the oldest religions in the world, has its roots in ancient India. It gradually developed from the religion of the Aryans, Indo-Europeans who first came into India around 1500 B.C. The four sacred books of Hinduism, the Vedas, date from the time of the Aryans. The oldest Veda, the *Rig Veda,* consists of hymns praising Aryan gods, who represented such aspects of nature as night and day.

Over the years, as the Aryans dominated India, Indian society became divided into what is called a caste system, a rigid social structure. This system, which included priests, warriors, peasants, and serfs, became a key part of Hinduism. The priests, or Brahmans, members of the highest caste, **implacably** (3) performed the rituals associated with Aryan beliefs; they were relentless in this task. However, because many people, including some Brahmans, did not find the Aryan rituals **compatible** (4) with their lives, they began to seek beliefs more in harmony with their experiences. As a result, a group of Brahmans developed other

sacred texts, including the *Upanishads,* that set forth important **axioms** (5) of what became known as Hinduism. One of these self-evident truths is that, despite the existence of many gods, there is a reality called Brahma that **encompasses** (6) everything. In other words, Brahma contains both the universal and the individual truth, and these truths are both the same and eternal. Another Hindu belief is that of reincarnation, or rebirth into another life after death. The Hindus understood the soul to be **indestructible** (7); they believed it could never be destroyed. The souls of people who do good deeds in this life are rewarded with a better existence in a future life, while those who do evil receive the **retribution** (8) of a less desirable life in a later rebirth. This concept of reward and punishment in future lives is known as karma. The Hindus believe that it is possible eventually to **transcend** (9) this cycle of rebirth—that is, to move beyond it and finally join Brahma through proper living, true understanding, and meditation.

Jainism: Peacefulness and a Respect for Life

Vardhamana Mahavira (c. 540–468 B.C.), the founder of Jainism, agreed with the Hindu ideas of karma and rebirth but added this crucial point: All things—living creatures and plants as well as **inanimate** (10) objects—have souls. Another **pivotal** (11) idea of Jainism is that all life is sacred, and this central concept forbids the destruction of any life, no matter how lowly. In fact, some Jains have been known to keep their mouths covered so as to avoid accidentally breathing in a small insect. Of course, absolute **compliance** (12) to this philosophy would mean that Jains would die of starvation. Jains, therefore, do not entirely submit to their philosophy; instead, they view humans as the highest life form, followed by animals, plants, and nonliving objects. As a result, although Jains do not eat meat, they allow themselves to eat plant life. The Jains also adopted the principle of nonviolence, an idea that spread throughout India and helped to explain why so many Indians, including Mohandas "Mohatma" Gandhi (1869–1948), refused to become **militant** (13) during their struggles for independence, even when violence in the name of self-protection seemed understandable.

Buddhism and the Eightfold Path

During the time Hinduism and Jainism were becoming established, an Indian named Siddhartha Gautama (c. 563–483 B.C.) founded Buddhism. Siddhartha, who was raised as a Hindu, earned the name Buddha, which means "Enlightened One," as a result of seeking religious answers through meditation. Buddha believed that humans were born with weaknesses. Furthermore, these **innate** (14) weaknesses lead to suffering and frustration.

Given the inevitability of human weakness, what **recourse** (15) do people have? Where can they turn for peace and enlightenment? The remedy Buddha offered was the Eightfold Path.

This code of conduct consisted of right views, right intentions, right speech, right conduct, right livelihood, right effort, right mindfulness, and right meditation. A person who reaches the eighth step attains a high level of **perception** (16). This ability to see and understand the universe is, according to Buddhist teaching, available to anyone who follows the eight steps. The ultimate goal of the Buddhist is to forego all attachments to things of the world. Buddha also stressed that nothing in the world is permanent; all is **transitory** (17), or ever-changing. Buddha did not emphasize the worship of gods, but he believed in an infinite power. Through his teachings, Buddha strove to provide the **incentive** (18), or encouragement, for each person to follow a spiritual path.

Buddha's death resulted in a split in Buddhism. One branch of Buddhism is very **stringent** (19). Its believers follow very strict rules and lead simple lives devoted to finding personal salvation. The followers of another, more liberal branch view Buddhism as **mutable** (20), like a house whose interior and exterior transform over time as new residents move in and fashions change. These Buddhists believe there are many paths to salvation, not just one unchanging one.

All three of India's great religions, though ancient in origin, survive today. Hindus make up the largest percentage of Indians; Jains and Buddhists make up one of the smallest. Buddhism today flourishes mainly in other parts of Asia. Nevertheless, the three great beliefs of India have claimed millions of devoted followers for hundreds of years.

EXERCISE 1   *Finding Synonyms* ✍

Directions. Reread the preceding passage. Then write on the line provided a synonym for each of the words in boldface. If you cannot think of an exact synonym, you may write a brief definition of the word.

1. prevalent _____

2. postulates _____

3. implacably _____

4. compatible _____

5. axioms _____

6. encompasses _____

7. indestructible _____

8. retribution _____

9. transcend _____

10. inanimate _____

11. pivotal _____

12. compliance _____

13. militant _____

14. innate _____

15. recourse _____

16. perception _____

17. transitory _____

18. incentive _____

19. stringent _____

20. mutable _____

EXERCISE 2 *Reading Strategically* ✍

Directions. Now that you have read the passage and thought about the words in boldface, circle the letter of the correct answer to each of the following items. The numbers of the items are the same as the numbers of the boldface vocabulary words in the passage.

1. When we read in the passage that India's three great religions became **prevalent**, we should realize that they became

(A) obsolete
(B) outlawed
(C) widespread
(D) overlooked
(E) understandable

2. In the passage, a **postulate** is a

(A) religious person
(B) distinct religion
(C) religious heritage
(D) common culture
(E) basic principle

3. In the passage, **implacably** means _____.

(A) with forgiveness
(B) relentlessly
(C) with humor
(D) spiritually
(E) without emotion

4. What strategy does the writer use to tell us that **compatible** is defined as able to get along, or agreeing?

(A) The writer links **compatible** beliefs with beliefs that are in harmony.
(B) The writer contrasts **compatible** with the antonym universal.
(C) The writer refers to the Brahmans' sacred texts.
(D) The writer refers to ritualized religion.
(E) The writer relates **compatible** to the word experiences.

5. When we read that the Brahmans developed their own important **axioms,** we should realize that they

(A) had unimportant ideas
(B) practiced hidden beliefs and practices
(C) set forth self-evident truths
(D) created obvious falsehoods
(E) devised new religious rituals

6. If Brahma **encompasses** everything, as the writer of the passage suggests, then Brahma

(A) is invisible but understandable
(B) stays separate from earthly life
(C) is not a part of anything living
(D) contains and encloses everything
(E) teaches but is otherwise uninvolved

7. In the passage, if the soul is **indestructible,** according to Hindu belief, then it

(A) cannot be explained
(B) is always changing
(C) cannot be destroyed
(D) is rewarded with a better life
(E) is punished with a less desirable life

8. We can infer from the passage that **retribution** is

(A) future rewards
(B) good deeds
(C) approval
(D) punishment
(E) true understanding

9. The writer provides a clue to the meaning of **transcends** by

(A) relating **transcends** to the word universal
(B) linking **transcends** to the phrase move beyond
(C) saying that **transcends** means everlasting
(D) telling us about karma
(E) relating **transcends** to the word cycle

10. The writer provides a clue to the meaning of the word **inanimate** by

(A) contrasting **inanimate** objects with living creatures and plants
(B) comparing souls to everything in the universe
(C) saying **inanimate** objects are living creatures and plants
(D) implying that **inanimate** means vegetarian
(E) saying that **inanimate** objects have souls

11. In the passage, an idea that is **pivotal** to Jainism is _____ to Jainism.

(A) unimportant
(B) destructive
(C) partial
(D) central
(E) unnecessary

12. We can infer from the passage that absolute **compliance** is _____.

(A) lack of control
(B) universal belief
(C) complete obedience
(D) unavoidable destruction
(E) social protest

13. In the passage, why did the Jains refuse to become **militant**?

(A) They did not believe in violence.
(B) They were more interested in warfare.
(C) They were against the draft.
(D) They adopted beliefs in violence.
(E) They struggled for independence.

14. We can infer from the passage that if a weakness is **innate**, it is

(A) developed
(B) useful
(C) inborn
(D) strong
(E) curable

15. In the passage, when we read that Buddha offers the Eightfold Path as a **recourse** for life's problems, we should realize that, according to Buddhism,

(A) Buddha offers little understanding
(B) following the Eightfold Path will lead to peace and enlightenment
(C) following the Eightfold Path results in suffering and frustration
(D) people cannot overcome inborn human weaknesses
(E) following the Eightfold Path is impossible for anyone but Buddha

16. What strategy does the writer use to tell us that **perception** is defined as discernment, or the ability to perceive?

(A) The writer says people never reach a level of perfection.
(B) The writer describes **perception** as permanent.
(C) The writer gives the antonym infinite for **perception**.
(D) The writer contrasts **perception** with the word perfection.
(E) The writer restates **perception** as the ability to see and understand.

17. If everything in the world is **transitory,** as the passage says Buddha suggests, then

(A) everything is permanent
(B) nothing is permanent or stable
(C) nothing ever changes
(D) things seldom change or move
(E) **transitory** means infinite

18. The writer provides a clue to the meaning of **incentive** by

(A) relating **incentive** to a belief in an infinite power
(B) saying an **incentive** is something that must be provided
(C) referring to Buddha's earlier teachings
(D) linking **incentive** to the word encouragement
(E) implying that an **incentive** can be achieved on spiritual paths

19. When we read in the passage that one branch of Buddhism is very **stringent,** we should realize that it

(A) is strict and rigid
(B) is very liberal
(C) requires much money
(D) allows much freedom
(E) has many followers

20. Because the liberal branch sees Buddhism as **mutable,** this branch of Buddhism is compared by a simile to

(A) people who build a new house to meet their needs
(B) people who trade in an old house for a newer one
(C) a house that changes over time to accommodate new residents
(D) a house that is built on only one path to salvation
(E) a house of people who are divided over their incompatible beliefs

READING NEW WORDS IN CONTEXT

The passage gives you an opportunity to expand your vocabulary. Below are twenty vocabulary words that are used in the passage and in the exercises that follow it.

appease	besiege	inclement	pretext
archaic	commence	invincible	vigilant
autonomy	devastation	latitude	vulnerable
balmy	espionage	perseverance	wane
beguile	facsimile	precarious	wreak

In Search of Troy and Ulysses

Just how far did the Greek poet Homer let his imagination roam? Were his epic poems the *Iliad,* about the Trojan War, and the *Odyssey,* about Ulysses (Odysseus to the Greeks) and his crew's return home after the war, simply myth and fancy? Homer gave himself plenty of artistic freedom, or **latitude** (1), in relating his famous epics. However, he also anchored his stories in truth. Modern research has established the Trojan War as a historical fact and has retraced the probable sea route followed by the fictional Ulysses.

The Trojan War: Fact and Fiction

In the 1800s, archaeologists located the site of ancient Troy on a hill in present-day northwest Turkey. An amateur German archaeologist, Heinrich Schliemann (1822–1890), thought that Homer's tales were at least partly factual. With **perseverance** (2), or persistence, Schliemann and other researchers discovered evidence of at least nine primary settlements that were founded at the site of Troy during the Early Bronze Age.

Archaeologists have determined that the Trojan War ended around 1250 B.C. What prompted the Trojan War and the eventual **devastation** (3) of Troy? According to Homer, love and a quarrel among the gods began the destruction of Troy. The Trojan War **commences** (4) when Paris, prince of Troy, steals Helen, wife of Sparta's king. Under the command of Agamemnon, the king of

Mycenae, armies from various Greek kingdoms wage war against Troy to **wreak** (5) vengeance and to recapture Helen. Historians, however, believe that disputes over trade routes may have been the real cause of the war. The **autonomous** (6), independent city of Troy was perfectly located to command trade routes in the Aegean and Black seas.

According to the *Iliad,* the bloody Trojan War lasted for ten long years. During this time, the Greeks and Trojans used **espionage** (7) to try to discover the other side's military secrets, yet neither side could gain an advantage. Troy was a small city and easily circled, but soldiers were not able to **besiege** (8) it, for the city was walled and well defended. Troy's defeat came through trickery. Acting on advice from Ulysses, the Greeks sent a huge wooden horse to the people of Troy. A Greek who pretended to be a traitor **beguiled** (9) the Trojans by telling them that the horse was a gift to Athena, the goddess of war, and that it would protect them. In fact, the horse made the misled Trojans completely **vulnerable** (10) to defeat. The false story was just a **pretext** (11) concocted by the Greeks, for concealed in the hollow horse were Greek soldiers. After the Trojans had brought the horse into Troy, the Greek soldiers hidden inside poured out of the horse's belly and captured the city.

The hero Ulysses, as far as we know, is strictly a mythological character. In the *Odyssey,* the **invincible** (12) Ulysses overcomes fantastic creatures and dangerous obstacles on his way home from Troy. His adventures are legendary and heroic. Homer chose what seems a short, safe route from Troy to Ulysses' home on the Greek island of Ithaca. According to the theory of explorer and author Tim Severin, a Greek warrior returning home from the Trojan War might also have chosen this less **precarious** (13) route. He would have wanted to avoid uncertainties and dangers that might have delayed his return.

Retracing an Ancient Route

In 1985, Severin and an international crew retraced Ulysses' route through the Aegean, Mediterranean, and Ionian seas. They sailed on the *Argo,* a 54-foot exact reproduction, or **facsimile** (14), of a Bronze Age galley, or single-decked ship. Like Ulysses, they encountered extreme weather conditions, from mild and pleasant—what we might call **balmy** (15)—to **inclement** (16) and severe.

The modern *Argo* crew identified land formations and local myths that correspond to those in the *Odyssey.* For example, at one point in the epic the normally alert Ulysses is not **vigilant** (17) and thus becomes trapped in the cave of the giant Cyclops. Homer says that the island on which the

Cyclops lived was inhabited by many goats. Severin reasons that the island was Crete not only because that island has many goats, just as Homer described, but also because people on the island still tell a Bronze Age legend of a Cyclops-like creature.

Severin argues that it was probably on the island of Paxos that Ulysses **appeased** (18) the sorceress Circe. She needed to be calmed down and pacified after she angrily turned all of Ulysses' men into animals. On his own voyage, Severin didn't find the ancient, **archaic** (19) leather bag in which Ulysses received the winds from the god Aeolus. However, he did find the island Grabousa, known to the ancient Greeks as Korykos, or "leather bag." Moreover, Severin's crew discovered what could be the famed Clashing Rocks near the island of Levkas. Severin thinks the Sirens probably lived on Levkas. According to Greek mythology, the strength of a man would **wane** (20) like a flower wilting in hot sun if he heard the sweet songs of the Sirens. Homer relates that Ulysses put wax in his crewmen's ears so that their strength would not decline in response to the Sirens' call.

It is unlikely that we will ever know the complete stories that lie behind Homer's *Iliad* and *Odyssey*. No written records of that time survive. But archaeologists and explorers have found proof that at least some of the places and events described in the *Iliad* and the *Odyssey* are based on historical fact.

EXERCISE 1 *Finding Synonyms*

Directions. Reread the preceding passage. Then write on the line provided a synonym for each of the words in boldface. If you cannot think of an exact synonym, you may write a brief definition of the word.

1. latitude _____

2. perseverance _____

3. devastation _____

4. commences _____

5. wreak _____

6. autonomous _____

7. espionage _____

8. besiege _____

9. beguiled _____

10. vulnerable _____

11. pretext _____

12. invincible _____

13. precarious _____

14. facsimile _____

15. balmy _____

16. inclement _____

17. vigilant _____

18. appeased _____

19. archaic _____

20. wane _____

EXERCISE 2 *Reading Strategically* 👆

Directions. Now that you have read the passage and thought about the words in boldface, circle the letter of the correct answer to each of the following items. The numbers of the items are the same as the numbers of the boldface vocabulary words in the passage.

1. If Homer gave himself plenty of **latitude,** as the author of the passage suggests, we may expect
  (A) Homer's writing to be limited to the facts
  (B) Homer to have been knowledgeable about geography
  (C) Homer to have given himself plenty of artistic freedom
  (D) Homer's writing to be difficult to understand
  (E) Homer to have written only about things he had experienced firsthand

2. What strategy does the writer use to tell us that **perseverance** is a continuous, patient effort?
  (A) The writer links **perseverance** to the synonym persistence.
  (B) The writer relates **perseverance** to the word located.
  (C) The writer implies that Schliemann was impatient.
  (D) The writer links **perseverance** to the word amateur.
  (E) The writer contrasts **perseverance** with an antonym.

3. We can infer from the passage that the **devastation** of Troy involved
  (A) six other settlements
  (B) great patience
  (C) rebuilding
  (D) unearthed evidence
  (E) destruction

4. In the passage, when a war **commences**, it

    (A) persists
    (B) begins
    (C) fails
    (D) is won
    (E) ends

5. When we read in the passage that the Greek armies went to Troy to **wreak** vengeance, we should realize that the armies went to

    (A) protect Troy
    (B) inflict punishment
    (C) kill Helen
    (D) display forgiveness
    (E) resolve a trade dispute

6. In the passage, a city that is **autonomous** is

    (A) dependent
    (B) a suburb
    (C) undefendable
    (D) independent
    (E) the capital

7. We can infer from the passage that someone involved in **espionage** is a(n)

    (A) prisoner
    (B) hero
    (C) Trojan
    (D) explorer
    (E) spy

8. According to the passage, why were the Greek soldiers unable to **besiege** the city?

    (A) The city was surrounded by walls and was well defended.
    (B) They were tricked by the Trojans.
    (C) The city was too large and populated to surround and attack.
    (D) The gods protected the city.
    (E) The Trojans came out of the city and surrendered.

9. According to the passage, when the Greek soldier **beguiled** the Trojans, he _____ them.

    (A) joined
    (B) misled
    (C) visited
    (D) helped
    (E) freed

10. The writer provides a clue to the meaning of **vulnerable** by

    (A) contrasting Ulysses with other mythological characters
    (B) telling us that Agamemnon was a traitor to the Greeks
    (C) including synonyms for **vulnerable**
    (D) describing what happened after the Trojans brought the horse into Troy
    (E) relating the horse to the goddess Athena

11. In the passage, the story about the wooden horse was a **pretext** because
   (A) it was meant to help the Trojans
   (B) it was meant to trick the Trojans
   (C) the story was true
   (D) no one was expected to believe it
   (E) the horse was made of solid wood

12. In the passage, Ulysses was **invincible** because he was _____.
   (A) entertained
   (B) overcome
   (C) defeated
   (D) swift
   (E) unconquerable

13. We can infer from the passage that if a route is **precarious**, it is
   (A) dangerous
   (B) safe
   (C) practical
   (D) long
   (E) narrow

14. In the passage, Severin's ship was a **facsimile** because it was a(n) _____ of a Bronze Age galley.
   (A) picture
   (B) improved version
   (C) faithful reproduction
   (D) poor imitation
   (E) forerunner

15. In the passage, **balmy** weather is
   (A) cold and windy
   (B) hot and humid
   (C) mild and pleasant
   (D) dark and threatening
   (E) wild and dangerous

16. What strategy does the writer use to tell us that **inclement** means rough and stormy?
   (A) The writer says weather at sea is always **inclement**.
   (B) The writer describes **inclement** weather as mild and pleasant.
   (C) The writer provides an example of **inclement** weather.
   (D) The writer uses **inclement** as an antonym for **balmy**.
   (E) The writer explains that Ulysses also encountered **inclement** weather.

17. When we read in the passage that Ulysses is not **vigilant**, we should realize that he is
   (A) not watchful and alert
   (B) very watchful and alert
   (C) always careless
   (D) often confused
   (E) selfish and uncaring

18. The writer provides a clue to the meaning of **appeased** by

(A) relating it to the story of the Cyclops
(B) suggesting that it means angered
(C) using the synonyms calmed down and pacified
(D) linking it to the use of Circe's magic
(E) implying that it means using enchantment to turn men into animals

19. In the passage, **archaic** means

(A) used
(B) old
(C) moldy
(D) new
(E) windy

20. To show that a man's strength would **wane** if he heard the songs of the Sirens, the writer uses the simile

(A) "leather bag"
(B) "a flower wilting in hot sun"
(C) "wax in his crewmen's ears"
(D) "Clashing Rocks near the island of Levkas"
(E) "the winds from the god Aeolus"

READING NEW WORDS IN CONTEXT

Lesson 7 | **CONTEXT:** Civilization

The passage gives you an opportunity to expand your vocabulary. Below are twenty vocabulary words that are used in the passage and in the exercises that follow it.

apex	edifice	juncture	ravage
bourgeois	hieroglyphic	meager	retainer
canine	inaccessible	obliterate	rivulet
coffer	influx	ossify	subsidize
defunct	innovation	perceive	tawny

Guatemala's Forgotten City

In the tropical rain forest of northern Guatemala, a great city once thrived by the Río Azul, or the Blue River. That city, now called Río Azul, was located at an important trade crossing, a **juncture** (1) reached by Mayans traveling from different parts of Central America. Although the area was settled before 900 B.C., the city did not reach the height of its influence until the eighth century A.D.

Probing the Secrets of an Ancient City

Modern archaeologists can **perceive** (2) Río Azul's greatness by observing and examining remains of buildings and other structures as well as the contents of excavated tombs. Individuals and organizations, such as the National Geographic Society, have **subsidized** (3) archaeological work at Río Azul through financial contributions. Without this support, the joint U.S.-Guatemala research project there might not have been possible.

Excavations at Río Azul, which today is in a nearly **inaccessible** (4) forest near the Mexico-Guatemala-Belize border, began in the 1980s. For the ancient Mayans, however, the urban community of Río Azul was not as difficult to reach as it is for modern travelers. The population of the city and its suburbs was approximately five thousand in the 700s. In addition, Río Azul probably had a steady **influx** (5) of traders and travelers entering the city to conduct business.

Architecture and Class Structure

Río Azul, an administrative center in the Mayan world, contained not only many residential houses but also palaces, temples, and other imposing structures. Some of these **edifices** (6) might amaze today's architects. One example is an enormous pyramid-shaped temple built in the fifth century. It is 155 feet tall, or 14 stories at the **apex** (7), which still can be seen above the treetops.

The layout of homes in Río Azul reflects the class structure of the city. The memorial temples were connected to homes of the upper classes by causeways, sometimes constructed over **rivulets** (8), or streams. Nobles lived in palaces with such modern conveniences (for the time) as built-in beds. Homes of the **bourgeois** (9), on the other hand, were smaller and often grouped around the nobles' palaces. The lower classes, which included **retainers** (10), had still smaller homes. Because these servants needed to be close to the houses in which they worked, their homes were built near the palaces and the homes of the **bourgeois**.

Outside the city, agricultural workers contributed to the well-being and overall success of the community. The farmers of Río Azul probably built soil platforms to grow crops in lowlands that flooded regularly. This traditional Mayan technique, new to the region, would have been an **innovation** (11) in the area of Río Azul. Also new to the lowlands area was the farmers' use of terraces, dams, and canals to irrigate crops. These new techniques benefited not only crops, but also the Mayans' domestic animals, which would have included fowl and members of the **canine** (12), or dog, family.

Unlocking the Mysteries of Tombs

Archaeologists have researched finds from several tombs at the now **defunct** (13) city, which finally fell to devastating military raids from the north about A.D. 830. Scientists have translated some of the **hieroglyphic** (14) writing in the tombs. The symbols and pictures that make up this system of writing have revealed information about rulers and important dates in the city's history. Scientists also have analyzed remains found in the tombs, such as the skeleton of an unusually tall man who died about fifteen hundred years ago. They also have studied artifacts such as **tawny** (15) or tan unpainted clay figurines. In one tomb, researchers

found pieces of cloth. The cloth had hardened like cartilage that has **ossified** (16), or changed into bone.

Unfortunately, some of the contents of the tombs that might have unlocked other mysteries about Río Azul have been **obliterated** (17). Time, of course, is one cause of the destruction; looters are another cause. Looters hired local workers at only **meager** (18) wages to tunnel into the tombs. Like an invading army **ravaging** (19) a city, the looters and their low-paid helpers destroyed many artifacts. What they did not destroy, they stole and sold to art and antique dealers. **Coffers** (20) full of stolen treasure were shipped out of the country. In these chests were jade gems and ceramic statues and pottery.

The ruins of Río Azul are now protected by the Guatemalan government. Archaeologists and historians continue to study the site to learn more about the civilization that once flourished there.

EXERCISE 1   *Finding Synonyms*

Directions. Reread the preceding passage. Then write on the line provided a synonym for each of the words in boldface. If you cannot think of an exact synonym, you may write a brief definition of the word.

1. juncture _____

2. perceive _____

3. subsidized _____

4. inaccessible _____

5. influx _____

6. edifices _____

7. apex _____

8. rivulets _____

9. bourgeois _____

10. retainers _____

11. innovation _____

12. canine _____

13. defunct   _____

14. hieroglyphic   _____

15. tawny   _____

16. ossified   _____

17. obliterated   _____

18. meager   _____

19. ravaging   _____

20. coffers   _____

EXERCISE 2 *Reading Strategically* ✍

Directions. Now that you have read the passage and thought about the words in boldface, circle the letter of the correct answer to each of the following items. The numbers of the items are the same as the numbers of the boldface vocabulary words in the passage.

1. How does the writer provide a clue to the meaning of **juncture**?
   (A) The writer uses **juncture** to describe the river.
   (B) The writer says that a **juncture** is a dead-end road.
   (C) The writer implies that **juncture** means civilization.
   (D) The writer relates **juncture** to the term tropical forest.
   (E) The writer links **juncture** to the word crossing.

2. According to the passage, why are archaeologists able to **perceive** Río Azul's greatness?
   (A) By observing and examining the remains of buildings and tombs, they understand how great the city was.
   (B) By studying books, archaeologists have learned about the city's history.
   (C) Archaeologists can recognize the greatness of a city without excavating its ruins.
   (D) The greatness of a city lies in its reputation and in the pride of its residents.
   (E) The city has remained a populous, thriving center of trade since the eighth century A.D.

3. We can infer from the passage that **subsidized** means
   (A) examined
   (B) financed
   (C) excavated
   (D) prohibited
   (E) admired

4. According to the passage, what does **inaccessible** mean?
   (A) It means easily reached by road.
   (B) It means impossible to reach.
   (C) It means hard to see.
   (D) It means in a treeless area.
   (E) It means the place where two rivers meet.

5. When we read in the passage that there probably was a steady **influx** of traders and travelers into Río Azul, we should realize that

(A) traders and travelers were unable to find the city
(B) the city contained only native residents
(C) the city's population has remained the same throughout history
(D) many traders and travelers probably entered the city
(E) people were constantly leaving Río Azul

6. In the passage, **edifices** are

(A) administrative centers
(B) especially imposing buildings
(C) things that amaze architects
(D) small houses in residential areas
(E) systems of underground pipes

7. We can infer from the passage that the **apex** of anything is the

(A) foundation
(B) side walls
(C) peak or top
(D) architecture
(E) front

8. How does the writer provide a clue to the meaning of **rivulets**?

(A) The writer links **rivulets** to class structure.
(B) The writer relates **rivulets** to memorial temples.
(C) The writer suggests that **rivulets** are a kind of bridge.
(D) The writer links **rivulets** to the synonym streams.
(E) The writer links **rivulets** to the antonym causeway.

9. What strategy does the writer use to tell us that **bourgeois** is defined as middle class?

(A) The writer links being **bourgeois** to the political system.
(B) The writer explains that the **bourgeois** live in palaces.
(C) The writer contrasts **bourgeois** with the antonym working class.
(D) The writer compares **bourgeois** to the servants' positions.
(E) The writer discusses the **bourgeois** as being between the nobles and the lower classes.

10. In the passage, **retainers** are _____ in the homes of the wealthy.

(A) ministers
(B) servants
(C) entertainers
(D) beds
(E) conveniences

11. If the Mayan technique of building soil platforms was an **innovation** in Río Azul, as the writer suggests, we know that it was

(A) a new technology in Río Azul
(B) an old tradition in Río Azul
(C) popular with the city's residents
(D) a time-consuming way of doing things
(E) prohibited by the landowners

12. In the passage, a **canine** is
(A) a member of the cat family
(B) any animal raised on a farm
(C) a member of the dog family
(D) a barnyard fowl, such as a duck
(E) any domestic animal

13. In the passage, what does it mean for a city to be **defunct**?
(A) It means it is thriving.
(B) It means it is overpopulated.
(C) It means it has been brought back to life.
(D) It means it no longer exists.
(E) It means it has changed forms of government.

14. What strategy does the writer use to tell us that **hieroglyphic** pertains to a system of writing that uses pictorial symbols?
(A) The writer explains that symbols and pictures make up this system of writing.
(B) The writer describes pictures of artifacts that revealed information about Río Azul.
(C) The writer translates a passage as an example.
(D) The writer defines **hieroglyphic** as writing in tombs.
(E) The writer compares **hieroglyphic** symbols to Arabic and Sumerian symbols.

15. In the passage, **tawny** means
(A) fossilized
(B) colorless
(C) tan
(D) dry
(E) dead

16. Because pieces of cloth had grown hard, the writer uses a simile to compare them to cartilage that has **ossified** or
(A) become flexible
(B) turned into wood
(C) become less rigid
(D) powdered into dust
(E) changed into bone

17. According to the passage, some contents of the tombs have been **obliterated** or
(A) protected
(B) hidden
(C) replaced
(D) destroyed
(E) kept secret

18. When we read in the passage that looters gave local workers **meager** pay, we should realize that
(A) the workers were very well paid
(B) the workers had long-term contracts
(C) the workers were paid very little
(D) the looters paid workers with jewels
(E) the workers could demand high salaries

19. The writer uses a simile that includes "Like an invading army **ravaging** a city" to illustrate the effects of

(A) looters
(B) artifacts
(C) archaeologists
(D) traders
(E) time

20. The writer provides a clue to the meaning of **coffers** by

(A) linking **coffers** to robbery
(B) referring to **coffers** with the words these chests
(C) relating **coffers** to open tombs
(D) linking **coffers** to looters
(E) using an antonym for **coffers**

READING NEW WORDS IN CONTEXT

Lesson 8 | CONTEXT: Civilization

The passage gives you an opportunity to expand your vocabulary. Below are twenty vocabulary words that are used in the passage and in the exercises that follow it.

abound	delectable	hors d'oeuvres	recur
aptitude	ensue	lapse	requisite
astute	erratic	palatable	steppe
buffet	expedient	pastoral	succulent
conducive	facilitate	quantitative	zenith

China's Ming Dynasty: A Dream Journey

What in the world will I dream about next? Lately I've found that my obsession with my world history course has not been **conducive** (1) to a good night's rest. It has, however, led to the strangest dreams. They are all related in some crazy way to history.

Dreaming of Ming

For example, for the past three days, my class has been studying China's Ming or "brilliant" dynasty. This dynasty began in 1368, when the Mongols were overthrown, and lasted until 1644. The time was a **zenith** (2) in Chinese history—a high point for Chinese arts and culture. As a result of my Ming dynasty studies, guess what **ensued** (3) last night? I went back to the Ming dynasty in my dreams!

After I fell asleep, I don't think any time had **lapsed** (4) or passed before I was dreaming that I was in China. First, I dreamed that I was flying over a **steppe** (5), a vast, almost treeless plain, in northwestern China.

At first, the dream, like an automated television that keeps changing channels at irregular periods, was **erratic** (6). From the **steppe,** I moved suddenly into a lovely **pastoral** (7) scene where farmers peacefully worked their rich plots of land. I had read that Hung-wu (1368–1398), the first

Ming emperor, **facilitated** (8) agriculture in China. His assistance took the form of land grants to peasants. From reading about his domestic and foreign policies, I think Hung-wu was an **astute** (9) leader. He was not interested in conquering other lands, but he was shrewd in his plans to rebuild the ailing Chinese empire.

Suddenly the farm scene disappeared, and I was attending a dramatic production on a bare stage. Drama was extremely popular during the Ming dynasty. The actors in the play I saw obviously had an **aptitude** (10) for singing. Their natural ability for music was a bonus, as the music they sang was difficult for a Westerner to fully appreciate. For a performer in Ming drama, singing ability was a **requisite** (11) because it was necessary to sing lines rather than say them. A small orchestra accompanied the singers.

A musician banged a gong during the play, and immediately I was transported to a museum. There, now-famous Ming porcelain and textiles **abounded** (12). For example, there must have been a thousand porcelain dishes and vases with colorful pictures of dragons. Ming potters obviously strove to produce quality products. And, judging from the staggering amount of pottery they created, they must have had **quantitative** (13) goals, too.

A Dream Feast

The highlight of my dream was a gigantic party given by Emperor Wan-li (1573–1620). He gave the party as a celebration of the completion of his enormous tomb near Peking, now called Beijing. (The tomb, which took Ming builders six years to construct, was uncovered in 1956.) I don't know what the party was really like, but in my dream it began with **hors d'oeuvres** (14). These appetizers were mostly vegetables. Then the emperor invited the guests to help themselves to the **buffet** (15), which included a variety of foods spread out on a thirty-foot table. This was the most **expedient** (16) way to serve all of the emperor's guests with as little fuss as possible.

The guests could sample all the foods they wanted. Of course, I didn't try everything. Because I was pleased with most of the dishes I tasted, though, I would have to say the foods were **palatable** (17). I liked the egg rolls, egg drop soup, dumplings, and preserved fruit. The sweet-and-sour fish was especially **succulent** (18), but the shrimp with rice was not as moist and flavorful as the fish. The noodles were delicious. In fact, they were so **delectable** (19) that I had four servings. I've never enjoyed a better **buffet**. Fortunately, because it was only a dream, I didn't gain any weight from my gluttony!

The emperor asked me back, but my dream about the Ming dynasty probably won't **recur** (20). Today, my world history class begins studying ancient Japan. I can hardly wait to see where my next dreams take me!

EXERCISE 1 *Finding Synonyms* ☞

Directions. Reread the preceding passage. Then write on the line provided a synonym for each of the words in boldface. If you cannot think of an exact synonym, you may write a brief definition of the word.

1. conducive _____

2. zenith _____

3. ensued _____

4. lapsed _____

5. steppe _____

6. erratic _____

7. pastoral _____

8. facilitated _____

9. astute _____

10. aptitude _____

11. requisite _____

12. abounded _____

13. quantitative _____

14. hors d'oeuvres _____

15. buffet _____

16. expedient _____

17. palatable _____

18. succulent _____

19. delectable _____

20. recur _____

EXERCISE 2 *Reading Strategically* ✍

Directions. Now that you have read the passage and thought about the words in boldface, circle the letter of the correct answer to each of the following items. The numbers of the items are the same as the numbers of the boldface vocabulary words in the passage.

1. In the passage, because the writer's obsession with a world history course has not been **conducive** to a good night's rest, we know that the writer
   (A) has been sleeping in class
   (B) has not been sleeping restfully
   (C) has been sleeping too soundly to dream
   (D) has been awake for a week
   (E) is taking a course in the history of dreams

2. In the passage, **zenith** means
   (A) dream
   (B) culture
   (C) dynasty
   (D) peak
   (E) light

3. We can infer from the passage that **ensued** means
   (A) preceded
   (B) stopped
   (C) followed
   (D) dreamed
   (E) lasted

4. In the passage, what does **lapsed** mean?
   (A) It means ended.
   (B) It means renewed.
   (C) It means learned.
   (D) It means arrived.
   (E) It means passed.

5. In the passage, **steppe** means
  (A) a big step
  (B) a polar icecap
  (C) a large, almost treeless plain
  (D) a vast swampy area
  (E) a grassy strip of beach

6. Because the dream was **erratic** at first, the writer compares it by simile to
  (A) an automated television that irregularly changes channels
  (B) a dream that switches from location to location regularly
  (C) a lovely countryside where farmers work the land peacefully
  (D) the **steppes** of northeastern Europe and southeastern China
  (E) neon signs that blink off and on with regularity

7. What strategy does the writer use to tell us that **pastoral** is defined as relating to a simple country life?
  (A) The writer explains that the land is fertile.
  (B) The writer tells of agricultural progress during Hung-wu's time.
  (C) The writer compares **pastoral** activities to foreign policies.
  (D) The writer describes farmers peacefully working their plots of land.
  (E) The writer compares **pastoral** to automated.

8. How does the writer provide a clue to the meaning of **facilitated**?
  (A) The writer compares **facilitated** to agriculture.
  (B) The writer links **facilitated** to the word assistance.
  (C) The writer contrasts **facilitated** with the antonym reading.
  (D) The writer explains domestic and foreign policies.
  (E) The writer relates **facilitated** to the word peasants.

9. In the passage, the word _____ provides a clue to the meaning of **astute**.
  (A) shrewd
  (B) interested
  (C) ailing
  (D) leader
  (E) conquering

10. In the passage, **aptitude** means
  (A) talented singer
  (B) Chinese drama
  (C) natural ability
  (D) musical accompaniment
  (E) comic character

11. When we read in the passage that singing ability was a **requisite** for a performer in Ming drama, we should realize that it was
  (A) unnoticed
  (B) unexpected
  (C) forbidden
  (D) required
  (E) not needed

12. In the passage, the Ming porcelain and textiles **abounded** because there were _____ of them.

    (A) none
    (B) many
    (C) few
    (D) some
    (E) photos

13. In the passage, if the potters had **quantitative** goals, they were interested in the _____ of pottery they produced.

    (A) selling
    (B) pictures
    (C) quality
    (D) patterns
    (E) amount

14. In the passage, **hors d'oeuvres** are

    (A) pottery
    (B) appetizers
    (C) parties
    (D) hot drinks
    (E) harvests

15. What strategy does the writer use to tell us that **buffet** is defined as a meal set out so that people may serve themselves?

    (A) The writer mentions the number of guests.
    (B) The writer describes such a meal.
    (C) The writer uses the synonym table for **buffet**.
    (D) The writer describes the servers.
    (E) The writer uses a metaphor for **buffet**.

16. When we read in the passage that the **buffet** was the most **expedient** way to serve the food, we should realize that it was the

    (A) most complicated way
    (B) slowest and most formal way
    (C) only way that was possible
    (D) easiest way
    (E) way all meals were served

17. The writer provides a clue to the meaning of **palatable** by

    (A) describing various foods made with eggs
    (B) describing foods that are not fit to eat
    (C) relating **palatable** to being pleased with the taste
    (D) contrasting **palatable** with the word royal
    (E) giving examples of foods the writer dislikes

18. In the passage, why did the writer think the shrimp with rice was not as **succulent** as the sweet-and-sour fish?

    (A) It was moist and flavorful.
    (B) It was the most delicious.
    (C) It was raw.
    (D) It was not as moist and flavorful.
    (E) It was dry and flavorful.

19. In the passage, the word that provides a clue to the meaning of **delectable** is

    (A) delicious
    (B) servings
    (C) noodles
    (D) spicy
    (E) preserved

20. We can infer from the passage that if something were to **recur**, it would

    (A) happen again
    (B) be invisible
    (C) occur once or twice a day
    (D) appear in a dream
    (E) be dangerous

READING NEW WORDS IN CONTEXT

| Lesson 9 | **CONTEXT:** Civilization

The passage gives you an opportunity to expand your vocabulary. Below are twenty vocabulary words that are used in the passage and in the exercises that follow it.

annihilate	diversion	insolence	protocol
clemency	evade	mandatory	purge
concession	flagrant	mannerism	sadistic
decimate	harass	meticulous	submission
disperse	inhibition	mettle	ultimatum

Japan's Samurai Warriors

Welcome to *Yesterday's News*. As your roving time reporter, I'm visiting Japan on June 3, 1183, the day after the famous Battle of Kurikara.

My guest is a man whose courage has just been tested, and his **mettle** (1) certainly was not lacking. He is Kiso Yoshinaka, a great samurai warrior and hero of the battle.

First, some background information about the samurai warrior is **mandatory** (2); it's required so that you can understand the highlights of the battle.

The Samurai: Honorable Warriors

The samurai, "those who serve," were originally warriors who defended various tribes or clans against other warring clans in old Japan. The term samurai later came to refer broadly to Japan's warrior class. From the late twelfth century to the nineteenth century, the samurai became powerful not only as warriors for clans and for the Imperial Palace but also as administrators. Because the samurai were so influential, other social classes remained in **submission** (3) to them. In other words, the other classes showed total obedience to the samurai.

"Kiso Yoshinaka, I hope that you won't consider my first question a sign of **insolence** (4). I certainly don't mean to be disrespectful. But I am wondering if your controlled, almost emotionless appearance is simply a **mannerism** (5)—by that I mean an exaggerated or unnatural style—that is cultivated by the samurai?"

"We samurai pride ourselves on our control of our emotions."

"Hmm. Would you care to tell us a bit about your costume?"

"It is traditional samurai armor, very strong but lightweight. Plates of iron scales have been **meticulously** (6) tied together with great care, using cords of silk or leather."

"Would you briefly explain the samurai code of conduct? What, if any, **inhibitions** (7), or feelings of restraint, do samurai have?"

"Our code of honor is called *bushido*. We fight for honor—especially for our clan's honor. For honor, there are no personal restraints. We never yield or give up; we make no **concessions** (8) to our enemies."

"The samurai have a reputation for being fierce. Do you agree with those who say that the samurai actually enjoy being cruel and are therefore **sadistic** (9)?"

"For honor, we samurai do what must be done."

"I see. Well, perhaps you will tell the viewers whether all of the samurai are men."

"Most are. My wife, Tomoe Gozen, however, is a samurai and fights in all battles with me."

"Now, please tell us what started this war."

"The Taira were too powerful in the imperial court. My clan, the Minamoto, are imperial descendants and by tradition should control the court. To our minds, the Taira were an undesirable element in court; as a result, we Minamoto vowed to **purge** (10) them from the court, to remove them completely."

"I see. So it was a clan war. But was there no **protocol** (11) to handle the situation and avoid war?"

"What do you mean?"

"I mean, wasn't there a code of conduct for important dealings and ceremonies? Could you not have handled the situation in a diplomatic way? Was it really necessary to **annihilate** (12) the Taira, to crush and destroy them like so many ants underfoot? . . . Your silence, Mr. Yoshinaka, may indicate to the viewers that you are trying to **evade** (13) or avoid my question."

"I believe I have already explained the samurai code of conduct."

"Very well, then. Please tell us more about the great battle."

The Battle of Kurikara

"After many years of battle, my cousin Minamoto Yoritomo and I joined forces to **decimate** (14) the Taira at the Pass of Kurikara. Our goal was to destroy them completely.

"The Taira were at the top of the pass. I **dispersed** (15) troops in three directions—to the rear of the pass, the foot of the pass, and the top of the pass. I needed to hold the Taira at the top of the pass until nightfall, when my other troops would be in position. I thought up a clever, entertaining **diversion** (16) to distract their attention. This game was a formal battle in the samurai tradition in which the samurai challenge each other to individual combat. We samurai are expert archers and swordsmen. The Taira enjoyed it!

"At nightfall, my troops in the rear appeared. My men planned a surprise for the Taira. They sent oxen with torches tied to their horns charging at the Taira. Of course, the Taira ran down the pass—right to my forces waiting in the dark. We didn't have to **harass** (17) them—one attack was trouble enough for them. The Taira were utterly defeated ."

"Will you grant **clemency** (18) to any surviving Taira?"

"For the samurai, honor has more importance than mercy toward an enemy. Taira samurai know that. To grant mercy after battle would be a **flagrant** (19), or outrageous, breach of the samurai code."

"I see. Well, thank you for talking with us, Kiso Yoshinaka.

"And thank you, viewers. Please join us next week when your roaming time reporter will visit Patrick Henry, just minutes after he delivers his famous **ultimatum** (20), in which he demands liberty or death, at the Virginia Convention in 1775. See you there."

EXERCISE 1   *Finding Synonyms*

Directions. Reread the preceding passage. Then write on the line provided a synonym for each of the words in boldface. If you cannot think of an exact synonym, you may write a brief definition of the word.

1. mettle _____

2. mandatory _____

3. submission _____

4. insolence _____

5. mannerism _____

6. meticulously _____

7. inhibitions _____

8. concessions _____

9. sadistic _____

10. purge _____

11. protocol _____

12. annihilate _____

13. evade _____

14. decimate _____

15. dispersed _____

16. diversion _____

17. harass _____

18. clemency _____

19. flagrant _____

20. ultimatum _____

EXERCISE 2 Reading Strategically ☞

Directions. Now that you have read the passage and thought about the words in boldface, circle the letter of the correct answer to each of the following items. The numbers of the items are the same as the numbers of the boldface vocabulary words in the passage.

1. How does the writer provide a clue to the meaning of **mettle**?
   (A) The writer links **mettle** to the synonym courage.
   (B) The writer says that **mettle** is a test.
   (C) The writer implies that **mettle** means to want.
   (D) The writer uses the expression "my guest."
   (E) The writer says that having **mettle** is a certainty.

2. In the passage, if something is **mandatory**, it is
   (A) original
   (B) masculine
   (C) informative
   (D) understood
   (E) required

3. In the passage, the word _____ provides a clue to the meaning of **submission**.
   (A) warriors
   (B) obedience
   (C) influential
   (D) classes
   (E) powerful

4. In the passage, **insolence** means
   (A) respect
   (B) dislike
   (C) understanding
   (D) disrespect
   (E) misunderstanding

5. What strategy does the writer use to tell us that a **mannerism** is an exaggerated or unnatural style?
   (A) An antonym is provided for **mannerism**.
   (B) The writer links **mannerism** to the word disrespectful.
   (C) A definition is provided for **mannerism**.
   (D) The writer gives several examples of **mannerisms**.
   (E) The writer uses figurative language.

6. When we read in the passage that plates of iron scales have been **meticulously** tied together, we should realize that
   (A) the scales have been tied with great care
   (B) the scales have been tied carelessly
   (C) traditional samurai armor is strong and light
   (D) samurai armor is traditional
   (E) samurai were very influential

7. How does the writer provide a clue to the meaning of **inhibitions**?
   (A) The writer describes the samurai code of conduct.
   (B) The writer restates **inhibitions** as feelings of restraint.
   (C) The writer uses the antonym conduct.
   (D) The writer describes types of samurai armor.
   (E) The writer uses the words feelings and honor.

8. If the samurai do not make **concessions**, as the writer of the passage says, we may expect them to
   (A) give up when surrounded
   (B) avoid fighting
   (C) never give up anything
   (D) negotiate with the enemy
   (E) surrender rather than kill another person

9. In the passage, someone who is **sadistic** enjoys being
   (A) captured
   (B) praised
   (C) cruel
   (D) kind

10. When we read in the passage that the Minamoto vowed to **purge** the Taira from the court, we should realize that the Minamoto

(A) planned to share control of the court
(B) wanted to learn from the Taira clan
(C) wanted the Taira to maintain power
(D) planned to rid the court entirely of the Taira
(E) often made vows they did not keep

11. In the passage, **protocol** is a

(A) list of clans with influence in government
(B) code of conduct for important dealings and ceremonies
(C) plan to protect the government from attack
(D) vow to change the way in which laws are made
(E) clan war

12. To illustrate the fate of the Taira clan when the Minamoto clan sets out to **annihilate** them, the writer uses the simile of

(A) people fighting a losing battle
(B) one group avoiding capture by another
(C) ants being crushed and destroyed underfoot
(D) cattle being brought to slaughter
(E) ships passing unseen in the night

13. In the passage, **evade** means to

(A) embrace
(B) fight
(C) give
(D) enjoy
(E) avoid

14. How does the writer provide a clue to the meaning of **decimate**?

(A) The writer links **decimate** to the word destroy.
(B) The writer says that to **decimate** is to survive.
(C) The writer provides the antonym battle for **decimate**.
(D) The writer uses **decimate** in a series of synonyms.
(E) The writer contrasts **decimate** with the word joined.

15. In the passage, what does it mean to **disperse**?

(A) It means to lose.
(B) It means to discuss.
(C) It means to restrict.
(D) It means to return.
(E) It means to spread.

16. We can infer from the passage that a **diversion** is

(A) a new, different way of doing battle in a lengthy war
(B) something that distracts, relaxes, or entertains
(C) a board game that uses cards, dice, and playing pieces
(D) a samurai tradition of using groups of people as targets
(E) a victory in battle

17. When we read in the passage that the Minamoto clan did not have to **harass** the Taira clan, we should realize that **harass** means to

(A) join
(B) cause no trouble
(C) attack repeatedly
(D) defeat
(E) withdraw from combat

18. In the passage, why would the Minamoto not grant **clemency** to the surviving Taira?

(A) The samurai believe honor is more important than mercy.
(B) The samurai often negotiate peaceful ends to their battles.
(C) The samurai treat their prisoners in a humane manner.
(D) The samurai prefer to show mercy.
(E) The samurai prefer dishonor to death.

19. The writer provides a clue to the meaning of **flagrant** by

(A) providing the antonym trouble
(B) using **flagrant** in a series of synonyms
(C) linking **flagrant** to the word surprise
(D) contrasting **flagrant** with the word defeated
(E) restating **flagrant** as outrageous

20. We can infer from the passage that an **ultimatum** is a

(A) last speech
(B) report
(C) demand
(D) question
(E) view

READING NEW WORDS IN CONTEXT

Lesson 10 | CONTEXT: Civilization

The passage gives you an opportunity to expand your vocabulary. Below are twenty vocabulary words that are used in the passage and in the exercises that follow it.

admirably	censure	destitute	mosque
affidavit	colloquial	diminutive	ornate
amnesty	consolidate	emancipate	prelude
bedlam	constituent	exultant	rift
bias	curtail	inalienable	timorous

A Letter from Nigeria

Dear Phoebe,
  Greetings from Nigeria! I promised you a letter, and here it is. The whole Kwanzaa Club is **exultant** (1) about being here for a month—jubilant, in fact! The sponsors and I wish you could have come on the trip, but we understand your situation.

  Because my great-grandmother was born in Nigeria, my opinion may be **biased** (2), but I find Nigeria a fascinating country; I am partial to it. **Admirably** (3), the government here is really encouraging tourism these days. Also deserving praise, I think, is the Nigerians' effort to invite African Americans to come here to discover their cultural roots.

The Nigerian Slave Trade
You probably know that many slaves in colonial America came from Nigeria. European slave traders had a thriving business. I don't see how anyone can say that liberty is an **inalienable** (4) right, one that can't be taken away, when slave traders obviously took away people's freedom and destroyed thousands of lives. They treated the slaves so cruelly that many of those who survived the voyage to the New World were **timorous** (5), or fearful, for the rest of their lives. Fortunately, the British Parliament abolished the slave traffic in 1807. Too bad the Parliament could not

emancipate (6) the slaves already sold; many would never see freedom again.

  Okay, I can hear you saying, "Lighten up!" I didn't mean to dwell on such an unfortunate time in history. Of course the slave trade should be **censured** (7), but I shouldn't take up all my letter criticizing it.

  What I want to do is describe Nigeria for you. First, you should realize that there is nothing **diminutive** (8) about Nigeria; everything is large. Our states of California, Arizona, and Nevada would almost fit in Nigeria's land space. Nigeria is Africa's most populated country, with about 121 million people.

Lagos: A City of Contrasts
I was overwhelmed by all the activity at the airport at Lagos, Nigeria's largest city. That was just an introduction, a **prelude** (9), to the energy of Lagos itself. Talk about a diverse community—the United States isn't the only country with a variety of people. There are about two hundred and fifty ethnic groups in Nigeria, and I think you could see them all on the streets of Lagos, the thriving urban heart of Nigeria.

  Like **bedlam** (10), a place or condition of confusion and noise, Lagos brims with activity both day and night. It's an exciting city, with a skyline similar to many major U.S. cities. The traffic here reminds me of U.S. cities, too. The people who live in Lagos call traffic jams "go-slows." That is an example of **colloquial** (11), or informal, language here. Nigeria is an oil-rich nation and has many other valuable resources. However, it has many social problems, too. Walking down the streets of Lagos, one sees tremendous contrasts: Some people are wealthy, while others are **destitute** (12).

Some of the architecture here is marvelous. I have especially enjoyed seeing the **mosques** (13). These Muslim houses of worship are quite **ornate** (14), like elaborately wrapped and decorated gifts. A large percentage of Nigerians are Muslims.

Lagos was for many years the capital of Nigeria, but now all the government offices have been **consolidated** (15) in the new capital, the Federal Territory of Abuja. This unification is part of Nigeria's change from a military to a democratic government. The **constituents** (16), or voters, with whom I talked are happy to have a voice in their government again.

Struggles with Independence

Nigeria received its independence from Britain in 1960 after being a British colony and protectorate for forty-six years. There wasn't a violent **rift** (17) between the two countries; actually, the separation was peaceful. Unfortunately, the West African nation's own government has been very unstable since independence was granted. Eastern Nigeria broke away and tried to form a new country, Biafra, in 1967, sparking civil war that lasted three years. I wonder if the Nigerian government granted **amnesty** (18)—that is, pardoned any political prisoners.

This letter is beginning to sound as if I had signed an **affidavit** (19) in which I made an oath to write or talk about only Lagos and Nigerian history to my friends back home. There is so much to tell you. I haven't even mentioned the National Arts Theater, the museums with fantastic bronze and brass sculptures from Benin and Ife and wood carvings from Yoruba. And I haven't told you about the country and the villages outside Lagos.

I will have to write you a series of letters. It's getting late. I'll try to find time tomorrow evening to write more.

Sincerely,

Daphne

P.S.
One of the sponsors just told us that our visit here might be **curtailed** (20), but she didn't explain exactly why it might be shortened. She said she would tell us later. See you soon—but not too soon, I hope.

EXERCISE 1 Finding Synonyms

Directions. Reread the preceding passage. Then write on the line provided a synonym for each of the words in boldface. If you cannot think of an exact synonym, you may write a brief definition of the word.

1. exultant _____

2. biased _____

3. admirably _____

4. inalienable _____

5. timorous _____

6. emancipate _____

7. censured _____

8. diminutive _____

9. prelude _____

10. bedlam _____

11. colloquial _____

12. destitute _____

13. mosques _____

14. ornate _____

15. consolidated _____

16. constituents _____

17. rift _____

18. amnesty _____

19. affidavit _____

20. curtailed _____

EXERCISE 2 — Reading Strategically 👉

Directions. Now that you have read the passage and thought about the words in boldface, circle the letter of the correct answer to each of the following items. The numbers of the items are the same as the numbers of the boldface vocabulary words in the passage.

1. In the passage, the word _____ provides a clue to the meaning of **exultant**.
   (A) promised
   (B) understand
   (C) jubilant
   (D) greetings
   (E) whole

2. In the passage, why might the writer be partial or **biased** in her opinion of Nigeria?
   (A) She has read much about Nigeria.
   (B) She immediately liked the country.
   (C) She prefers the United States.
   (D) Her great-grandmother was born in Nigeria.
   (E) She is a tourist.

3. What strategy does the writer use to tell us that **admirably** is defined as in a worthy manner?
   (A) The writer compares **admirably** with really encouraging.
   (B) The writer says that everyone in Nigeria behaves **admirably**.
   (C) The writer contrasts **admirably** with an antonym.
   (D) The writer uses the word also to link **admirably** to the words deserving praise.
   (E) The writer uses **admirably** in a clause with several examples.

4. In the passage, what does it mean to have **inalienable** rights?

(A) It means to have rights that cannot be taken away.
(B) It means to have rights that are presented in writing.
(C) It means to have rights you have voted for.
(D) It means to have rights given by aliens.
(E) It means to have rights you do not deserve.

5. When we read in the passage that some slaves who survived the journey to the New World were **timorous** for the rest of their lives, we should realize that

(A) the slaves became angry and rebellious
(B) the slaves felt very small
(C) the slave trade would be abolished by Parliament in 1807
(D) the slaves would never see freedom again
(E) the slaves were fearful

6. In the passage, since the British Parliament did not **emancipate** the slaves that had already been sold, the slaves were still

(A) free
(B) enslaved
(C) fortunate
(D) sponsored
(E) abolished

7. How does the writer provide a clue to the meaning of **censured**?

(A) The writer describes Nigeria today.
(B) The writer compares **censured** to the word admired.
(C) The writer links **censured** to the word criticizing.
(D) The writer contrasts **censured** with the word sold.
(E) The writer links **censured** to the synonym described.

8. We can infer from the passage that something **diminutive** is

(A) fragile
(B) large
(C) African
(D) small
(E) cloudy

9. In the passage, **prelude** means

(A) introduction
(B) following
(C) dissatisfaction
(D) explanation
(E) rejection

10. If Lagos is a **bedlam**, as the writer of the passage suggests, we may expect it to

(A) be a beautiful city
(B) be noisy and confusing
(C) be quiet, but exciting
(D) have the busiest airport
(E) make visitors welcome

11. What strategy does the writer use to tell us that **colloquial** is defined as informal language?
  (A) The writer gives an example of formal speechmaking.
  (B) The writer gives an example of a **colloquial** expression and uses the synonym informal.
  (C) The writer contrasts **colloquial** with informal speech.
  (D) The writer translates ancient Nigerian terms that are now examples of **colloquial** speech.
  (E) The writer explains that **colloquial** is a local word.

12. When we read in the passage that some people are wealthy, while others are **destitute,** we should realize that
  (A) everyone in Lagos belongs to the middle class
  (B) some people are rich and others are middle class
  (C) Lagos contains many different nationalities
  (D) people cannot be judged by the way they dress
  (E) some people are rich and others are penniless

13. How does the writer provide a clue to the meaning of **mosques**?
  (A) The writer uses the antonym gifts.
  (B) The writer defines the word **mosques** as "Muslim houses of worship."
  (C) The writer compares world religions and states that many Nigerians are Muslims.
  (D) The writer describes one specific **mosque** in detail.
  (E) The writer uses the word marvelous.

14. To describe the appearance of the **ornate** Muslim **mosques** in Lagos, the writer compares them by simile to
  (A) marvelous architecture in the United States
  (B) old capitals in foreign countries
  (C) valuable books in a library
  (D) elaborately wrapped and decorated gifts
  (E) a large percentage of religious Nigerians

15. We can infer from the passage that when the government offices were **consolidated,** they were
  (A) separated
  (B) vacated
  (C) united
  (D) enlarged
  (E) multiplied

16. In the passage, **constituents** means
  (A) voters
  (B) voices
  (C) territories
  (D) governments
  (E) mergers

17. When we read in the passage that there was not a **rift** between Nigeria and Britain, we should realize that
  (A) there was a long war for Nigerian independence
  (B) there was never a break in friendly relations
  (C) Nigerians voted to remain a British colony
  (D) Britain forced Nigeria to seek independence
  (E) Nigeria and Britain are hostile toward each other

18. In the passage, what happens to prisoners who are granted **amnesty**?

    (A) The prisoners are executed.
    (B) The prisoners are imprisoned.
    (C) The prisoners are given money.
    (D) The prisoners are pardoned.
    (E) The prisoners become politicians.

19. If the writer had signed an **affidavit,** she would have

    (A) written only short letters
    (B) signed her letter using a different name
    (C) read all the material about Lagos, Nigeria
    (D) become a government official
    (E) signed a written statement made under oath

20. The writer provides a clue to the meaning of **curtailed** by using the word

    (A) series
    (B) visit
    (C) explain
    (D) shortened
    (E) time

READING NEW WORDS IN CONTEXT

Lesson 11 | CONTEXT: The Environment

The passage gives you an opportunity to expand your vocabulary. Below are twenty vocabulary words that are used in the passage and in the exercises that follow it.

bestride	enjoin	livid	reprieve
casement	fluctuate	melancholy	requiem
clangor	gloat	mortify	theoretical
debut	indict	patent	vehement
documentary	legacy	patriarch	wheedle

Editorial: Can the Elephant Be Saved?

Elephants, real and fictional, survive in our imaginations and in our memories from childhood on. There's Jumbo, the six-ton African elephant that made its first public appearance, its **debut** (1), in the United States in P. T. Barnum's "Greatest Show on Earth" in 1882. There's Horton, the gentle elephant who heard a Who and hatched an egg. He is an inheritance, a treasured **legacy** (2) from the imagination of the late Theodor "Dr. Seuss" Geisel (1904–1991). Then there's Dumbo, the flying elephant from the Disney Studios, and the curious Elephant's Child from Rudyard Kipling's *Just So Stories*. Last but not least is the wonderful Babar. How many times have children **wheedled** (3) their parents into telling them the Babar stories? Many parents need little coaxing, however; they fondly remember these stories from their own childhoods.

Many people have cherished memories of zoo elephants. I remember going to the elephant house at the zoo one morning and being surprised because there were no elephants there. Suddenly, the hinges of a large **casement** (4) window creaked open, and an elephant stuck its trunk out the open window. I heard a **clangor** (5) coming from inside the house. The loud ringing sound must have been an alarm. Then the doors of the elephant house swung open, and five newly washed elephants walked out to greet me. It was as though I were receiving a special welcome. **Bestriding** (6) or

straddling the fence around the elephant yard, I watched these amazing animals for a long time.

Yes, such memories survive. But will the mighty elephant itself survive? This is not just a **theoretical** (7) question; the world must be shown that such a catastrophe could very well occur.

Population and Greed: The Elephant's Enemies

Elephants are in trouble. Their numbers are decreasing, mainly because of increasing human populations. Elephants in both Africa and Asia are now competing with people for food, water, and land. As populations grow, people are taking the elephants' traditional grazing lands for crops, pasture for cattle, and timber. One can only reach the **patent** (8), or obvious, conclusion that the elephants are going to be the losers in this competition.

A few statistics will illustrate what has been happening. There were perhaps two hundred thousand Asian elephants in 1900; in 1991, there were only an estimated thirty-five thousand to fifty-four thousand left in the wild. In Africa, there were five to ten million elephants in 1930; there were only about six hundred thousand in 1989. One can imagine an old male elephant weeping over these figures, like a **patriarch** (9) reacting to the death of his tribe.

Poachers who hunt elephants for their tusks also continue to pose a threat to elephants. Some countries have strict laws that **enjoin** (10) people to stop killing elephants for their tusks. These legal commands have greatly diminished the raw ivory trade. Poachers may be **indicted** (11)—that is, charged with a crime. Still, there are poachers who take a mean pleasure in their work. As a result, they **gloat** (12) while killing the elephants and selling the ivory. If poachers aren't shamed by their destructive deeds, I am sure they are not **mortified** (13) by anything else they do.

More than just a **reprieve** (14) is needed for the elephants; they need permanent relief from humans, their deadliest predators.

What Can We Do?

Because the elephants' situation makes me so angry, I easily become **livid** (15) when discussing it. However, just becoming furious will not help.

Giving in to **melancholy** (16) will not accomplish anything, either. Nevertheless, I become sad and depressed whenever I read about the plight of elephants or watch a **documentary** (17) on television that shows actual instances of those sensitive, family-oriented creatures being killed by poachers.

Are we hearing the first notes of a **requiem** (18), a funeral hymn for these beloved animals? If so, let's all help stop this music from being played. I strongly, **vehemently** (19) urge all governments and peoples to do their share to help the living elephants. Governments and world wildlife organizations must continue to provide suitable grazing lands for wild elephants. Also, governments should continue with or adopt new bans on the ivory trade. For future generations of elephants and humans, our commitment must not **fluctuate** (20). Rather, we must hold to a steady course of conservation.

| EXERCISE 1 | *Finding Synonyms* |

Directions. Reread the preceding passage. Then write on the line provided a synonym for each of the words in boldface. If you cannot think of an exact synonym, you may write a brief definition of the word.

1. debut _____

2. legacy _____

3. wheedled _____

4. casement _____

5. clangor _____

6. bestriding _____

7. theoretical _____

8. patent _____

9. patriarch _____

10. enjoin _____

11. indicted _____

12. gloat _____

13. mortified _____

14. reprieve _____

15. livid _____

16. melancholy _____

17. documentary _____

18. requiem _____

19. vehemently _____

20. fluctuate _____

EXERCISE 2 Reading Strategically ✍

Directions. Now that you have read the passage and thought about the words in boldface, circle the letter of the correct answer to each of the following items. The numbers of the items are the same as the numbers of the boldface vocabulary words in the passage.

1. In the passage, **debut** means
   (A) final public appearance
   (B) first private appearance
   (C) appearance with a circus
   (D) first public appearance
   (E) memory of first private appearance

2. According to the passage, why is Horton a **legacy** from Dr. Seuss?
   (A) Horton appears in a popular book.
   (B) Horton is a treasured inheritance.
   (C) Dr. Seuss abandoned Horton.
   (D) Horton inherited a large sum of money.
   (E) Dr. Seuss never wrote about anyone else.

3. What strategy does the writer use to tell us that **wheedled** is defined as persuaded by flattery or sweet words?
   (A) The writer defines a synonym of **wheedled**.
   (B) The writer says **wheedled** means forbidden.
   (C) The writer links **wheedled** to the word coaxing.
   (D) The writer uses the word therefore to link **wheedled** to the word fondly.
   (E) The writer links **wheedled** to the synonym remembered.

4. We can infer from the passage that a **casement** window is a window that
   (A) slides up and down
   (B) is always open
   (C) opens on hinges
   (D) only elephants can open
   (E) cannot be opened

5. In the passage, a **clangor** is a(n)
   (A) loud ringing sound
   (B) soft humming noise
   (C) elephant house
   (D) herd of elephants
   (E) piercing scream

6. In the passage, what does **bestriding** mean?
   (A) It means standing next to.
   (B) It means running.
   (C) It means walking around.
   (D) It means leaning against.
   (E) It means straddling.

7. How does the writer provide a clue to the meaning of **theoretical**?
   (A) The writer contrasts **theoretical** with the words could very well occur.
   (B) The writer links **theoretical** to the words such memories.
   (C) The writer provides an antonym for **theoretical**.
   (D) The writer implies that **theoretical** means unproved.
   (E) The writer uses a series of synonyms in the sentence.

8. We can infer from the passage that something that is **patent** is
   (A) sincere
   (B) obvious
   (C) leather
   (D) projected
   (E) lost

9. To illustrate the way an old male elephant might feel, the writer uses the simile of a **patriarch**
   (A) gathering his troops to fight
   (B) reading history to his tribe
   (C) looking for help from outsiders
   (D) living in a forest of young saplings
   (E) mourning the death of his tribe

10. If strict laws **enjoin** people to stop killing elephants for their tusks, as the writer of the passage states, we may expect
   (A) the elephants to be in danger of being killed
   (B) people to be permitted by law to kill elephants
   (C) it to be illegal to kill elephants for their tusks
   (D) that poachers will find a legal way to sell ivory
   (E) laws to be designed to protect poachers

11. When we read in the passage that poachers may be **indicted**, we should realize that they may
   (A) be rewarded
   (B) be charged with a crime
   (C) never be punished
   (D) be freed
   (E) diminish the ivory trade

12. In the passage, what does it mean to **gloat**?

    (A) It means to take a mean pleasure in something.
    (B) It means to be ashamed of something.
    (C) It means to work quickly.
    (D) It means to poach ivory legally.
    (E) It means to be careful.

13. How does the writer provide a clue to the meaning of **mortified**?

    (A) The writer provides an antonym for **mortified**.
    (B) The writer defines **mortified** as pleased.
    (C) The writer compares **mortified** to glorified.
    (D) The writer links **mortified** to the synonym shamed.
    (E) The writer implies that **mortified** means satisfied.

14. When we read in the passage that more than a **reprieve** is needed, we should realize that a **reprieve** is

    (A) permanent relief
    (B) a wrong solution
    (C) too expensive
    (D) never possible
    (E) temporary relief

15. In the passage, the writer is **livid**, or _____, about the elephants' situation.

    (A) confused
    (B) excited
    (C) furious
    (D) curious
    (E) quiet

16. In the passage, why are some people **melancholy** about the elephants' situation?

    (A) They are excited about the progress being made.
    (B) They are sad and depressed because the situation is serious and getting worse.
    (C) They are resentful of government interference with the elephants.
    (D) They are uninterested in television coverage of the elephants' situation.
    (E) They are happy that elephants are doing well in zoos.

17. The writer provides a clue to the meaning of **documentary** by

    (A) implying that a **documentary** is fiction
    (B) linking **documentary** to the words family-oriented
    (C) telling about other programs on television
    (D) relating **documentary** to the words actual instances
    (E) contrasting **documentary** with the word television

18. In the passage, a **requiem** is a(n)

    (A) funeral hymn
    (B) wildlife organization
    (C) serious discussion
    (D) song of celebration
    (E) beloved animal

19. In the passage, the word that provides a clue to the meaning of **vehemently** is

(A) steadily
(B) funding
(C) strongly
(D) honor
(E) share

20. According to the passage, **fluctuate** means the opposite of holding on to a(n) _____ course.

(A) legal
(B) steady
(C) limited
(D) approved
(E) wavering

READING NEW WORDS IN CONTEXT

Lesson 12   **CONTEXT: The Environment**

The passage gives you an opportunity to expand your vocabulary. Below are twenty vocabulary words that are used in the passage and in the exercises that follow it.

arbiter	closure	impartial	rectify
botch	condole	imperceptible	stipulate
breach	convene	inertia	stratagem
cant	crony	momentum	subsidiary
clientele	equilibrium	oblivious	substantially

The Destruction of the Rain Forests

Mark Glass, an independent public relations specialist, couldn't decide how to begin his report about the rain forest of western Brazil. After spending a month in the rain forest, Glass was no longer the **impartial** (1) observer he had been hired to be. As a result, he was having difficulty writing an objective report.

A paper company, one of several **subsidiaries** (2) of a large timber company, had hired Glass to study the effects of development in the Brazilian rain forest. Some of the company's **clientele** (3) were concerned that the timber industry was destroying the rain forest. Of course, neither the parent company nor its secondary company wanted to lose these customers because of bad publicity.

Glass had been recommended to the company's president by one of the president's **cronies** (4), or friends, on the company's board. The president instructed Glass to analyze the pros and cons of developing the rain forest and harvesting its timber. Glass agreed, but he refused to play the role of **arbiter** (5) to decide disputes between environmentalists and developers.

Glass didn't want to **botch** (6) his job; he had a reputation for good work. He knew that the report should consist of his observations, but Glass also wanted to give his opinions and recommendations. After observing the effects of development in the rain forest, he wanted to recommend the **closure** (7) of the company's plant in Brazil. But

he knew the company's president would never consider shutting down the plant. Glass strongly believed that the timber industry could no longer be **oblivious** (8) to the rain forest's condition; it could no longer close its eyes and avoid responsibility for the destruction.

How Have People Harmed the Rain Forest?

Glass reminded himself to stick to the facts. And the facts clearly showed that recent developments and commercialization of the rain forest had upset the area's natural **equilibrium** (9). Glass felt strongly that it was up to people to restore this ecological balance.

Human intrusion into the rain forest gained **momentum** (10), or force, with the paved, two-lane Amazon highway known as BR-364. This road, completed in 1984, made it possible for thousands of settlers to move into the rain forest region of western Brazil. Land began to be cleared for farms and ranches as well as for logging businesses. The fragile landscape changed **substantially** (11) in a very short time. For example, it is estimated that twenty percent of the rain forest may have been destroyed within just four years after the highway opened. The growth of agriculture and industry was virtually unplanned and unregulated at first, Glass discovered, although the Brazilian government later attempted to protect the region.

Rain forests receive at least eighty inches of annual rainfall. Biologists believe the rain forests are home to more than half of all the plant and animal species on earth. Many of these species have not yet been identified or studied. While damage to the environment of the rain forest is easily seen, other damage to plant and animal life is **imperceptible** (12). At scientific conferences that **convened** (13) throughout the world, scientists met to discuss the rain forest. They began working to develop successful **stratagems** (14), or schemes, to win the war being fought on the environmental front.

Many people **condole** (15) the loss of the rain forest, mourning not just because of the effects on plants and animals but also because of its worldwide effects. Some scientists fear that continued destruction of the rain forests will result in a loss of oxygen as well as create climatic changes, such as global warming, throughout the world.

Can the Rain Forests Be Saved?

When he finished recording his observations, Glass felt that he had fulfilled his task. He knew he would not be cited for **breach** (16) of contract—that is, for violating his agreement with the paper company. However, he decided to go further with his writing.

Glass reasoned that he had to let the company know what he thought should be done to **rectify** (17) its mistakes. First, he argued that the company should correct some of its errors by changing its method of harvesting trees in the rain forest, since trees grow back faster if they are removed following the natural outlines of the land. Second, he said that the company should **stipulate** (18) that it will cooperate with scientists to help preserve the bulk of the rain forest. Making such a guarantee would be good public relations, he noted. Finally, Glass stated that the company's effort must be sincere, because the public will not be fooled by **cant** (19), or insincere words and empty promises.

On finishing his report, Glass felt that he had done his part to help the rain forest. He was hopeful because he knew that the company that hired him did not suffer from **inertia** (20). The very fact that it had sent him to study the rain forest was an indication that the company was willing to act on the facts and to change its methods. Glass hoped that other companies and developers would also learn to use the resources of the world's rain forests wisely.

EXERCISE 1 *Finding Synonyms*

Directions. Reread the preceding passage. Then write on the line provided a synonym for each of the words in boldface. If you cannot think of an exact synonym, you may write a brief definition of the word.

1. impartial _____

2. subsidiaries _____

3. clientele _____

4. cronies _____

5. arbiter _____

6. botch _____

7. closure _____

8. oblivious _____

9. equilibrium _____

10. momentum _____

11. substantially _____

12. imperceptible _____

13. convened _____

14. stratagems _____

15. condole _____

16. breach _____

17. rectify _____

18. stipulate _____

19. cant _____

20. inertia _____

EXERCISE 2 _Reading Strategically_

Directions. Now that you have read the passage and thought about the words in boldface, circle the letter of the correct answer to each of the following items. The numbers of the items are the same as the numbers of the boldface vocabulary words in the passage.

1. What strategy does the writer use to tell us that **impartial** may be defined as unprejudiced?

(A) The writer says that Mark Glass was independent.

(B) The writer links **impartial** to the word objective.

(C) The writer tells of Mark Glass's difficulty in writing.

(D) The writer relates being **impartial** to expressing an opinion.

(E) The writer links **impartial** to the rain forest.

2. According to the passage, what does it mean for a company to be a **subsidiary**?

(A) It means that a **subsidiary** is a large company that controls several other companies.

(B) It means that a **subsidiary** is totally independent, unconnected to any other company.

(C) It means that a **subsidiary** is a smaller company that is controlled by a larger one.

(D) It means that a **subsidiary** is an independent public relations firm.

(E) It means that a **subsidiary** is a timber company operating in Brazil.

3. We can infer from the passage that **clientele** are

(A) customers

(B) owners

(C) specialists

(D) settlers

(E) companies

4. How does the writer provide a clue to the meaning of **cronies**?

(A) The writer contrasts **cronies** with the antonym board.

(B) The writer uses an antonym for **cronies**.

(C) The writer relates **cronies** to the word observer.

(D) The writer uses the word and to link **cronies** to the word develop.

(E) The writer links **cronies** to the synonym friends.

5. In the passage, what does it mean to be an **arbiter**?

(A) It means to write and complain.

(B) It means to observe and report.

(C) It means to be a developer.

(D) It means to decide disputes.

(E) It means to reject answers.

6. In the passage, why did Mark Glass not want to **botch** his job?

(A) He wanted to maintain his reputation for good work.

(B) He wanted to turn the work over to someone better.

(C) He cared more about the rain forest than his reputation.

(D) He wanted to destroy the company with a bad report.

(E) He wanted to do a poor job because he disliked the company.

7. How does the writer provide a clue to the meaning of **closure**?

(A) The writer links **closure** to his observations.

(B) The writer compares **closure** to recommendations.

(C) The writer relates **closure** to the development of the rain forest.

(D) The writer implies that **closure** means opens.

(E) The writer restates **closure** as shutting down.

8. We can infer from the passage that if you are **oblivious** to something, you are

(A) not aware of it

(B) aware of it

(C) concerned about it

(D) objective about it

(E) opposed to it

9. According to the passage, when people upset the natural **equilibrium** of the rain forest, they disturb the _____ of nature.

(A) variety

(B) development

(C) balance

(D) facts

(E) movement

10. In the passage, **momentum** means

(A) intrusion

(B) force

(C) reason

(D) barrier

(E) excuse

11. What strategy does the writer use to tell us that **substantially** may be defined as considerably?
   (A) The writer uses the word greatly.
   (B) The writer relates **substantially** to the word destroyed.
   (C) The writer implies that **substantially** means slowly.
   (D) The writer gives an example of considerable change.
   (E) The writer contrasts **substantially** with an antonym.

12. When we read in the passage that some damage is **imperceptible,** we should realize that it
   (A) is very noticeable
   (B) is unimportant
   (C) cannot easily be seen
   (D) is easily seen
   (E) is easily repaired

13. How does the writer provide a clue to the meaning of **convened**?
   (A) The writer links **convened** to the word met.
   (B) The writer defines **convened** as dismissed.
   (C) The writer compares **convened** to the word scattered.
   (D) The writer relates **convened** to reported.
   (E) The writer uses **convened** to mean not used.

14. Because the problems with the environment are very serious, the writer draws an analogy between **stratagems** and
   (A) the schemes to engage in and win military battles
   (B) schemes used to make money quickly
   (C) the development of plans to take over major corporations
   (D) the work that scientists do in a laboratory
   (E) scientific conferences

15. In the passage, **condole** means to
   (A) control
   (B) create
   (C) enjoy
   (D) console
   (E) mourn

16. If, as the writer of the passage suggests, Mark Glass is not cited for **breach** of contract, it means that he
   (A) did not complete the work assigned
   (B) did what the contract required
   (C) did not understand the contract
   (D) refused to sign any contracts
   (E) agreed to work only near oceans

17. The writer provides a clue to the meaning of **rectify** by
   (A) restating **rectify** as mistake
   (B) saying to **rectify** is to make worse
   (C) relating **rectify** to the word correct
   (D) linking **rectify** to the word harvesting
   (E) saying that to **rectify** is to be wrong

18. In the passage, **stipulate** means
  (A) preserve
  (B) guarantee
  (C) discuss
  (D) require
  (E) deny

19. When we read in the passage that the public will not be fooled by **cant,** we should realize that
  (A) the public is easily fooled
  (B) **cant** cannot be understood by the average person
  (C) the public will not be fooled by insincere words and empty promises
  (D) the public doesn't appreciate sincerity
  (E) the public is powerless

20. When we read in the passage that the company did not suffer from **inertia,** we can expect it to
  (A) make excuses and refuse to change
  (B) listen to developers and continue damaging the rain forest
  (C) stay the same and discredit Glass's findings
  (D) be willing to act and change
  (E) reject suggestions made by Mark Glass

READING NEW WORDS IN CONTEXT

Lesson 13 | CONTEXT: The Environment

The passage gives you an opportunity to expand your vocabulary. Below are twenty vocabulary words that are used in the passage and in the exercises that follow it.

abdicate	immaculate	mull	sardonic
debase	imposition	naive	sporadic
effervescent	inadvertent	quibble	stimulant
episode	infallible	rankle	synthesis
explicate	itinerary	resonant	translucent

The Ocean Source

"Ocean, who is the source of all."
—The *Iliad*, Homer

The Assignment

The science assignment was difficult at best. The class was told to **explicate** (1) how people have used the ocean for food and other resources throughout history. There was another requirement: The explanation had to be in the form of an original play. As you might expect, we **mulled** (2) over the assignment for a long time. Our thoughts finally led to a series of short scenes for a play we call *The Ocean Source*. The play is a **synthesis** (3) of the class's efforts: a complete treatment of the subject put together from many individual parts. Descriptions of some of my favorite scenes from our collaborative effort follow.

Scene 1

The play opens in a prehistoric time more than two hundred thousand years ago. Two **naive** (4) people are standing on the ocean shore, praying for fish to jump into their hands. Two more-experienced people stand nearby, using simple harpoons made of bone to catch fish in the shallow water by the shoreline.

"How many fish have you caught like that?" the second couple asks the first couple in a sarcastic or **sardonic** (5) tone. The success of the harpooners **rankles** (6) the first couple. Angrily, they run off stage and soon return with their own bone harpoons.

Scene 3

Around 300 B.C., the king of a small country on the Mediterranean Sea tells his advisors that he plans to **abdicate** (7) the throne. "I will no longer have the responsibilities of a king. As a result, I will be free of the burdens of power," he tells them. "Then I will become the sailor I've always wanted to be. I'll give those Phoenicians, the first true seafarers, some real competition!"

After hearing the petty objections of his advisors, the king says, "I won't listen to you **quibble** (8) any longer. Leave me now, for I must plan the **itinerary** (9) of my first trip. The route must be carefully thought out."

Scene 7

The deep, rich tones of a bell are heard offstage. As the **resonant** (10) sound fades, the curtain opens to reveal two whalers talking on the deck of a whaling ship. It is around 1900, during the golden age of whaling.

"This captain is just like the last one, who didn't think he could make mistakes," says one of the men. "Well, you and I know that he's not **infallible** (11)."

"Yes, many events this past month prove it, but this latest **episode** (12) is the best example," remarks the other man.

"Right you are. Our whale sightings have been **sporadic** (13) lately, unlike the days when we saw them regularly. And what do we find out when we finally spot a whale? That the captain **inadvertently** (14) unloaded the harpoons with explosive heads at the last port. Now, I ask you, how does a person unintentionally unload explosive harpoons?" the first man asks with disbelief.

"Very carefully," replies the other sarcastically.

Scene 10

An **effervescent** (15) young woman rushes in, as bubbly as a gurgling fountain. She has a string of beautiful pearls draped around her neck. The pearls seem to act as a **stimulant** (16) to her actions, for she whirls around the stage with great excitement. Suddenly, the woman stops and holds up the pearls to inspect them one by one. The pearls are shiny but not **translucent** (17), since no light shines through them.

The woman carefully places the pearls on an **immaculate** (18) cloth on a table center stage. The cloth is so perfectly clean that it almost glows. She then starts to sing about pearls, which have been used as adornments for more than five thousand years. Of all the gifts from the sea—

sponges, seaweed, sea minerals—the pearl is the most treasured, she sings.

Scene 12

A modern panel debates whether offshore drilling for oil **debases** (19) the ocean by lowering its long-term worth.

"The costs of such drilling are an **imposition** (20) on the public," one speaker argues.

"I disagree," another speaker says. "The costs are not forced on people. They want the oil for their automobiles and for other uses. The oceans are yielding yet another valuable resource, as they have for centuries."

"Yes, but for how long?" another panelist asks, and the debate really heats up.

The Conclusion

When we had first been told that our science project was not only to explain the historical importance of the ocean as a natural resource, but also to transmit the information in the form of a play, we were doubtful that we could accomplish such a task. But we discovered that we could present scientific information in a way that was creative and entertaining. We learned a great deal from our collaboration, and I think our audience did, too. In the future, it will be hard to go back to doing traditional science reports.

| EXERCISE 1 | *Finding Synonyms* |

Directions. Reread the preceding passage. Then write on the line provided a synonym for each of the words in boldface. If you cannot think of an exact synonym, you may write a brief definition of the word.

1. explicate _____

2. mulled _____

3. synthesis _____

4. naive _____

5. sardonic _____

6. rankles _____

7. abdicate _____

8. quibble _____

9. itinerary _____

10. resonant _____

11. infallible _____

12. episode _____

13. sporadic _____

14. inadvertently _____

15. effervescent _____

16. stimulant _____

17. translucent _____

18. immaculate _____

19. debases _____

20. imposition _____

EXERCISE 2 *Reading Strategically* ✍

Directions. Now that you have read the passage and thought about the words in boldface, circle the letter of the correct answer to each of the following items. The numbers of the items are the same as the numbers of the boldface vocabulary words in the passage.

1. Which word in the passage provides a clue to the meaning of **explicate**?

   (A) requirement
   (B) difficult
   (C) assignment
   (D) people
   (E) explanation

2. In the passage, what does it mean when the writer says the students **mulled** over the assignment?

   (A) It means the students loudly argued about it.
   (B) It means the students carefully thought about it.
   (C) It means the students misunderstood it.
   (D) It means the students refused to do it.
   (E) It means the students did it immediately.

3. When we read in the passage that the play is a **synthesis** of the class's efforts, we should realize that a **synthesis** is

(A) a single scene that attempts to summarize many other scenes

(B) a play written by amateurs

(C) a whole made up of many separate parts

(D) a script for a television episode

(E) a description written by one person

4. What strategy does the writer use to let us know that **naive** may be defined as inexperienced?

(A) The writer contrasts **naive** with the words more-experienced.

(B) The writer says a **naive** person is very experienced.

(C) The writer relates **naive** to being a prehistoric person.

(D) The writer uses the word are to link **naive** to the word shallow.

(E) The writer links **naive** to two synonyms.

5. The writer provides a clue to the meaning of **sardonic** by

(A) contrasting it with an antonym

(B) comparing it to fishing practices

(C) describing a fishing contest

(D) linking it to the synonym sarcastic

(E) relating it to relationships between couples

6. In the passage, **rankles** means

(A) succeeds

(B) harpoons

(C) depresses

(D) angers

(E) pleases

7. According to the passage, how can the king become a sailor if he decides to **abdicate**?

(A) When a king **abdicates**, he becomes an admiral in the navy.

(B) To **abdicate** means to choose more power and responsibility.

(C) When a king **abdicates**, it means that he maintains power but joins the royal navy.

(D) When a king **abdicates**, he moves to a new country and becomes its ruler.

(E) When a king **abdicates**, he gives up power and responsibility.

8. In the passage, **quibble** means to

(A) make an important decision

(B) sign a contract

(C) make petty objections

(D) make encouraging comments

(E) make flattering comments

9. When the king plans his **itinerary**, as the author of the passage suggests he is about to do, he will probably use

(A) maps

(B) bells

(C) food

(D) rivers

(E) trips

10. We can infer from the passage that the bell's **resonant** sound is
  (A) thin and high
  (B) deep and rich
  (C) quick and bright
  (D) hard to hear
  (E) slow and harsh

11. What strategy does the writer use to tell us that **infallible** may be defined as incapable of making mistakes?
  (A) The writer says that anyone who is **infallible** is able to make mistakes.
  (B) The writer implies that since the two captains have made mistakes, they are not **infallible**.
  (C) The writer uses several examples of the captain's being **infallible**.
  (D) The writer uses **infallible** to refer to the golden age of whaling.
  (E) The writer contrasts **infallible** with the way ordinary sailors act.

12. According to the passage, the latest **episode** is just one in a series of _____ that prove the captain makes mistakes.
  (A) rights
  (B) whales
  (C) months
  (D) plays
  (E) events

13. How does the writer provide a clue to the meaning of **sporadic**?
  (A) The writer contrasts **sporadic** with the word regularly.
  (B) The writer relates **sporadic** to the word lately.
  (C) The writer compares **sporadic** to sightings.
  (D) The writer also uses the word irregular.
  (E) The writer uses **sporadic** to mean constant.

14. In the passage, why do the whalers doubt that the captain **inadvertently** had the harpoons unloaded?
  (A) They believe that no one could do that intentionally.
  (B) They doubt that the captain ever sailed the ship into port.
  (C) They think that the captain is not able to make a mistake.
  (D) They know that the captain can only act unintentionally.
  (E) They believe the captain would never tell anyone a lie.

15. Because the young woman with the pearls is **effervescent,** the writer describes her with the simile of
  (A) foam in the waves
  (B) the sea at high tide
  (C) a gurgling fountain
  (D) soapsuds in a sink
  (E) a carbonated drink

16. If, as the writer of the passage suggests, the pearls are a **stimulant** to the woman, we may expect her to be
  (A) crying
  (B) excited
  (C) hopeful
  (D) sleepy
  (E) unhappy

17. The writer provides a clue to the meaning of **translucent** by
  (A) implying that light shines through **translucent** objects
  (B) saying that pearls are the only truly **translucent** gems
  (C) relating **translucent** to objects that are white and shiny
  (D) using **translucent** as a synonym for bright lights
  (E) contrasting shiny pearls with **translucent** black sapphires

18. In the passage, **immaculate** means
  (A) colorful and shiny
  (B) wrinkled
  (C) soiled and dirty
  (D) perfectly clean
  (E) slightly soiled

19. When we read in the passage that the panel questions whether offshore drilling **debases** the ocean, we should realize that
  (A) no activity can affect the worth of the ocean
  (B) the worth of the ocean lies in the value of its oil
  (C) some activities can decrease the worth of the ocean
  (D) offshore drilling would increase the long-term worth of the ocean
  (E) the ocean can recover from any sort of abuse

20. We can infer from the passage that an **imposition** is something that is
  (A) forced upon someone
  (B) agreed to by everyone
  (C) wanted by everyone
  (D) voted on in elections
  (E) charged to taxpayers

READING NEW WORDS IN CONTEXT

Lesson 14 | CONTEXT: The Environment

The passage gives you an opportunity to expand your vocabulary. Below are twenty vocabulary words that are used in the passage and in the exercises that follow it.

demure	intuition	merge	rendezvous
detonate	irrational	pallid	seethe
edify	irrelevant	potency	sequel
eject	jostle	redundant	simulate
intermittent	lexicon	reminiscent	synopsis

Is the Earth Alive?

Our part of the earth certainly was alive during the city's first Gaia Festival last weekend. In last week's column, I said **intuition** (1) had told me that the festival would be a great success. This week, I'm glad to say my insight was accurate.

For those of you who missed either the publicity or the festival itself, I'll first try to enlighten and **edify** (2) you about Gaia and the "Gaia hypothesis," which inspired the festival.

The "Gaia Hypothesis"

You will find Gaia's name in a **lexicon** (3), or dictionary, of Greek mythology. Gaia is the Greek goddess of the earth. The modern "Gaia hypothesis" is a theory developed by British scientist and inventor James Lovelock and American microbiologist Lynn Margulis. Their theory was first presented to the public in 1979. Because it would take a full-length book to completely explain the theory, I will offer a summary, or **synopsis** (4), of the "Gaia hypothesis."

The earth itself is a superorganism, a living thing, according to the theory. Like other living creatures responding to environments and conditions, the earth makes necessary adjustments to stay alive. These adjustments are accomplished through the earth's microorganisms, plants, and animals adapting to their surroundings. These organisms **merge** (5) to form the superorganism

earth; they combine to control earth's climate and environment. It is as though all living things, taken together, become one gigantic life form.

Now, some people may think the Gaia hypothesis is **irrational** (6), but I, and speakers at the festival, think it makes a lot of sense. Unlike some critics, we don't consider the idea **irrelevant** (7) either, because it clearly applies to today's concerns about the planet's future.

"The Gaia idea is **reminiscent** (8) of Buckminster Fuller's 'Spaceship Earth,'" one festival speaker said, "because it suggests that we must all help care for the earth. The Gaia hypothesis implies that all creatures must work together for the good of our superorganism."

How Has Gaia Been Harmed?

The next speaker's remarks were somewhat **redundant** (9), more frosting on an already frosted cake. Nevertheless, I found them interesting. He said, "The **potency** (10)—strength, if you will— of the Gaia hypothesis is not its scientific truth, which is debatable, but its influence on people. Gaia's real importance is in helping to bring about a global awareness of people's environmental responsibilities. People are the superorganism's most powerful element. Gaia is trying to take care of herself, and human beings are hurting her efforts."

I strongly agree. If we think of the Earth as an organism, it is clear that we are wounding her by damaging such vital organs as rain forests, the ozone layer, and the oceans and rivers. Imagine how Gaia must feel every time we **detonate** (11) nuclear bombs for testing purposes. Such explosions must cause hideous wounds on her fragile body.

We should be careful. Mother Earth is far from **demure** (12); we should not think of her as being shy and reserved, like a modest maiden. In fact, she is a powerful, assertive woman. She may **seethe** (13) for a while over the way we're abusing and polluting her and then let her agitations explode in our faces. It's not a pleasant thought, but it is one that **intermittently** (14), or occasionally, goes through my mind.

As for the festival, the crowd was large and enthusiastic. Most people seemed to enjoy the speakers, information booths, games, rides, and food. I'm happy to report that we earthlings were well-behaved. Police told me that they didn't have to **eject** (15) anyone from the festival; no one had to be forcibly removed. There wasn't even any rude shoving, or **jostling** (16), at the food booths.

A crowd pleaser was Judge Ethel Walters, who **simulated** (17) the imagined appearance of Gaia herself, right down to a long, flowing, green dress and colorful flowers in her hair. She told me that she enjoyed playing the role of the guest of honor at the festival. However, by the end of the festival's two-day run, the judge looked rather **pallid** (18) and exhausted. I told her I hoped that her paleness did not reflect Gaia's true condition.

Will the Gaia Festival continue? Yes. The promoters assured me that there will be a **sequel** (19) next year—every bit as good as the original.

I wish the promoters could arrange a **rendezvous** (20) for me with one of the originators of the Gaia hypothesis. I would jump at the chance for such a meeting!

EXERCISE 1 · *Finding Synonyms*

Directions. Reread the preceding passage. Then write on the line provided a synonym for each of the words in boldface. If you cannot think of an exact synonym, you may write a brief definition of the word.

1. intuition _____

2. edify _____

3. lexicon _____

4. synopsis _____

5. merge _____

6. irrational _____

7. irrelevant _____

8. reminiscent _____

9. redundant _____

10. potency _____

11. detonate _____

12. demure _____

13. seethe _____

14. intermittently _____

15. eject _____

16. jostling _____

17. simulated _____

18. pallid _____

19. sequel _____

20. rendezvous _____

EXERCISE 2 — Reading Strategically

Directions. Now that you have read the passage and thought about the words in boldface, circle the letter of the correct answer to each of the following items. The numbers of the items are the same as the numbers of the boldface vocabulary words in the passage.

1. In the passage, the word that provides a clue to the meaning of **intuition** is
   (A) certainly
   (B) insight
   (C) column
   (D) publicity
   (E) festival

2. What strategy does the writer use to tell us that **edify** is defined as to instruct or improve?
   (A) The writer contrasts **edify** with two antonyms.
   (B) The writer uses a simile to explain the meaning of **edify**.
   (C) The writer links **edify** with the synonym enlighten.
   (D) The writer gives an example of an edifice.
   (E) The writer uses an analogy for **edify**.

3. In the passage, a **lexicon** is a
   (A) speaker
   (B) mythology
   (C) goddess
   (D) Greek name
   (E) dictionary

4. In the passage, why does the writer give a **synopsis** of the "Gaia hypothesis"?
   (A) The entire hypothesis is too long to present fully.
   (B) The hypothesis is too short in its original version.
   (C) The writer does not fully understand the hypothesis.
   (D) The writer prefers to translate directly from Greek.
   (E) The writer is not very interested in the hypothesis.

5. When we read in the passage that organisms **merge,** we should realize that they

    (A) separate

    (B) change

    (C) explode

    (D) combine

    (E) control

6. People who think the "Gaia hypothesis" is **irrational** think it is

    (A) adequate

    (B) factual

    (C) not sensible

    (D) very rational

    (E) incomplete

7. In the passage, an idea is **irrelevant**

    (A) when it applies to today's concerns

    (B) if it makes sense in a senseless world

    (C) if it is related to current events

    (D) when is it not serious enough

    (E) when it does not apply to today's concerns

8. We can infer from the passage that if an idea is **reminiscent** of an earlier idea, it

    (A) proves both ideas are right

    (B) suggests the earlier idea

    (C) proves both ideas are wrong

    (D) contradicts the earlier idea

    (E) replaces the earlier idea

9. To illustrate how **redundant** a speaker's remarks were, the writer uses a metaphor to compare them to

    (A) taking the same trip again

    (B) excess frosting on a cake

    (C) two ideas that mean nothing

    (D) Greek and Roman myths

    (E) eating the same food at every meal

10. In the passage, the **potency** of the "Gaia hypothesis" is the _____ of its influence on people.

    (A) lack

    (B) debate

    (C) strength

    (D) awareness

    (E) denial

11. In the passage, what does it mean to **detonate** bombs?

    (A) It means to cancel them.

    (B) It means to create them.

    (C) It means to airlift them.

    (D) It means to explode them.

    (E) It means to defuse them.

12. In the passage, why shouldn't we think of Mother Earth as **demure**?

 (A) She is not shy and reserved; she is powerful and assertive.
 (B) She is wounded by nuclear bomb test explosions.
 (C) She always reacts in ways that are shy and reserved.
 (D) She appreciates the concern people have for rain forests.
 (E) She is not capable of protecting herself from harm.

13. What strategy does the writer use to tell us that **seethe** means to boil or be highly agitated?

 (A) The writer defines **seethe** as a soothing reaction.
 (B) The writer relates **seethe** to pleasant thoughts.
 (C) The writer links **seethe** to the word agitations.
 (D) The writer also uses the words abusing and polluting.
 (E) The writer uses **seethe** to mean calm down and think.

14. In the passage, **intermittently** means

 (A) informally
 (B) occasionally
 (C) triumphantly
 (D) never
 (E) continually

15. In the passage, if the police had had to **eject** someone from the festival, the writer of the passage would have known that person was

 (A) making a long speech
 (B) feeling sick
 (C) enjoying the food
 (D) not well-behaved
 (E) eager to be there

16. In the passage, the word that provides a clue to the meaning of **jostling** is

 (A) talking
 (B) eating
 (C) throwing
 (D) behaving
 (E) shoving

17. When we read in the passage that the judge **simulated** Gaia, we should realize that she

 (A) really was Gaia
 (B) pretended to be Gaia
 (C) spoke about Gaia
 (D) dressed in judge's robes
 (E) protested against Gaia

18. The writer provides a clue to the meaning of **pallid** by

 (A) contrasting **pallid** to the word pretending
 (B) comparing **pallid** to the color green
 (C) restating **pallid** with the word paleness
 (D) relating it to Gaia's condition
 (E) saying **pallid** means seriously ill

19. We can infer from the passage that a **sequel** is a

- (A) continuation
- (B) publication
- (C) promotion
- (D) discontinuation
- (E) restoration

20. In the passage, the word that provides a clue to the meaning of **rendezvous** is

- (A) originator
- (B) festival
- (C) meeting
- (D) promoters
- (E) assured

READING NEW WORDS IN CONTEXT

Lesson 15 **CONTEXT:** The Environment

The passage gives you an opportunity to expand your vocabulary. Below are twenty vocabulary words that are used in the passage and in the exercises that follow it.

carp	incendiary	negligible	protrude
caustic	inconsistent	obligatory	rebuke
coincidental	irksome	odious	scenario
decrepit	jargon	parody	sordid
farce	malignant	pertinent	transition

Where Does All the Garbage Go?

People have always asked me that most annoying of **irksome** (1) questions: What do you want to be when you grow up?

I used to give **inconsistent** (2) responses, depending on my most recent interests. Lately, however, my response doesn't change.

"I want to be a garbage archaeologist," I state. Then I wait for the expected **scenario** (3), the predictable outline of what will happen next.

One of three responses will always follow. Some questioners believe my answer is a **farce** (4) because they think it is so ridiculous. They give me strange looks. Others say something like, "Oh, that's nice," and quickly change the subject. A few, however, ask to know what I mean, and I gladly tell them.

What Is Garbage Archaeology?

Two years ago, I was giving a lot of thought to my future for an assignment in my careers class. During that time, while waiting at the doctor's office one day, I read a *National Geographic* article titled "Once and Future Landfills." You could say that it was just an accident that I read that particular article while working on the assignment. I don't think it was **coincidental** (5), however. It was fate.

The article was written by William L. Rathje, a professor of anthropology at the University of Arizona in Tucson. In 1973, he and his students formed the Garbage Project to study the nation's garbage problem. I immediately realized that it was a **pertinent** (6) article, truly important to our time. And it described an interesting job, too, I thought.

I've always been interested in garbage, even though my parents used to **rebuke** (7) or scold me for not taking ours out. What people throw away is fascinating and really says a lot about them, I think.

My older sister told me she didn't like the idea of her brother spending his life looking through garbage. "It's a disgusting idea," she said. "I can't think of a more **odious** (8) job."

When I first told my father about my decision, he wasn't impressed, either. He said, "It seems like that would be a **sordid** (9) job—dirty and degrading."

"Oh, no," I responded. "It'd be an unusual job but a really helpful one."

There definitely is too much garbage in the world. People constantly **carp** (10) about it, but their complaining doesn't do any good. Recycling is the key to solving the garbage dilemma. A garbage archaeologist can look at what has been thrown away over the years to get a better idea what people should recycle and how our society is being wasteful. For example, every piece of decrepit (11) furniture doesn't have to be thrown away. Sometimes old, worn-out furniture can be fixed and sold at garage sales or thrift stores.

By reading the article, I learned what material goes into landfills. The Garbage Project dug through 11 landfills, including the enormous Fresh Kills landfill on New York City's Staten Island. Paper accounts for 50 percent of a landfill's contents. Newspapers alone make up 18 percent of a landfill's space. Plastics, you may be interested to know, fill up to only 10 percent of a landfill's space because they are so easily crushed. Tires, however, are a problem in landfills. Rising to the surface and sticking out, they **protrude** (12) like capsized life rafts in a sea of garbage. Yet some of the items we generally think of as being overabundant in landfills may actually be taking up **negligible** (13) space. For example, disposable diapers make up only 0.8 percent of a landfill's total contents.

For an English assignment, I wrote a short story about landfill contents called "Gone with the Garbage." This story was a **parody** (14), or humorous and satirical imitation, of Margaret Mitchell's classic novel *Gone with the Wind*. I made fun of her story to show a society invaded by its own **malignant** (15) garbage. The image of life-threatening garbage is comical but disturbing.

Recycling Is a Solution

There should be more recycling programs for papers, plastics, and other household items. People generally don't mind being required to do something if it is for a good cause. In fact, I think people would gladly accept more **obligatory** (16) community recycling programs. In our community, we moved from having no recycling program at all to having a very active one. The **transition** (17) was very smooth and quick.

I've found that people just need to be educated about recycling. For example, many people don't realize that they shouldn't throw away batteries. Batteries are **caustic** or corrosive (18) in landfills, and dangerous chemicals leak out into the soil and water. Of course, **incendiary** (19) substances, those capable of causing fires, shouldn't be put into landfills, either. I've helped people become familiar with specialized language used in the recycling field—**jargon** (20) such as the words biodegradable and hazardous waste.

Garbage archaeology is an exciting field. Much still needs to be learned about the role of trash in American society. With this new information, we can make this world a cleaner, safer place for the generations to come. I'll be happy to help make the world more garbage-conscious.

EXERCISE 1   *Finding Synonyms*

Directions. Reread the preceding passage. Then write on the line provided a synonym for each of the words in boldface. If you cannot think of an exact synonym, you may write a brief definition of the word.

1. irksome   _____

2. inconsistent   _____

3. scenario   _____

4. farce   _____

5. coincidental   _____

6. pertinent   _____

7. rebuke   _____

8. odious _____

9. sordid _____

10. carp _____

11. decrepit _____

12. protrude _____

13. negligible _____

14. parody _____

15. malignant _____

16. obligatory _____

17. transition _____

18. caustic _____

19. incendiary _____

20. jargon _____

EXERCISE 2 *Reading Strategically* 👈

Directions. Now that you have read the passage and thought about the words in boldface, circle the letter of the correct answer to each of the following items. The numbers of the items are the same as the numbers of the boldface vocabulary words in the passage.

1. In the passage, the word that provides a clue to the meaning of **irksome** is
  - (A) questions
  - (B) always
  - (C) response
  - (D) annoying
  - (E) adults

2. When we read in the passage that the writer's answers used to be **inconsistent,** we should realize that the answers
  - (A) were not always the same
  - (B) always focused on the same career
  - (C) changed only one time before
  - (D) never fit the question
  - (E) never made sense

3. In the passage, why can the writer give the **scenario** of the responses to his choice of careers?
  (A) The writer expects all people to respond in the same way.
  (B) The writer has never had anyone react to the career choices.
  (C) The writer knows people always respond in one of three predictable ways.
  (D) The writer is accustomed to everyone being very interested.
  (E) The writer never tells people the truth about his interests and ambitions.

4. In the passage, the writer's answer about a career is not a **farce** because he is _____ about it.
  (A) joking
  (B) uncertain
  (C) ridiculous
  (D) unhappy
  (E) serious

5. What strategy does the writer use to tell us that **coincidental** is defined as occurring together by accident?
  (A) The writer defines **coincidental** as an assignment.
  (B) The writer links **coincidental** with the word accident.
  (C) The writer contrasts **coincidental** with the word article.
  (D) The writer relates **coincidental** to a particular article.
  (E) The writer compares the assignment to a disaster.

6. The writer provides a clue to the meaning of **pertinent** by
  (A) contrasting it with the antonym study
  (B) giving an example
  (C) linking it with the words important to our time
  (D) defining it as useless
  (E) relating it to garbage

7. In the passage, **rebuke** means
  (A) ask
  (B) praise
  (C) scold
  (D) joke with
  (E) answer

8. We can infer from the passage that if a job is **odious**, it is
  (A) exciting
  (B) high-paying
  (C) unusual
  (D) disgusting
  (E) interesting

9. In the passage, why did the writer's father think his child's choice of a career might be **sordid**?
  (A) He thought the career would be too difficult to train for.
  (B) He thought that there were better-paying careers.
  (C) He thought there must be something illegal about it.
  (D) He supported whatever career his child decided on.
  (E) He thought working with garbage was dirty and degrading.

10. In the passage, people **carp** about garbage, but they need to do more than _____ about it.

(A) complain
(B) shout
(C) be happy
(D) laugh
(E) be silent

11. In the passage, what does it mean for something to be **decrepit**?

(A) **Decrepit** means it is not completely paid for.
(B) **Decrepit** means it is still like new.
(C) **Decrepit** means it has been resold.
(D) **Decrepit** means it is old and worn out.
(E) **Decrepit** means it is a piece of furniture.

12. To illustrate how old tires **protrude** from landfills, the writer uses a simile to compare them to

(A) trucks and cars in a used car lot
(B) weeds floating in a lake
(C) capsized life rafts in a sea of garbage
(D) life rafts hanging from hooks on a ship
(E) cereal flakes floating in a bowl of milk

13. What strategy does the writer use to tell us that **negligible** means insignificant?

(A) The writer uses the synonym disposable.
(B) The writer cites a specific example.
(C) The writer uses the antonym total.
(D) The writer uses the analogy of a sea of garbage.
(E) The writer uses a simile.

14. In the passage, why was the writer's short story a **parody**?

(A) It was a serious article about garbage.
(B) It was a humorous imitation of another work.
(C) It was a new and different form of a popular folk tale.
(D) It was written in class as an English assignment.
(E) It described things that could never happen in school.

15. In the passage, **malignant** means

(A) life-threatening
(B) healthy
(C) angry
(D) death-defying
(E) painfully comical

16. We can infer from the passage that if something is **obligatory**, it is

(A) optional
(B) punishing
(C) useful
(D) required
(E) exciting

17. If a **transition** occurs smoothly and quickly, we may expect
  (A) nothing to be changed
  (B) change to take place easily
  (C) people to be opposed to change
  (D) new ideas to be forced on people
  (E) arguments that prevent any change

18. The writer provides a clue to the meaning of **caustic** by
  (A) contrasting it with the word closing
  (B) also using the synonym corrosive
  (C) referring to different chemicals
  (D) relating it to reusable car parts
  (E) linking it to the word landfills

19. When we read in the passage that **incendiary** substances should not be put into landfills, we should realize that
  (A) it would be dangerous for a landfill to burn
  (B) burning would be very helpful to large landfills
  (C) **incendiary** substances are illegal everywhere
  (D) **incendiary** substances pose no threat to land or people
  (E) **incendiary** substances can spread disease

20. In the passage, **jargon** is
  (A) the jokes made up by garbage archaeologists
  (B) the specialized language of a trade or profession
  (C) a dialect of the English language
  (D) a special kind of body language
  (E) one of several languages spoken in Central America